Wild Holy Love
A True Mystical Adventure
Kye Crow

For my mother Brenda with her big open heart. Thank you for the gift of the animals.

And for my father Philip, who however far away he is, is always in my heart. xxxxx

Wild Holy Love

contact-www.kyecrow.love

First Published 2014 as Ghosts & Ghoumas

Copyright text @Kye Crow

Cover art by @Kye Crow

Copyright cover image @Kye Crow

Wild Holy Love is also available as an e-book

All rights reserved. No part of this publication may be reproduced whole or in part, stored in a retrievable system, or transmitted
in any form or by any means, electronic, mechanical, photocopying, recording, or otherwise, without permission of the copyright holder or publisher, other
than for 'fair use' as brief quotations in articles and reviews.

One

Let the Current Take You

One of the best lessons I ever learnt was at the top of a forty-four metre bungee tower, stomach churning as I waited for the person in front of me to jump. She had already been counted down from five to one and hadn't moved, and after a second countdown, was still standing quaking at the top. I felt wrung out with anxiety watching every tortured countdown, and I swore then that I would jump first time. There was no way I would need a second go, or a third, which is what she'd needed before she finally jumped. If you've got something shitty to do, whatever it is, do not falter; get it over and done with. There is far less stress in life when you do!

And that's why I was walking boldly toward the market even though I felt anxious and totally uncool, clutching my almost-new Dr Marten boots that I didn't wear because they pinched my toes. I was a woman on a mission!

This is a journey that began over twenty years ago in 1991, when my life—a big old mess until then— cracked open. It began in Goa, India, on the shores of the Arabian sea in the already sweaty hours of the early morning as the sun turned everything amber. It began in the colourful cacophony of early dawn, as I walked up the beach, passing the menfolk taking their early morning shits; bums hanging over the ocean as they clung to the rocks that buttressed the shallow waters of the sea, whilst cows that looked to be cut from card, sat chewing their cardboard cud.

Even though it was early, the beach was already throbbing with life. The beach sellers were busy, poking and prodding sleeping party-goers that had crashed on the beach somewhere during the night and looked up, dazed, when a man with yellowed teeth and apricot turban tried to sell them a piece of juicy watermelon. There were women wearing brightly coloured saris with huge baskets of mirrored sarongs balanced on their heads, and those dodgy men I'd already been warned about—the ear cleaners who often dropped a tiny stone into someone's ear to entice them to pay to remove it—they wouldn't get anywhere near me!

There was no doubt I felt nervous as I entered the Anjuna market, with its smells of cumin and spice and the sizzle of samosas and bhajis cooking in oil; the smell of cow shit and pigs and sweet chai bubbling endlessly and everywhere on single gas burners and mud earth stoves. The market was a feast of colour: lurid green saris next to shocking pinks, piles of embroidered and mirrored blankets, the apricot robes of a sadhu who had a long grey beard that trailed to his knees.

As I walked up the aisle, a couple of bony-yet-holy cows sat chewing their cud, blocking the flow as people waited to walk reverentially around them, whilst a gypsy seller, wanting me to buy some beads, jabbed me so aggressively in my arm with her finger she left a small pea-sized bruise.

I was looking for somewhere I could sit and I finally found a tiny patch of free ground between two stalls. On one side, three younger women with huge, elaborate nose rings, wearing ornately mirrored and embroidered choli tops looked down at the ground giggling shyly whenever I looked their way. They sat, bums in the dirt with their tribal wares spread out on sarongs in front of them.

I felt so foolish as I placed my Dr Marten boots on the sand in front of me, arranging my hand-drawn 'for sale' sign at their toes. I only had one thing to sell and all the other stalls were laden with goods. To make matters worse, I had become the centre of attention. Nothing happens in India without an audience, and more often than not, it's men.

A group had gathered around me. They stared at my boots and then at me, almost as if they were waiting for my show to begin, only I didn't have one. This is it folks, one pair of boots! I felt ridiculous for even thinking I could sell them for a decent price in India, but I had to trust; the feeling to sell them had been so strong. This was not how I'd imagined my first week in India to be, yet if I wanted to stay I had to sell something and the only thing I had left of value besides my boots was my camera, and I was not parting with that.

Even though I felt vulnerable and unsure of what was going to happen next; even though I felt way out of my depth and very much alone, I could feel I was sitting on the pulse of an experience that was too big to ignore or run away from, and everything in my life was whispering softly, *Just let go, just let go, Kye*, and as I surrendered to the moment I had never felt so free.

I was so absorbed by the scenes around me it was hard to focus on what I needed to do—and that was sell my boots! There was a tiny pig rolling in the dirt, playing with a scruffy puppy. A holy man walked past wearing bright saffron robes, his long, grey dreadlocks trailing below his bum, his body lithe and muscled. He was carrying a three-pronged trident and a bright red shiny bucket, which made him look as if he was on his way to fight a fire.

As the sun rose higher, the tourists began to leak in, some looking as if they'd come straight from one of the dance parties that Goa was famous for, with their faces painted, trailing glitter and wearing psychedelic body suits. A couple of gruff-looking men, black-leathered and testy with grey pouchy faces, were parking their hired Enfield motorbikes at the back of someone's stall whilst some other tourists haggled over the price of a sarong. My audience had soon dispersed and apart from the odd glance, most people walked past as if I wasn't there, which didn't exactly reassure me, as I was hoping to make a fast sale.

The wafts of curries and other Goan cuisine being cooked in all the ramshackle huts that edged the market was making me ravenous, but I couldn't eat until I'd sold my boots, and no one had shown the slightest interest yet.

When I had originally booked my ticket to Delhi, an older man in the travel agency had asked me if I'd ever been to India before. When I replied no, he offered the best advice anyone could have ever given me: 'It's like a river,' he said. 'You just have to throw yourself in and let the current take you.' And that's what I was doing, sitting on the sand hoping to sell my lonesome pair of Dr Marten boots. I had thrown myself into the river but I hadn't expected the current would be so strong.

I had been in India less than a week when my bag was stolen. It contained my travellers' cheques, a large amount of cash, the opals I'd brought to trade and every single rupee I had. I was left with nothing, except my camera. I had been washing at a well, with my bag right beside me, and as I lifted up the bucket to rinse my hair, someone must have slithered in and snatched it.

The moment I realised my bag had gone I went into a panic. I raced around hysterically for half an hour, searching everywhere I'd been, asking everyone I knew if they'd seen it—even people I didn't know— and the whole time I had this knowing ache in my gut that told me it had gone! As I collapsed onto the sand, I had no idea what I would do, and for a while I sat there feeling absolutely stunned.

Then I became aware of someone standing near me. I have no idea who; I was totally submerged within myself. As they spoke, I listened —'You must feel terrible losing everything'—and something within me began to change. I thought about their words for a while, really letting them sink in. I knew how I was *supposed* to feel. Most of us divide experiences into 'good' or 'bad'— a common language we all understand. But what I discovered once I got past how I was programmed to react was that I didn't feel terrible at all. In fact, I felt absolutely amazing! I was astonished to discover this.

Getting in touch with how I felt, instead of how I was expected to feel, opened a doorway to one of the most treasured experiences of my life—one that I would not have given up for anything. Yes, adversity *can* be transformed. What I was to discover was that having all your money stolen in India can be a wonderful experience if you are open to letting go of programmed responses that simply block the flow of abundance in your life.

One thing was certain: I didn't have to worry about my bag anymore. The stories I had been told about how some Indians parted travellers from their cash included sending monkeys in to steal while you slept, drugging food to knock you out then taking everything as you lay unconscious, and putting bamboo poles with pads soaked in ether through your window as you slept to etherise you, then breaking in and taking everything. Stealing in India was a fine art and I had begun to feel so paranoid, as if I was dealing with a corrupt Spiderman who had all these magical abilities he could use to relieve me of my cash. I would not have been at all surprised to be told they could slither through bars on a window and manifest like a freaky apparition inside. Every moment, every second of every day, so far, had been heavily laced with the fear of being parted from my bag. Well, it was over; the deed had been done, and I felt utterly and deliriously free!

I could have travelled by bus or bike the forty kilometres to the nearest phone and put one of my loved ones into a panic as they tried to stretch funds I knew they didn't have to help me. Or I could have spent two days travelling to Bombay to get my travellers' cheques replaced. But I didn't feel I wanted to do that. I only had a couple of hundred dollars in cheques anyway; the rest was in cash. For sure that money would have helped, but I found myself feeling so deeply immersed in the moment, nothing existed outside the reality I was in. And in that space, for the first time in my life there was absolutely no fear.

I sat on the warm sand at the market trying to ignore the endless stream of nomads all touting their wares, trying to separate me from cash I no longer had. I could feel the innocence of the sun on my face, the smell of chai and spice and sweaty bodies basking on the beach, and I felt infused with a knowing that I was looked after. In the next moment, holding up my boots was a smartly dressed Indian woman calling excitedly to her husband and kids. For many Indian people West was always best. I had experienced this several times already in only a week. The first time was when I'd gone to buy some Ayurvedic soap and toothpaste. The shopkeeper had been mortified that I didn't want Lux or Colgate. He had tried, rather emphatically, to dissuade me from my choice, and much to his distress, without success. As I'd paid for my purchases he had looked at me with such pity, completely unable to equate my choice with that of a rational human being. It was the same with my Dr Marten boots. They were from the West and therefore revered like the Holy Grail. Hubby eagerly pulled out his wallet and with barely a haggle freed me of my market stall.

I was elated as I headed off to find myself something delicious to eat. I had done it, I'd braved my insecurities, sat feeling foolish and trite and lonely for hours on end, but I had damn well done it! I'd sold my boots! Nothing about my trip was turning out like I'd hoped. I had expected to be immersing myself in the sacred chants and sanctuary of an ashram and instead I had landed right in the midst of the Goan party scene. And even though I didn't like parties and always tried to avoid crowds, everything in my life felt perfect—even losing all my money. I was exactly where I was meant to be and I knew that because I felt full of love.

Selling my boots had been my initiation on the miraculous path of living a life of trust. I thought it was all about love; all innocent and balmy like a meadow of flowers swaying in the breeze and I had no idea then that my journey ahead would take me straight into the depths of darkness from which I would return with jewels so bright they would be a guiding light in all my years to come.

Two

Only This Moment Exists

So many different layers of my life were beginning to unravel in Goa and I had every reason to feel as light and free as an eagle soaring in the thermals. For the first time in six years I was living away from a relationship that had strangled and choked everything joyful within me. But it hadn't only been my partner that had betrayed my trust. I had been so deeply let down by close friends that I began to wonder if I would ever trust people again; and yet here I was making new friends and feeling safe. Simply being away from all the lies and manipulations had me feeling like I'd healed myself of a chronic disease. I had left my old relationship with such low self-esteem, believing all the things he'd said were wrong with me—and none of them were true. I could be happy; I WAS happy!

My partner, Dan, was a charismatic social butterfly, a Mr Nice Guy who wanted to be loved by all, and had turned our home into a transit lounge for all his fans. He brought everyone and anyone home to stay, regardless of whether they nicked the silver, shit on the carpet or sucked the life out of all that was good, and I was seen as the person who spoilt everyone's fun.

Miserable old me, heartbroken by all his affairs, let down by friends who had seen the abuse and turned away, and betrayed by endless women who valued a quick fuck with him over their friendship with me. I was devastated at the life I had created, which had snared me like a fly in a spider's web.

I know how hard it is to break free. I know how lies and manipulations defended as truth weaken and disable our own abilities to think clearly, act wisely or do something loving for ourselves. I struggled for so long to break free, I became weak. I had prayed and pleaded, even getting down on my knees and begging, 'If there is some humanity in this universe, please help me end the hell I am in.'

And here I was in India. Finally, I'd been spat out the other end of that murky tunnel, and I'd landed in a reality that was *all mine*. This was *my* world now, and what I could create was totally up to me. The possibilities were exciting.

I had manifested a home of my own; a rickety little hut made from the fronds of coconut leaves with a delightful wonky door that opened straight onto the beach—a prime beachfront property. I felt so proud of myself. I was pushing past all my comfort zones and facing my fears.

And for those of you who may be wondering about the bathroom, well ... er ... there wasn't one! Basically India is a poo free-for-all. When I needed the toilet, the best place was the bushes at the back of the beach. Prayers answered, there wouldn't be too many squatting tourists and the biggest bush would be free. I had to get there before the pigs though, who kept the whole place clean by gobbling all the faeces and paper, but could often be impatient. They had no capacity to wait!

Showering involved buckets of icy water at the well, yet despite my basic lack of comfort, I had no desire for anything more.

Selling my boots only gave me a couple of weeks' grace with my cash, but I didn't feel stressed. I didn't have a single thought about how to get more money, even though I was financially on my own with no close friends around to help. Some kind soul had actually given me three very beautiful t-shirts when he'd first heard of my plight. They were of Lakshmi, goddess of wealth and prosperity, sitting in a hot pink lotus in full bloom! How fitting! He'd suggested I sell them, but I'd tucked them in my bag, not feeling ready to let go of Lakshmi and her gracious vibes just yet. After all the excitement of selling my boots, I began to feel like doing something; in fact, I had an overwhelming desire to create—but with what?

I had no sooner thought this than the answer arrived. Someone dropped off a white t-shirt and a bag of fabric paints. They'd gotten up that morning and felt compelled to bring me these things. I was over the moon, seeing such instant results from my heartfelt desire to create was empowering. This was one of my first little lessons in going with how you *feel* and not with what you *think* you should do.

I immediately threw myself into this new project and spent the next week meticulously painting pictures all over the shirt. The artwork was colourful and inspired by India's lurid and dazzling colours, and on the back, I painted a clock with the word NOW on its face. Why? Because life was constantly showing me that the only point of power was the 'now', and nothing else outside this moment existed.

I didn't think about what I would do with the shirt. I was so immersed in the process of painting. I even felt a little distracted when someone suggested I raffle it. 'You've put so much work into it,' they said. 'Most people would love a chance to win it.' It resonated immediately as the perfect idea.

Within a few days, I was out and about at the bars and cafés, my finished t-shirt displayed on a pole, with a new friend carrying one end and me the other. I sold so many raffle tickets that I made more money than if I'd sold my shirt at a plush Sydney art gallery. I felt exhilarated. Talk about escalating self-esteem! (Oh, and a really lovely French guy won the T-shirt. He was so ecstatic! He put it on immediately and ran around all the cafés on the beach showing off his prize. I was delighted that my t-shirt had gone to such an appreciative home!) After this personal victory, I felt I could cope with anything, and it was just as well, as there was another element about to enter my life that nothing could have prepared me for.

Goa is a place where everything exists and anything is possible, from the highest, most angelic spheres to the darkest and most sinister shadows. I met some amazing people who lived totally from their hearts, but I also met others who were so dark they made my blood run cold. The chills that radiated from them were terrifying. Before Goa I did not know such people existed. This idyllic beach resort was a paradise for black magicians and highly skilled energy vampires to prey psychically upon others. It was also a haven for those running from heinous crime.

One such woman kept seeking me out. She was German with a very strong accent and she spat her words out with such hate and contempt that I felt like I was being sliced by a knife every time she spoke. She despised India, its people, its food and its 'loathsome and disgusting ways'. She was barely in her fifties, with short cropped hair. Her face was white and sickly-looking because she went everywhere with an umbrella up, big shades on and never saw the sun. She felt as though she was rotting from within.

She seemed to be attracted to me and kept on seeking me out, even though I didn't encourage her in any way. I had no idea why she kept doing this. One day she told me she would be leaving in a day or two, as she hated this place. I asked her where she was going, trying to hide my relief, and she replied 'I do not know; I go where the bus takes me.' She had been travelling like this around India for seven years. Most of us on the beach had surmised she was on the run from something, and I had not the faintest desire to know what.

Several days later I was lying on the beach, feeling the sun on my body after a swim, when she turned up. 'You'll get skin cancer and die,' she hissed. *Dammit.* She hadn't left. I had hoped I'd seen the last of her! I immediately sat up, looked at her and said calmly and clearly, 'Go away.' I had made a matter-of-fact statement, telling her what I wanted her to do. There's no time for bullshit in India; you are who you are.

Every day you get poked and prodded by people wanting your money. You get asked a thousand times what is your country, where are you from and are you married. I heard so many travellers say they felt like hitting someone. If you like your life neatly folded, if you hide under a constant veneer of being nice, or you're a control freak, you'll crack under the strain. When she continued to ignore me and stayed there, it was I who got up and walked away.

I was mortified when I discovered later that she had rented the hut next to mine for the night. It was so close and built of flimsy cane. I knew I wouldn't sleep a wink. Col, my affable little mate from Manchester who called everyone 'petal' or 'love' and lived in the hut next door, was freaked out too at the prospect of this woman staying a night so near to us.

Later in the evening she came and sat in my doorway, once again ignoring all the times I had told her to leave me alone. She usually had some evil tidings to share, but this time she was silent, so I didn't jump down her throat telling her to leave. For a long time she didn't speak.

Everything she did always made me feel uneasy. It didn't matter how much love I was manifesting in my own life, or how much I was learning to trust, I was not capable of feeling any compassion or love for her. Every moment she was near me, I was on guard, and nothing could have convinced me to let it down. Even her silence was making me uneasy.

When she finally spoke, she surprised me; it was not her usual vitriol. 'Do you believe in forgiveness?' she asked. Her voice was hoarse.

'Yes,' I said.

She thought about my answer for a while. When she finally broke the silence, she replied slowly, spitting and hissing each word, 'It's too late for me. I have done terrible things.'

'You can change anything in a second if you choose,' I said, feeling like a Girl Guide leader giving advice to a psychopath.

'It's too late, much too late,' she spat. She got up and walked to her hut.

There would be no restful sleep for me that night, I was certain. I kept trying to change my state of mind, but I couldn't. I knew from experience that when that happens, there is a reason and I need to trust what I am feeling. As I sat in my hut, I could hear her breathing just a few feet away from me. It was like a ticking clock. After several hours of discomfort, I must have dozed off for a second or two because I was woken by Col urging me to get up and leave with him NOW! I'd been sitting up, trying to stop myself from falling asleep and it was an abrupt awakening, but every single alarm bell inside me was going off and telling me to run.

We got out of there so fast, well as fast as we could! Col was carrying his prized possession, a newly purchased Indian drum, which was too big to haul on a fast get away but he was adamant he wasn't leaving it behind! We ran as if we were escaping a fire, down to the shoreline before stopping to look back.

'She was creeping around outside your hut,' Col told me breathlessly.

We sat in the shadows, hearts pounding. There was a rise behind my hut and she was standing on it, illuminated by the moonlight. I knew she was looking directly at me and I could feel her evil intent like a knife.

Neither of us had a doubt that she had something awful planned, and that's why she'd moved in on her last night. In the morning, by the time her crime was discovered, she would have been long gone. Col and I wandered around all night and didn't return to our huts until late in the morning. Even then we circled from a distance and watched for a long time to make sure she had left. I only began to breathe normally when I knew that she had indeed gone. I was not being paranoid. I was honouring the gift I'd been given of my life—I was keeping myself safe.

Only once before in my life had I felt in similar danger. I had been walking down a long road that joined two outer suburbs in Brisbane. There were trees on each side, but no houses. I was happily daydreaming away when I was hit by a strong wave or force so terrifying it almost disabled me completely. When I looked up, there were two men sitting in a van, just a few feet in front of me, and every muscle in their bodies was tensed, ready to pounce. I had been completely unaware of their presence, and in just a few more steps I knew the life I treasured would have been gone. My heart was beating so fast as I quickly crossed over the road. I physically felt the wave of disappointment that came from them as they saw me get away. I had been so close. If I had not responded to how I'd felt, I'd be dead; I am sure of it. I don't ignore these feelings now.

While this level of danger had been rare for me, the German woman was not the only person I met like this in Goa. Things happened that I had never experienced before—animals harmed, people fighting in vile and hateful ways—the details of which I'll spare you. Why give such evil acts any more power? They were sick people doing sick things, and while some of those people were crazy, some were very powerful black magicians that were masters at the art of manipulating large crowds of people.

The first time I became aware of a dark malevolent presence was at a party that unfolded right on the beach in front of my hut. It started sleepily in the afternoon; a small group of people painting the trunks of the coconut trees with psychedelic paints. Then massive sound systems were brought in and throughout the afternoon the energy built as more and more people arrived. People erected fire sculptures and wildly painted tipis, stages and circus hoops. Hundreds of Indian women came, unrolling their cane mats and setting up their pots of spiced chai and cakes for all the party goers who slowly began to arrive as the sun went down. By late evening the energy was really starting to pump. There was so much to look at and I lay with a couple of friends, unable to move for hours, completely riveted as we watched it all unfold. No conversation, just constant exclamations from us all. It was surreal and we were mesmerised.

There were people wearing holographic body suits and face paints in amongst beggars with stumps for arms. One Indian man with a huge dagger would leap in front of Westerners and slice the dagger back and forth, really fast, through a hole in his chin. He had such a dark and sinister look on his face; the whole experience was macabre and shocking. Another man, with his own unique party trick, would lie under the front feet of an enormous bull, its horns and body ornately painted and jangling with fluorescent tassels and bells, with its whole weight on the man's chest!

It wasn't until the early hours of the morning that I felt the presence. I had climbed down from my hut to go to the dance floor, and as I approached I felt as if I was about to be vacuumed up. The suction was so intense I knew if I went any further, I would be unable to turn back. People were skipping excitedly past me, throwing themselves into what felt to me like a black hole. I had no idea what was happening. I'd never experienced anything like this before. It was incredibly seductive and persuasive, and while I could feel myself being enticed, I also felt repelled. It whispered to me in soft and sensual tones of love that were hypnotic and sickening all at the same time.

I remember thinking that all the aspects of myself that I treasure—my kindness and compassion, my love and gentleness—were all the things I would have to let go of to become a part of what was unfolding here. That price was one I was not willing to pay. It was in that moment, when I turned my back on the party, that I felt terror and if I'd ever thought I'd been terrified before, I had been wrong. Those vile and hateful people that I had met since arriving in Goa were mere soldiers of a force so black, so creeping and loathsome and vile, I felt utterly sick it had seen me. Because I had turned to walk away, I had become its focus, and there were no escapees here.

I had no logical explanation for the events of that night. I tried a few times in the morning to communicate what I'd felt with people I knew, but it sounded mad, even to me, and I soon gave up. For several days after the party I felt paranoid something bad was going to happen to me, but nothing did. Maybe it HAD been my imagination. On the surface everything looked like paradise, the ocean sparkled in the sun, the days were balmy and bright. Was I going mad? Everyone else was having fun! No one else I spoke to had felt the darkness luring people into its folds, tempting them with its vices. I tried over and over again to convince myself I'd imagined it, but I couldn't. I knew, I felt it in my body; something had happened at that party that masked itself in pleasure and fun, yet felt evil—and evil was a word I had only begun to use since arriving in Goa.

Was it weaving its spell on me? I convinced myself that I simply wanted to understand what it was and if I was fooling myself, I was unaware. Whatever the reason, I sought it out. I had this incredible curiosity and maybe an innate knowing that once I learnt to stand in my own light everywhere, anywhere, even in total darkness, I'd be free.

I went to the next party with Col. I wanted to see if it would happen again. We were sitting on one of the chai mats, once again soaking up the visual display. We chatted occasionally but mostly sat silent. All around the dance floor was darkness, and as my eyes adjusted I noticed an Indian man squatting on a low branch of a small, wizened tree that reached out towards the dance floor. He was poised like a leopard ready to pounce on its prey. The more I looked, the more men I saw creeping around in the shadows, waiting for people to lose themselves in the party, and, even if it was just for a moment, to forget they were in India and prey to such hungry, desperate men. Then something very strange happened.

Col and I suddenly found we were both crouched down so close to the ground that our heads were almost on the mat! It was a position no one would have assumed naturally unless they were trying to hear the sounds of beetles in their burrows or listen to what the earthworms had to say. Our bodies were responding to a force we were completely unaware of.

'What the fuck,' Col said, looking at me sideways with his head on the ground. It was then the words of the music registered: *You are under control, you are under control, pull the trigger, pull the trigger.* On and on it went, over and over. Whilst I still didn't have any answers that explained what was happening in these parties, I didn't doubt that in some of them, people were being manipulated in dark ways. It wasn't until several years later that a Romany gypsy, who was an elder and witch, helped me understand not only why I had been so perceptive to this energy, but what was really going on. But I'll tell you about that later.

Those initial few weeks were very lonely for me. I had asked a few people I trusted if they had felt the dark energy at the parties, and they had said no. Not every party was like it. Some were so beautiful they awakened love on every level, and the journey they took you on throughout the night until sunrise dipped deep into the divine. But I found these to be rare.

Even though Col had experienced the strange way our bodies responded that night, he put it down to imagination. About six weeks passed before I began to hear other people say they felt like their heads were being messed around with. They felt paranoid and worried they were losing the plot or had taken too many drugs! The drugs were definitely an element of vulnerability, and one of my greatest concerns about people being manipulated. Drugs made it so easy; every barrier was down. Many people arrived in India, straight off the plane from Europe, thinking they had landed in some idyllic tropical beach paradise (which in many ways they had). They threw themselves into partying and drugs with no awareness of their vulnerability. There were so many predators and to them these ignorant people were fodder.

During the day in my beach paradise, it was often easy to forget the currents that prevailed during the nights. I felt, though, that something always simmered just below the surface, and the longer I stayed, the more sinister it got. I had learnt basic protection like how to cast a circle and bring up my shields, but here in India I found myself weakened. I often felt directly in the line of attack. There were too many times I dropped to my knees and repeated over and over, 'I know no fear; I know only love. I know no fear; I know only love.'

Once, after not going out at night for several weeks, I was coaxed to a small party, reassured that the people holding it were loving and kind. They were, but in the early hours of the morning it was invaded by people I can only call vampires. They fed on people's fears, and the hungrier they were, the more horrific the deeds they would do to ignite fear. These people were the opposite of Love and nothing to them was sacred. I found myself in a circle of three, arms around each other, shields up repeating the mantra over and over,

'I know no fear; I know only love.' It was a long time before I felt safe to go out at night again. I had seen enough to know this was not the world I chose to inhabit, and why put myself in harm's way?

But the damage had already been done and my whole immune system was weakened. I caught golden staph virus and every little mosquito bite, every cut, every little nick in the surface of my skin got infected. I tried everything I could think of and nothing got rid of it. I even got the help of a kind Indian woman, Marta, who knew I had lost all my money and mothered me as if I was her own.

Every morning Marta got up at the crack of dawn to bake her delicious banana breads and cakes that she sold to the tourists on the beach. One particular morning, I was standing outside my hut with a few others. We had lit a fire and were standing around it, laughing and being silly, completely removed from the struggles of the people whose lives we had briefly inhabited. When

Marta turned up, she suddenly broke down crying. Between sobs she told us her children had been sent to live with her sister because she couldn't afford to feed them. My beautiful Californian surfie friend, Flash, who is all heart, went over and put his arm around her and reassured her it would be okay. It was a very sobering moment and I felt quite ashamed. Marta had been coming to the beach for a long time, yet none of us really knew her. How could we tell her it would be okay, and how could we even create a bridge that would help us understand how doing everything she could was still not enough? I was appalled at the decadence of my own reflection; I lived on the surface like a tick!

I know how easy it is to get disillusioned with people in India. Some people can be very cunning. You think they are being kind to you when, actually, they have one thing on their mind, and that's parting you from your money. A dear friend of mine was completely taken in by a family. They had welcomed her, embraced her as their own and cooked for her. She had been so moved that she had even given the mother her own deceased mother's gold wedding ring! She'd showered them with gifts, yet when she went to say goodbye for the last time, they turned on her like rats chewing at her flesh. They jabbed at her with their fingers and blocked her as she tried to leave. All they had wanted was her money and they would not let her go until she paid the *baksheesh* that they said she owed them. She broke down crying when she told me.

She had given them the one thing she treasured, and it was much too late to get it back.

I knew Marta, however, was different. I didn't have anything of value I could give her, but I knew that when I could, I would do everything to help her get her children back. Of course, I didn't tell her this; I didn't want to make promises until I knew how I could honour them. But that was not the only reason. I valued that our relationship was not built on cash.

Every morning she sought me out. Sometimes I'd wake up and she would be sitting by my side, a hand gently and lovingly resting on me. She fussed around me like a clucky hen and always turned up in the most unexpected places. I had no idea how she found me. I'd be at a market or on the beach and she'd come walking towards me, scolding me as she waggled her head from side to side. 'Where have you been? I've been looking everywhere for you. I have your dinner. Now sit down.' And she would begin to open her stainless steel canisters of rice with roti breads and make me sit on the ground like a naughty child and eat. It was simple fare, but Marta shared everything she had. She had even brought me some medication to try to kill my staph virus.

I had been given so many different things from people to clear up that virus but nothing had helped; I was starting to feel desperate. As a last resort, I began to eat copious amounts of raw chillies and garlic and play hacky sack for hours, praying I'd sweat it out. Hacky sack had become my meditation and my discipline in staying centred. It's a game played with a small, soft ball and the aim is to keep it off the ground using everything but your arms and hands. It's usually played in a group, but I'd got so fed up trying to find people to play with, I began to practise by myself. When I stayed totally present, I danced with the ball. It was only when an outside thought passed through me that I would drop it. The more I practised the longer our dance became. There were times I forgot about the world completely. All that existed was me and my ball. I would say quietly to myself, in sync with my breath, 'Centre, centre, centre.' While I wasn't great at tricks, I could keep the ball in the air in a controlled way for over a hundred hits.

But however much I played and however much I sweated out those chillies and garlic, it didn't stop or even slow down the progress of my virus. I was a weeping, infected mess, and it was everywhere on my body, including my face. I knew I had to get out of Goa. There were too many psychic predators hanging around, and if I stayed, I would be really vulnerable. I had no resources left and my body needed a complete break. But in order to give it one, I had to take another leap of faith.

The money I had made from my hand-painted shirt had sustained me so far, but was now getting low. I had enough left for a train ticket and a night or two, and that was it. If there was one thing I had learnt in my time so far, it was that when I honour myself and go with what feels right, life always looks after me. As I booked my train ticket to Hampi, a temple town twelve hours away, I felt very vulnerable. Yet I also felt that I was once again back in my flow. My energy had fallen since I'd been sick, and I was desperate to rid myself of this virus. It had affected me on every level: my self-esteem, my trust in being looked after and my ability to cope. It was only when I decided to leave Goa that I realised how all the dark undercurrents had crept into my core and weakened me from within, not just emotionally but physically too.

Now it might seem crazy that with such little money I had booked to travel first class, but honestly, to sit twelve hours in a carriage that was so jam-packed full of people they were almost sitting on your lap was beyond me.

My previous journey on an Indian train had been hell even if it had contained one revelatory experience. When the train had finally pulled into the station, little Miss Polite that I was had been completely unprepared for the fight that ensued to board it. By the time I'd got on it, all that was left was squatting space in the aisle, already crammed with people. It was a ten-hour trip and the woman I was wedged up against was not making my life any easier. I was so thin at this time; the soles of my shoes took up more space than my bum. As I squatted I had my bag resting on my knees, which were wedged up against my chest. It wasn't possible for me to take up any less room and yet the huge woman next to me in her dirty beige sari with lots of rings in her nose was snarling aggressively at me, whilst jabbing me nastily in my side with her elbow. It really hurt. I had tried several times to reach out to her, but she wouldn't even look at me. There was nowhere I could go and I didn't know how I would survive the train trip being hurt like this.

After one particularly aggressive jab, which left me with a black bruise on my ribs, I stood up. I tapped her on the shoulder and pointed at the tiny bit of space my standing up had made available and offered it to her. I then took my woollen shawl and wrapped it around her shoulders and offered her my bottle of water. I placed my hand on my heart and as I looked directly into her eyes, I called her sister. There was nothing else she could attack me for; she had what she wanted, and I had nothing else to give.

I didn't expect what unfolded next. I simply hadn't the strength to fight her, surrender had seemed like my only choice and it was a powerful lesson for me on the path of least resistance. As she struggled to her feet she appeared to shrink in size, her head was down and she did not look at anyone as she squeezed her way through the tangled knot of passengers, out of our carriage and out of my life. She had let my shawl fall from her shoulders and it descended like a welcome mat in the space she had left for me. I had been on the edge of tears, I couldn't believe she had gone and those around me who had been watching the drama unfold cheered!

Yes, I had learnt a valuable lesson from my previous train trip but I was not prepared to travel squashed up in the intestines of an Indian train again. I wouldn't have been able to let my guard down for a second. There would be at least one person trying to extract from me the little of value I had left.

I'd had a tiny debate with myself over the rationale of this and came to the conclusion that my priority *had* to be looking after myself; so first class it was. As I climbed onto the train I could feel that something wonderful was about to happen. If I had lost my power, well, I was about to reclaim it.

Three

The Gods Must be Crazy

'What a beautiful shirt you're wearing. I love it.' I was sharing my plush, first class carriage with a German couple, and this was the first thing they said to me. I was wearing one of the three Lakshmi goddess t-shirts I'd been given to sell when I first lost my money. When I told them I had a couple of extra ones to sell, they were delighted. My mind flashed back to how I'd felt when I'd been handed the shirts. I was learning so much about observing my feelings and going with them—using them as a guide. I remembered that when I'd been given the shirts, I didn't feel a push to take them to the market to sell with my boots. I'd been aware that the timing hadn't felt right; now I knew why. Even though I loved them, I had only just decided to keep one for myself and once again I was seeing how when I honoured me, everything flowed. It seemed verging on miraculous that my two remaining shirts were the perfect size for my keen customers, and when they paid me, they gave me extra cash.

As you can imagine, I was over the moon. As I thanked this couple I shared with them my story of how I'd had all my money stolen and the amazing journey of trust I was on. I was learning that when you truly let go and trust, you never have to ask for anything. Unlike some other travellers who had experienced bad luck in India, there were many in Goa begging or going round with hats and a sad story of how everything they owned had been lost or stolen. They looked hungry and pathetic as they pleaded with others to give them money so they could eat. They were doing 'poor me' fabulously well, and while I certainly could relate to their plight and how desperate that situation had the potential to make you feel, there was another way, and I was loving finding it.

Everywhere I went in India I carried a water pistol. I'd found it so challenging dealing with all the tiny children that came towards me with big, sad faces and their grubby palms outstretched to beg. I couldn't give them money and even if I had it, I couldn't have fed them all. But I knew there had to be some other way I could transform this experience, not just for me, but also for them. When I came across the most amazing shop that sold ONLY water pistols, I knew I'd found a wonderful solution. They came in every shape and form. There were animals, deities and angels, and birds of every kind. I was in water pistol heaven and it took me ages to choose, but I finally selected a white dove.

I'd had so much fun since I'd bought it. Children would approach me in the usual way, their palms outstretched begging, some of them were so tiny, barely more than toddlers and yet they all knew the word 'rupee'. The look of surprise on their faces when I gave them an unexpected squirt from my water pistol was so funny. It took a moment for them to get over the shock and then their faces would light up with a huge smile and before you knew it, I would have a crowd of little children screaming with laughter, playing as all children should as I chased them with my water pistol. It wasn't just them having fun; I was too. There would be screeches of laughter every time the train pulled into a station. The kids would run over to my window begging for money and instead they'd get the unexpected squirt. My white dove water pistol was one of the best investments I ever made!

Playing with the kids on the train trip to Hampi was so rejuvenating I soon began to feel so much lighter and the closer I got to Hampi the happier I felt. This was always a sign that I was doing the right thing.

After a final leg of the journey in a rickety old bus full of people with their chickens and pigs, I arrived in Hampi. I now had enough money to last for a week or two and I couldn't have felt richer. As the sun went down over this ruined temple town, once a thriving city, I took a steep climb to the top of a hill to observe what was to be my new home. I sat on a huge boulder feeling happy, and looked out over this ancient, crumpled town that existed in the midst of a landscape of big round boulders and rocky outcrops, with a wide river snaking its way through the valley. In the last rays of the setting sun everything glowed like molten lead, even me. I could hear the sounds of bells and monkeys and people's voices, and the wafts of spice, incense and jasmine made the air pungent and intoxicating to breathe. I could not imagine how my day could get any better when a one-legged holy man hopped over, settled down beside me and began to open his stainless steel canteen full of absolutely divine Indian cuisine and offered it to me!

When night came I opted for the cheapest accommodation I could find, and not because of the price. Sleeping on the roof of any building, outside, under the stars, with the streets of India smoking and chanting around me, was always preferable to a flea bitten, dingy old room. I woke the first morning to see the wild monkeys sneaking amongst the other sleeping travellers who shared my boudoir, looking for things they could steal. I soon learnt to sleep with my bag under my head. They were so sneaky, they crept around like cat burglars and I saw one pull a bottle from someone's bag then run to the edge of the roof and dangle it over the edge. It sat for a long time debating whether or not to drop it, and then it did. It sat peering over the edge watching that bottle fall the two storeys to the street below where it exploded. Monkey mayhem.

There was so much to explore in Hampi. I walked for miles alongside the Tungabhadra River, seeing water buffalo, with only their heads poking out of the water, being scrubbed with a coarse brush by men standing on their backs. I sat for a long time watching the circular woven boats that looked like a huge basket being paddled down the river, and I cut through terraced fields of crops growing on a hillside, lush and green.

I found myself following a small, well-worn track that wound up and over some boulders and came to a small, ruined temple with a sunken pond that had water and lilies in it. It was so serene and hypnotic I couldn't resist sitting down. I hadn't been there long when a holy man wearing saffron robes appeared and sat beside me. He had long, grey dreadlocks down to his bum and a beautiful radiant face. He told me through drawing in the dirt that he was over seventy years old. He was so lithe and youthful, it was hard to believe. It was only the wisdom and depth in his eyes that told me he spoke the truth.

He didn't speak English, so I pulled out my How to *Speak Kannada* book. After searching through it for something relevant to say and not finding anything, I finally settled on asking him how his elephant was. We laughed so much over that. We both knew we didn't need words to understand each other.

He beckoned me to be quiet, sat himself in the lotus position and began to meditate. Everything around us became more vivid. It was if I'd suddenly been plucked from the lower frequencies and I was soaring in his realm. I closed my eyes and let the bliss and stillness take me. This was exactly what I had come for, and if I needed another sign when I opened my eyes, it was there. A magnificent bird that looked as if it had flown in from paradise was sitting right beside him. It was only small, but its tail fanned out in the most brilliant blue; it didn't look real. Something very special was happening. I felt I'd found the person that, unknowingly, I'd actually come to see, and so for the next three weeks this holy man became my meditation buddy. I spent most of my nights sleeping on the roof with the monkeys, and every day with him.

When I showed him the sores that had become the bane of my life, he nodded, smiled and disappeared for ten minutes. When he came back, he was carrying a bowl of paste he'd made with dried turmeric and water. He began to plaster it all over my face and arms, and then gave it to me to finish the rest. While I certainly had a few reservations about my bright orange face, it worked! The following morning all of the infection had gone and my skin began to heal.

I was ecstatic!

I never knew what would happen in our days or where we would go. He naturally assumed I would follow him, and I did, which is something I rarely do. I have never comprehended following a musician, a movie star or a guru, but for these three weeks I was a well- behaved little lamb.

Many times I watched him tell stories to a large crowd, and while I couldn't understand them, I could see people held him in high esteem and listened to his every word. His tales were always theatrical. Sometimes his voice would disappear into a whisper and then there would be a long pause laden with intrigue before he spoke again. Then with a big unexpected boom he was back.

Once he took me to a temple in a cave, which was packed with people sitting patiently, waiting for something to begin. People spilled from the entrance and stood on tippy toes to get a better view, but since I was with a holy man, we were led towards the front where we plonked ourselves down on the ground.

I'm completely unable to give any logical explanation for what happened next. A wild-looking holy man, who looked as if he had the devil inside him, was leading everyone in praying and chanting. Periodically he would throw a hard, brown coconut at full force into the congregation. The only bonus to being at the front was that they all went over our heads, though I was constantly ducking, just in case. I found it quite terrifying. I had no idea when a new missile would be launched or if the people that fell to the ground wailing and screaming had been hit and needed help or were in the throes of holy rapture. It was a crazy world that was opening up to me through my holy man, but I loved every single second.

Once we were walking down the street when a very drunk and angry man came towards us. He was yelling and shouting, and as we approached he went up to my holy man's face and started screaming at him, with spittle spraying from his mouth. I have no idea what had upset him, but my holy man put his hands on each side of his face and kissed him long and slow on the lips. All the man's anger fell away and he began to cry. By choosing to love, my holy man had helped open a door for the angry man's pain to flow in tears.

Many times I saw my holy man transform situations like this that could have become nasty. For example, I saw a similar situation with an angry, drunk man who shouted in his face. This time, in mid-rant, he popped a sweet in the man's mouth. Every day with this gentle, loving man I was learning potent lessons about the power of love.

Over time I could feel the strength returning to my body. The infection had gone, and being away from Goa was like a breath of clear, fresh air. As much as I had tried, I failed to comprehend the party mentality. They were happening everywhere; at the top of mountains where holy men lived in isolation, on the banks of sacred rivers, and in the temples and the crypts. In response to this trend, almost every café and bar in almost every Indian town played doof music all day long. It did occur to me that I was a sour puss, unable to let myself go, and I may have been. But, really, it was much more than that.

I had seen donkeys worked so hard their sores had become a permanent, weeping mess. I had seen heavily pregnant women looking like skin and bones with huge, towering baskets of rocks on their heads, and children with their limbs twisted and broken, so young and yet the cloudy yellowness of their eyes told me they were already full of disease. I'd seen beggars grovelling in the filth of the streets, begging for money while their owners herded them on like sheep, jabbing them with a stick. If you're a feeling person like me, sensitive to the plights of others, poverty and despair slashes at your heart almost every minute of every day, unless you hide. I felt self-indulgent focusing on my pleasure, here.

I couldn't be part of the tribe. I was a loner and a fringe dweller, and while I'd certainly made a few close friends, it didn't give me any sense of belonging. I loved climbing mountains to meditate and washing in the river and drinking chai by the side of the road. I especially loved traipsing around in the dirt and the dust with my sadhu friend, whose eyes lit up with merriment and laughter every time he saw me.

Then Ollie joined us, and the harmony began to change, through no one's fault. Ollie was an overweight, red-headed German man who was gentle, kind and incredibly shy. When he arrived, he was wearing a Walkman. Well, when our holy man heard the sound of music leaking from the earphones, he wanted to listen. It was a The-God's-Must-Be-Crazy moment. But neither Ollie nor myself had any idea how destructive this little gadget was going to be.

Mr Holy Man would not give the Walkman back and wore it always. Even when we climbed up mountains to meditate, not once was it turned off. Our meditations were now distracted by the hissy sounds of Jimi Hendrix or Deep Purple. Ollie tried to reclaim his Walkman, but our holy man almost rugby-tackled him to get it back. I prayed the batteries would run out, but Ollie told me he'd only just replaced them.

Our sadhu had never heard music like this before or experienced a Walkman, so who could blame him. He listened not with judgement of good or bad but with childlike fascination of a new experience. Someone must have been supplying him with batteries because for the next couple of weeks, he never took it off his head. It didn't even appear to affect his meditations; it seemed as if he went as deep as before. But in other areas I began to notice a change in this old man who had lived a life of simple yogic discipline. He began to react to things out of frustration and impatience and was no longer the centred, loving being I had first met.

One day he took us around to meet another holy man who lived in one of the ancient temple ruins. He was sitting cross-legged on the ground, and Ollie and I couldn't believe it: he had a Walkman on too! We hadn't been there long when a third holy man joined them. We were told he lived as a hermit in the hills and only came to town once every couple of years. He was mesmerisingly beautiful, with the longest, lily- white beard and white dreadlocks that fell almost to the back of his knees. He shone like a lantern. The holy man we were visiting spoke good English and explained that the visitor was well past a hundred. He wasn't sure exactly how well past a hundred, but he settled roughly on a hundred and thirty!

The old holy man settled himself down on the ground before noticing the Walkmans. It was obvious by his outstretched hand that he wanted a go. The other two were shaking their heads vehemently, which only intrigued him more. He got back up and walked over to them and tried to tug the Walkman from our holy man, who put up a good fight. Before we knew it, there were three ancient and wise holy men rolling around in the dirt, fighting to either keep or get a Walkman. It was so shocking that my first reaction was to laugh; yet on so many levels it was tragic seeing my lovely, radiant holy man degenerate in such a short time.

Afterwards, Ollie and I thought long and hard about what had happened and could only conclude that until then, our holy man had only ever heard the sacred devotional music of India or a Bollywood- style pop song and certainly no heavy metal. I would be pretty unstable after five minutes of heavy metal, and our holy man had listened non-stop for a couple of weeks. We felt it had certainly derailed him.

It was a potent lesson in not only valuing the tests of life but also in discerning what influences we allow in. There had been times, sitting at the tops of mountains with my holy man, that I had thought how easy it would be to live in peace and stay connected to the divine in the simplicity of this life. There was nothing to bog you down. No worries about the overdue electricity bill; no working for a living; no shopping at the supermarket or even having to remember to put the wheelie bin out. On the surface my holy man appeared to wander through life as free as a bird. He didn't have to provide for himself in any way. When he was hungry, he was given food, and he slept wherever he was when he was tired.

He spent a lot of time in the lotus position, deep in meditation, and I had felt his connection with the divine and been moved by it. But I wanted to find that space within myself, despite the challenges of my modern life, and I knew for me that however much I felt I was learning in this ancient land where the gods and the goddesses were honoured and the sacred imbued every breath, where sexuality was not a dirty word but a temple art, the real test for me would come when I left India and returned to the West.

I knew it was time for me to leave Hampi. I felt nourished and renewed by my break but I could feel that a final initiation awaited me in Goa, and it was time to put all I'd learnt to the test. He had tears in his eyes as I kissed him goodbye, my crumpled little holy man. In only a few weeks he had become smaller, sadder and older. Our worlds had not collided without casualties. I prayed he would find his way again, but I didn't think it would be long before some other Westerners came along thinking they were doing good by giving their latest gadget away and upsetting the balance once again. I had already heard stories about the total disruption created when a holy man, and not a very stable one, had been given a knife.

As I pulled out the money to pay for my train ticket back, I realised I was once again dancing on the edge—I had not a single rupee left! Ollie was my travelling buddy on the trip and we were, of course, travelling first class! As the train was pulling out of the station, he reached over and gave me an envelope, telling me he'd been asked to give it to me when I was on the train, so I couldn't give it back. It was from the two German tourists who'd bought the t-shirts. They'd written me a note that said they had been so inspired by my trust that they wanted me to have the money enclosed. There was forty dollars (US).

I was speechless. Once again the universe had provided for me in a way that had been completely unexpected. I knew then that I could let go of apprehension and fear. There was not a remaining doubt in my mind that when we live totally from our hearts and honour what feels right in each moment, whatever we need will be there.

Four

The Day I Met God

Marta was so happy to see me back and immediately demanded that I sit down and eat. She looked diminished, as if life was slowly erasing her edges, and I feared that if it got much tougher, there would be nothing of her left, she'd simply fade away.

While she served me up some rice, tears rolled down her face as she told me she still hadn't gotten her children back. Her husband had gone somewhere to find work, so her lean-to of a home was empty of even love. I was simply a floating plank in an ocean for her to cling to, and I prayed I could make a difference and change the flow of this woman's life.

Broke or not, we travellers were incredibly self-indulgent. Marta got up in the middle of the night to start baking the cakes she sold, her price usually bargained down to a pittance by some decadent tourist who had no idea the rupees they saved to fritter away somewhere else meant a mother lost her children and those kids, their mum.

Now I have to say there were many people I came to love in Goa. I shared friendships that I carry like jewels to this day. We were all gathering the pieces of our lives and trying to make some sense of the madness. One dear friend was going cold turkey from smack addiction; another was struggling to come to terms with his mother who'd had a sex change when he was a kid and overnight had morphed into his dad. I made friends who were battling depression, and I was finally unveiling the good things about myself after six years that had only mirrored the bad. I shared intimately and deeply, but the stories of others are not mine to tell. While our paths wove together, other people didn't consume my life. A lot of the time I was on my own, but there were always people around if I needed them.

One morning I was visiting friends in their cane hut when a very excited Indian man, whose enthusiasm was brimming over like a waterfall, called in to see us. As his head bounced merrily from side to side he told us he had the most remarkable news. 'You won't believe it,' he said, 'but God will be visiting a town nearby this very afternoon and we must, at all costs, go and see him. He will solve all our problems.' We sat there looking astounded. It certainly was remarkable news. 'Abandon everything,' he continued. 'Go and find God; he will be waiting for you.'

Well, he convinced me and I couldn't let an opportunity like that pass. We were given scrawled instructions on how to get there, and my blue-eyed, gorgeous Californian surfie friend Flash, who had earned his nickname from bungee jumping in the nude, grabbed his bag and said he was coming too.

It took us several bumpy hours of travel before we arrived at a dusty little ramshackle town that—even though it was hosting God himself—I can't remember the name of! I got off the bus to complete sensory overload. I loved this country; I could sit in the dusty, rubbish-strewn streets of India for hours and hours, just watching life unfold around me in all its unexplained madness. Everywhere you looked there was something to mesmerise and it was no different here—except there was no time to either sit or catch a breath. A sea of people stretched as far as we could see in every direction, and they'd all come in the hope of seeing God.

I was hanging on to Flash so I didn't lose him. We were the only Westerners there and everyone wanted to claim us. Over-zealous devotees grabbed and pulled us in every direction, wanting to take us to meet their guru. We were taken to a small podium on a slight rise. Except for the very long queue, it would not have occurred to me that we'd arrived at God's place. On the podium was a steel hospital bed and propped up with pillows was a very frail old man. We were told he was a hundred and forty, and I didn't doubt it.

I never liked the opulent Western privilege of going straight to the front of a queue, but our Indian hijackers wouldn't listen to my objections and, pushing others out of the way to get us through, they urged us to tell God our problems and he would solve them all. Try as I might, I was unable to come up with even one. Flash on the other hand had a few things on his mind and began to explain them to God, who waved him aside mid-dialogue and said in a weak voice, 'Come back at five o'clock.'

I wasn't at all sure I wanted to stay that long. There was nowhere to sit and relax, and every minute we had to defend ourselves from some enthusiastic group of men who had something very important to show us and wouldn't take no for an answer. I didn't think I could take much more. When the transgender dancers, all jewelled and dazzling with their black, heavily kohl-smudged eyes and their elaborately sequined costumes danced up to us and sneered as they pushed their faces into mine, all I wanted was to get on a bus and head home. They had such dead, yellow eyes and their actions felt menacing. If their intention was to intimidate, they had succeeded.

There were so many times in India when I just had to remind myself to throw myself in and let the river take me, and this was definitely one such time. We were mobbed and were in the midst of a crowd that was determined to show us something. If we had known that this was Indian hospitality at its best, throwing ourselves in may have been a little easier. We found ourselves being swept along towards two long tents in a river of hospitality that split off into two tributaries as we were separated. I felt anxious leaving Flash, but I was assured we would meet again very soon. The tent I was pushed into was full of women either sitting, eating or walking around with huge pans of food, ladling it out onto banana leaf plates. They beckoned me to come and join them. I spent the next hour eating and laughing with women who were as fascinated by me as I was by them. They were horrified to learn that Flash wasn't my husband and at the grand old age of thirty-three I had neither husband nor children. Some of these women had been betrothed when they were twelve!

India was a man's world. Everywhere I travelled I saw women working in the fields, or on the roads breaking up rocks to make gravel. It wasn't unusual to see a heavily-pregnant woman carrying a huge metal bucket on her head, full of chips of stone, while the men would be sitting, smoking and drinking under a shady tree.

I'd even wondered how the women dealt with basic bodily needs as every chug of every train journey exposed yet another Indian man having a shit on the edge of the track. On the train trips that arrived in a town at sunrise there would be so many men alongside the tracks squatting to shit that it was commonly known as the 'dawn chorus'. But where did the women go? In six months I never saw a woman having a shit; and they certainly didn't have their own personal toilets. I could only surmise they rose in the dark so that no one would see them. A hard day's work and up early too!

It was impossible for these women not to be shocked at the indulgent and decadent life I lived, just as it was impossible for me to even begin to comprehend all the complexities that governed an Indian woman's life. But at least for a moment in time we all tried.

When I met up with Flash again we both felt so tired we decided to catch the bus back to Goa. But once again we were surrounded by men trying to take us in a different direction. They would not listen to a word we said, and I was beginning to feel quite desperate, when a midget of a holy man with a cheery garden gnome face beat everyone off with his trident and demanded we follow him. He seemed like the best option at the time, so we followed him like little lambs, certain we had been rescued and innocent of the fact that our saviour was actually a mini dictator.

The only consolation was that he took us to a walled garden full of flowers and apricot-robed holy men who sat smoking their chillums or lotus positioned in divine contemplation. It was a haven from the crowds outside and I thought I could finally relax, but I was wrong. Our holy man ordered us to smoke a chillum with him. It was the last thing I wanted to do. It appeared he was going to hit me with his trident if I went to say no, so to appease him, I agreed. I noticed some of the other holy men giving us pitying looks when we first entered the garden. It was an '*Oh Shiva, what poor suckers has he kidnapped now?*' kind of look. Now I understood why.

It didn't take us long to realise this holy man was not only a despot, but quite mad. Unfortunately, after only one chillum I was completely at his mercy. I lost any ability to negotiate basic physical tasks, like walking away fast, and I no longer had the capability to decipher what I wanted to do. His tyranny continued. We were force-fed chillums for the next hour or two and if we tried to resist, out came his three-pronged trident in a menacing way. If we hadn't had a prearranged appointment with God our chances of escape would have been remote. I have vague recollections of hearing shouting from outside the garden wall and several sadhus coming over to help us up while our holy man waved his trident and yelled at them. I felt as if I'd been lying bound up and gagged, and as I stood up I swayed, I felt quite dizzy. One man gave me some water, pretending he was splashing it over his face in a bid to get me to do the same.

I'm always so touched by the kindness of strangers, little insignificant moments that could pass unnoticed or be forgotten so easily. When he saw I was still having difficulty, he soaked a cloth in the water and held it up against my head. I found myself laughing when, with a wry grin, he pointed at our still fuming holy man and then at his own head. The universal language to express someone's mental instability was understood here, and while a couple of holy men held our despot back, others led us off to the knot of men who were ready and willing, and jolly excited, to be privileged to take us to see God.

This time he was in a big, beautiful, crumbling mansion, with faded paintwork and hot pink bougainvilleas. We were led with all the pomp of arriving at the gates of heaven, which in this case was a huge, old, carved front door that was opened only wide enough to allow Flash and me in. We were told to wait in a big room where several other families sat on the floor, wringing their hands in anticipation of meeting God. We sat for a time, watching one door open and shut as things and people went in and out: pitchers of water, steaming bedpans with wads of paper on top, piles of dirty linen replaced with fresh, until, finally, God's toilet regime was complete and we were guided in.

He sat this time on a throne of a chair and looked impatient and irritated to see us. If I'd had a problem, I wouldn't have wanted to share it with him. I'm certain that after our forced chillum session, Flash was still a long way from being anchored to his physical body, but he always did throw himself into life and didn't hold anything back. Yet even I was surprised when he approached God, bowed, then reached for his hand and kissed it.

Well, God looked as if he'd been given some deadly disease! For the rest of our session, the kissed hand dangled disdainfully at a distance from his body. It didn't occur to me why he'd been so horrified until much later on, when I found on several occasions Indian people gasping in horror because I was eating with the wrong hand. In this culture your left hand is your dirty hand, the one you use for the toilet, so why would you use the same hand you clean your bum with for eating food? It's just not done! While I was pretty certain Flash had kissed God's right hand, he may have held it with his left, and that would have been a huge faux pas. After we left the throne room, God would have conducted some sort of hygiene ritual for sure.

So even after a bad start, nothing was holding Flash back, and in his Californian drawl off he went: he didn't know whether to continue travelling or not; his parents wanted him to go home and finish college but he wasn't sure he was ready for that; he was trying to separate obligation from getting in touch with what felt right for him. He'd like to see Europe, but should he go now or after college? He felt confused about everything and went on and on and on. Finally, there was silence—on both sides. There was a long, painful pause before God spoke. 'You have no problem,' he said and dismissed us with an irritable flick of his un- kissed hand, the soiled one still dangling in the air.

We had waited a whole day to hear something we already knew. How could we not know it? We were surrounded by poverty. It was everywhere. There would have been people in that queue who were dying or riddled with disease; some would have been starving, living life in the gutters of despair. Meeting God would have meant everything to them and yet that privilege was frittered away on us. But I did not waste the lesson.

My 'Day I met God' gauge has served me well over many years. Whenever I think I have a problem, I imagine standing before God, his kissed hand still dangles and he still looks impatient—nothing has changed. I tell him what's on my mind and each time he dismisses it with his impatient wave. God puts everything into perspective!

We were escorted out of Gods Mansion, and as the front door opened to the rabble outside we found ourselves in a scene from Monty Python's *The Life of Brian*. Before us was a crowd of people as far as the eye could see and people were yelling questions at us, as if we had inside information.

'Will God be coming out again today?'

'What spirit do you find him in?'

'Will he be seeing anyone else today?'

We stood there telling the crowds he looked well-ish and we didn't think he would be coming out again that night and we thought he still had several families to see that were waiting inside.

We finally made it to the bus. Flash was a little contrite from his kissing God's hand and ranting on for so long—he couldn't understand what on earth made him do it. But he soon saw the funny side and we both laughed.

Personally, I blamed it on those chillums!

Five

Money is Just Like Love

A few weeks later I decided to catch the bus to Mapusa and do some shopping with the money I had left. Like all Indian towns it was hectic and at the end of the day, ready to go home and feeling totally worn out, I made my way to the bus stop. As I stood waiting for the bus I suddenly found myself with the option of taking two completely different choices and one of these, in my current financial situation, seemed rather radical, if not foolish.

On one side was the bus. Two rupees and three hours of crazy, bumpy, packed-like-sardines travel with distorted Bollywood music loud enough to burst an eardrum, and on the other side a taxi looking so sweetly serene it was almost purring. Seventy rupees and thirty minutes of comfort and I would be home. But I only had seventy-five rupees left and once that was gone I had nothing. I thought about it for a second and it didn't take longer than that. Once again I went with my feeling. That little taxi with its lace curtains and plastic roses decorating the dash was just too attractive to resist. As

I sat in the back, this conversation was running in my head:

'You're a fool.'

'No I am not; I'm honouring myself.'

'But you can't afford to; you've almost spent all of your money.'

'Yeah, but it's by honouring myself that I manifest money.'

That little voice just wanted to fill me with doubt and fear, and while I was trying not to listen, I did feel a little shaky about how exactly my next miracle would manifest. So what did I do then? That night, feeling I needed to get as close to the edge as I could, I spent my last five rupees on dinner and savoured every morsel!

When I woke up in the morning, it took me a few minutes to remember that I was once again completely broke. I sat there pondering what to do when as clear as a bell I heard a voice within say, *Go to the café as usual, Kye.*

The nearest café was a short walk away through the tall coconut palms that edged the beach. Built of cane, it was a haven for chocolate everything— porridge, pancakes, lassis and shakes—and most mornings it was where I went for breakfast. As I started to walk to the café I was full of doubt. It was only a two-minute walk, which didn't give much time for a miracle to manifest, and yet *voila*, one did. It absolutely, unbelievably did! I found a fifty-rupee note lying on the path! I was in India and I had found money lying on the ground right in front of me! What were the chances of that? This was a country where nothing of value went unnoticed and every tiny scrap of waste was recycled into something.

I was fast learning that money is energy, just like LOVE and it's attracted to us when we love ourselves and honour our needs as they arise. So often we hold on to money because of fear. Now I'm not suggesting that we become reckless with it but if the night before I had said to myself, I had better miss dinner even though I'm hungry because I only have five rupee left and if I spend it now I won't be able to buy breakfast, I would have been coming from fear and fear is what blocks the flow. I was learning in Goa to experience money in the same way I would an expression of love. If there was someone I really wanted to hug, it wouldn't occur to me to think I'd better not, I've already hugged several people today and I don't want my hugs to run out. When I treated my money in the same way, it never ran out and it always manifested miraculously just as I needed it.

I was feeling so empowered by everything I was learning I even began to venture into the shadowy realms of the night, but this time, I wasn't looking for anything, I was purely having fun. One evening there was a party on the beach outside a café. It had happened spontaneously and there wasn't a huge crowd, only about thirty people dancing on the grass, and I joined in. I felt so at one with the music as I danced; every beat pulsed through me as I entered another realm. I was the music and the music was me. There was no separation. I have no idea how long I danced for before I felt alarm—something was pulling me out of my trance.

It was hard for me to come back to the reality of my surrounds. I had thrown myself into the music and in doing so disconnected temporarily from the reality going on around me. Yet, when I needed to come back, some innate knowing had warned me and I was able to pull back. I realised then that when we embrace the moment, we are always aware and can sense danger before it comes. Over the years I've taken great comfort from this experience.

As I stood looking around, trying to figure out what it was that I'd felt, I became aware of what looked like a smoky thread trying to wrap itself around me. It was an energetic tentacle, and as I looked closer, I saw that there wasn't just one, there were many creeping their way around me, trying to ensnare me like a net. When I followed them to their source, they led to a man simmering in the shadows who was watching me with a gloating look on his face, certain he'd hooked his prey. I felt so enraged! How dare this man try to violate me. A powerful tidal wave of energy surged from the earth, up through my feet. Instinctively, I flicked my hands towards him and saw energy like electricity shoot out the tips of my fingers, race up the threads he'd been trying to wrap me in and hit him like a bolt of lightning. I even heard him scream. Hey, energy flows both ways!

In that moment I had no doubt that the most potent protection is a loving and gentle heart. When we live our lives in an honourable way, are kind and compassionate, there is nothing to fear and nothing to protect ourselves from because we have become our own bright light. As soon as darkness approaches light, it is not only transformed by it, but it can be seen for what it is. This is why I could see the snake- like threads of evil energy. Ultimate power comes from within and is the manifestation of a loving heart in action, but we have to give, honour and cherish our sacred self first. While I honour the rituals of protection where we invoke the Goddess as we cast our circle of salt or create mirrors for shields, quite honestly, if we cheat on our friends, betray those we love or shit on others to get to where we want to go, we leave our psychic doors wide open. We can create a walled circle of salt, even a tower out of the stuff, but if we are not living honourably or we are unwilling to bring our fears into the light and face them, any shadowy felon can wander in. We need to know this; we need to be aware that every action, however seemingly inconsequential has a consequence. The only natural protection we have is our innocence, but as soon as we are aware of the impact of our actions, we lose that shield.

Until my time in Goa I'd had the innocence of a meadow flower living in a field of poppies and clover with absolutely no idea that a conscious force of darkness existed, sucking everything vulnerable and willing into its black, hellish hole. It offered everything attractive on the physical realm—bodily pleasure, power, indulgence and decadence on every level. But it was all so short-lived and illusory, and it neglected to mention that there was a price to pay, and that price is devastation. Decadence soon turns to decay; indulgence to disease, and you might as well forget about peace of mind.

After this experience I wanted to leave Goa. People were breaking down all over the place. If they hadn't lost their money or their health, they'd lost their minds. While I felt I'd come through the whole experience pretty well, I did feel fragile. I'd lived in a cocoon for so long, and I felt as if I'd been broken down and reassembled so many times, I wasn't quite sure who I was anymore. The prospect of going back out into the world, dealing with real things like flights and stolen passports, did seem daunting, especially on my own. Even so, I could feel my time in Goa was coming to a close. My money, once again, had come to an end and I had no idea what sort of miracle would occur next.

I sat in my flimsy cane hut looking out over the ocean. It looked so beautiful, but like everything here, it was a double-edged sword with all the shit that went into it. You swam in the ocean at a cost, though most people, including me, did so. It was too hot not to.

I was sitting there trying to decide my next move and nothing was coming. No magical inner voice telling me with clarity what my next step would be. I was feeling a little lost. Then I heard a familiar voice call my name, a voice from the past. In the next breath of the sea air, there was Dan, my ex-partner, standing in the doorway of my hut. The past had come into my present.

I had lived each day for the last five months learning to love and trust in myself again. I wasn't the person I'd once been.

After all the predators I'd faced in Goa and blitzed with my own inner light, here stood my ultimate test.

Six

Cosmic Joke

I'd had an inkling Dan might turn up, but I'd hoped I would meet up with Tui first. Ah, beautiful gentle Tui. I haven't told you about him, have I? He was another reason for coming to India. I'd met him two months before I'd left for India. Some new friends, Tyler and Lucy, were going to a festival and they insisted I go with them. There was no debate, they would not take no for an answer. I was going with them to the festival and that was that. At the time I was recovering from a sickness that had had me hovering on the edge of death. Nothing that Dan and I shared nurtured well being. If I was going to get better, I had to get away, and the two new friends that had just entered my life were determined to make sure I did.

I wasn't aware until later how seriously ill I'd been. I simply existed in a reality that was much more elusive and less demanding than the physical one I'd left. I was drifting in a dreamlike vale beyond hurt and pain and if I so chose, one snip of the fragile cord that kept me hovering above my wasting body and I'd be gone. My life and the choice to live or die was the only control I felt I had left.

My demise into ill health had begun with a kidney infection. My doctor had been treating me each day at home with penicillin injections, but when I took a turn for the worst, he told me I would have to go into hospital as he could no longer treat me. In his opinion I had meningitis and could easily slip into a coma.

I vaguely remember asking him what they would do to me in hospital and him replying that they would give me a lumbar puncture and take fluid out of my spine. My friend and neighbour Jen was going to drive me to the hospital and was busy gathering things together for me to take when I told her I wasn't going. She was horrified and tried several times to get me to reconsider, but nothing would make me change my mind, and I was much too weak to explain.

I had not given up, I had woken up. It was in that very moment when my doctor told me the hospital would give me a lumbar puncture that something inside me yelled, 'ENOUGH!' I had lost my will to live *because* of all the pain. I had put myself through enough suffering and nothing would convince me to intentionally choose more—and having a lumbar puncture would be more pain. I did not think about death. It never even crossed my mind, but I could see on the shocked and teary faces of those that came to see me that it had. As I lay inside myself, wafer thin, I felt totally detached from the emotions of others, but I was finally back in my own orbit. Yes, I had skimmed death, but one thing had become crystal clear: I wanted to live—only this time it had to be happily. I didn't know how to create that, but I was damn well going to try. As soon as I acknowledged that to myself my temperature began to abate.

I was determined to end my relationship with Dan. He had never made this easy for me. Whenever I tried to leave, he would sob and plead with me, promising that things would change. I was always so easy to sway. Innocent me always wanting to believe the best, but the best never came.

Up until my illness, my desperately wounded self had prayed for help so many times, but it was always with conditions. The outcome always had to be some fairy tale scenario of Dan and I living happily ever after. Not anymore. I asked only to be shown the way to create a life for myself that I loved, and help came, and I don't think the people that gave it knew the impact it had. Truly, there were times when a few kind words from a stranger grew like an oak tree inside me, giving me much needed strength, and I don't know where I would have been without Tyler and Lucy.

They helped me make the break from Dan and when they insisted I go to the festival with them I had no idea I was about to step through a doorway that would reawaken love. I had so much respect for them. They faced each other in honesty and love and always with a willingness to grow and learn. To Tyler and Lucy their shadows were not a place to ignore but a treasure trove for growth. I could never have reached that depth with Dan, and to be honest, I wasn't there myself. I often found Tyler and Lucy, and their relationship, confronting. There was nothing hidden. You got it all, raw and unedited and real, and I wasn't willing to expose myself in that way ... yet!

I had tried to make a few feeble excuses about why I couldn't go to the festival, but neither of them would listen. I was going whether I liked it or not.

'You can even have a stall and sell your clothes there,' Lucy had cajoled. I couldn't help smiling when she told me with a cheeky grin that she'd already booked my spot. Lucy kept all her friends organised! 'You'll do really well there,' she'd said, 'Everyone loves your clothes.'

I had only just begun to create my own range of hand-dyed clothing to sell and it was proving to be really popular. Whilst I was hesitant about going to the festival the prospect of making some money was certainly enticing. If I had some cash, a few more doors would be opened and it would be easier to part from Dan.

The festival was several days' drive away on a beautiful property at Bellingen. Black bamboo grew in a tall, creaking forest on the edge of a wide river. Tents and tipis, marquis and stages had been erected for this week-long event. The whole place buzzed with energy and as soon as I jumped out of the car I felt light and free.

I had only been there a few hours when I saw two guys playing hacky sack and I asked if I could join in. Approaching strangers was something I would never normally have done. Moving completely out of the sphere I shared with Dan had instant results. All the love I had denied myself was suddenly showered upon me. I had stepped out of the stagnant and stinking mud and now swam in a crystal clear, lily-filled pool.

I was radiant at the simple pleasure of making two new friends. We tossed the ball around between us for an hour or two, chatting and laughing as we did before the game broke up and I found myself wandering around the festival with Tui, one of the guys. He was so tall and willowy, with huge, deeply mesmerising hazel eyes that sparkled joy. Everything about him was gentle and poetic; the grace with which he moved, his long fingers, the passionate way he spoke. When he looked at me, he gazed deep into my eyes and didn't need to fill the silence. He was unafraid to bare his soul or laugh at himself. I was hypnotised by this soulful bard.

We sat together that night sharing a fire. Just a vast, starry sky and us. The festival was happening all around us, but I didn't notice a thing. It was crisply cold and we were rugged up. Tui had previously told me there was something he wanted to ask me, then we started talking about something else and forgot. By the time it came up again. I was so lost in this man that nothing else existed.

'Oh, I remember,' he said, 'I wanted to ask you if you know a guy called Dan. He lives somewhere near you and people tell me I'm like him.' My mouth fell open in shock. This was the first time I had been even close to being romantic with anyone and here was Dan, thrusting himself in between us. I was almost two thousand kilometres away from him and he was still in my life!

It took me a while to answer. When I did, I explained who Dan was and told him I was leaving him and why. I also told Tui he was nothing like Dan unless being tall with long hair was the only criteria for being similar because that was where it ended. What was blossoming with Tui and I was so beautiful; Dan coming between us did little to hinder the flow. For the next three weeks I shared a love that put me back up on the throne of the Goddess. I felt beautiful. I emanated. Everything in my life flowed with grace and ease.

One freezing night Tui and I returned to his tent. The ground was stiff with frost. It was so cold we didn't even take our clothes off. After much struggling to get into our sleeping bags, I was finally comfortable and warm when it suddenly hit me. I couldn't remember arriving at Tui's tent with my purse. I had been selling my clothes for several days and it had over three thousand dollars in it. Our last call had been the chai tent, where we had sat outside on the mat huddled for warmth over our steaming cups. The last thing I wanted to do was to get up and go back out into the bitter night to find my purse. I felt so lulled by the snug and loving cocoon I was in I decided to leave it until the morning.

In the morning, Tui and I were sitting around the fire having a cuppa when I suddenly remembered my purse. I felt a slight panic. I had been so detached from its whereabouts and I ran back to the chai tent at top speed. The mats outside were crowded with people and yet when I went to where we'd sat, there was my purse, sitting on the ground, completely untouched. It felt as if it had a shield of love all around it. I felt ten foot tall as I picked up my purse and went to find Tui. I knew it was the miracle of love, and not the love for another. It was the love I was finally giving myself.

In that sacred space I was living in trust. I had allowed myself to be put down and denigrated for so many years; I had begun to believe all the terrible things I'd been told about myself were true. Yet the first opportunity I'd had to break free, life had rushed in to caress and love, cajole and care for me.

My time with Tui was coming to an end, and although I loved being with him, I was beginning to crave time for myself. I wasn't ready to be consumed by any love... yet. His ticket to India had already been booked by the time we met, and his flight was to take off in less than a week. He asked me to come to India with him.

I had to return home; there were things I had to do. I had three dogs that would need to be looked after, and I had to settle things with Dan. I told Tui I would think about it. He was going to be in India for six months, so there was plenty of time for me to join him.

One night I spoke with Dan on the phone, checking my dogs were okay and letting him know when I'd be home.

'You've had an affair, haven't you?' he accused. 'Yes,' I replied, 'and it's absolutely beautiful!'

I had never understood Dan's need to love in the shadows and then bury the evidence as if it was a crime scene. I had gone through hell over all his betrayals and had often felt like a victim of this abuse, but in many ways he denigrated the women he loved more than he did me. To be unworthy of acknowledgement to me seemed even more appalling than being cheated on.

Dan was so abusive on the phone, I hung up. I couldn't believe the hypocrisy of his rage. In all the years I had been with him, I had never had another lover. Anyway, what I shared with Tui was no betrayal; it was me finally breaking free.

The night before Tui left I asked him how I would find him if I decided to go to India. He cupped my face so gently and lovingly in his hands and looked at me. 'You'll hear me,' he replied, with absolutely no doubt. 'You will hear a voice deep within calling you, and it will be me.' I didn't doubt it for second.

A week later I arrived home. Dan had done everything he could to woo me back. The inside of the house had been painted, my kombi van was now a lovely bright purple, a colour I had wanted to paint it for a long time. Everything had been made perfect for my return. I was slightly alarmed to see Dan had set up a romantic dinner for two, outside under the stars, by the fire. I had made my feelings clear to him; as far as I was concerned the romantic aspect of our relationship was over. When I voiced this again, Dan flew into a rage and stormed off, leaving me sitting by the fire alone. I felt exasperated by his childishness and how could he be so hypocritical?

Dan's anger at me did not abate, and it wasn't until a day or two later that a woman who was staying at the house told me there was something I should know. 'Dan has been having an affair while you were away!'

It was so incredulous, I began to laugh. I couldn't believe it. Surely not? After the guilt trip he'd just put me through! Something inside me began to unravel. It was tragic and funny all at the same time. The cosmic joke had been on me. I was the crazy one, the mad woman and the fool. I could have left and been happy a long time ago. I fell onto the ground and laughed so much I had tears rolling down my face and an ache in my gut. When I got up, the phone rang. It was the travel agent ringing with the great news that I was no longer on a waiting list and now had a confirmed flight to India, leaving in two weeks. 'Tui,' I whispered, 'I'm coming.'

Seven

Come to Pushkar

Maybe I had imagined my relationship with Tui to be more than it was. I had come to India certain we would find each other, but as the weeks had rolled into months, I'd given up hope. For all I knew, Tui could have returned home to England.

I know it didn't make any sense, but I was happy to see Dan.

I remember a time just after we'd taken a break from each other. I looked him in the eyes and told him how difficult it was living with someone who did not value truth or honour. He said he was sorry. When I asked him how he saw me, I was astounded when he told me I was his rock. I felt at the time he was sincere in saying he was sorry, but he couldn't have meant it because he never changed. He still kept on lying and cheating. It may have been the only time I could say this about Dan, but when he arrived in Goa, he was my rock.

I had been through so much transformation. I had shed so many skins, and I didn't even recognise myself.

Having someone familiar turn up was exactly what I needed. We had spent so long apart it didn't occur to me that our past could sneak back in again.

I had disconnected from him physically a long time ago and I didn't intend to have a sexual relationship with him ever again. As far as I was concerned that aspect of our relationship was over. I was relieved to hear he was in a new relationship. The woman he'd had the affair with when I'd met Tui was now his partner and was even looking after our home and dogs while we were both away; a strange situation that had yet to show its darker side. I find it hard to believe that at the time, it simply had not even occurred to me that it would have a darker side. With everything I was learning I could still be incredibly naïve!

Dan had six hundred dollars that he owed me, so once again I was provided for. Finally, I had the funds to leave, but before I did so, I wanted to help Marta although I hadn't seen her for several weeks and I was worried. I had no idea where she lived. She had described her home as small and told me she was embarrassed by it. But despite my reassurances she had never invited me to visit. I had asked at all the cafés on the beach, but no one had seen her or knew where she lived. I prayed she would turn up before I left.

Like most new arrivals in Goa, Dan was enthralled and the last thing he wanted to do was leave. But I was desperate to go. I honestly couldn't take much more. All the dogs I'd come to know and love on the beach were dying of disease; there was madness everywhere. The party season was almost over and after several months of psychic predation there were many people—their life force sucked out of them— wandering around like zombies. It would soon be the wet season, when the heavy monsoon rains fell, and the whole place felt in dire need of that cleanse. With six months of people shitting everywhere, the whole place felt filthy. But I knew I couldn't demand that Dan leave right away. I had to make a compromise and reluctantly I agreed on three weeks.

Not long after, I took Dan to a party and somewhere during the night I lost him. The darkness had no power over me anymore, and while I spent the night at one with the music, dancing, Dan was having a totally different experience. When I found him in the early hours of the morning, he looked as if he'd gone through hell. He is usually immaculate in his appearance and I'd gone through years of frustration over how much time he spent on his hair. It was long and curly and every day he spent ages combing it through with his fingers—a big job as there was a lot of it. Then he would scrunch the ends in coconut oil. He is very tall and has a presence about him that makes people take notice. He was always stylishly dressed in well-cut linen shirts and pants. But when I saw him coming towards me, I almost didn't recognise him; he was dishevelled and white as a ghost.

Someone had certainly been having an energetic feed on him, and he was aware of it—he was freaked out. He wanted to leave Goa, not in three weeks but that very day. I was so relieved. I ran around saying goodbye to my companions of the last few months, promising to meet a few further down the track and asking people to keep looking for Marta as I desperately wanted her address, which, sadly, I never did find.

When Dan had arrived, I had moved from my small cane hut into a room we were to share with twin beds. Although at the time I was sad to leave the fragile little home that had been my haven for almost five months, I was ready for a little more indulgence, and a cold shower seemed like the epitome of luxury after five months of bucket washing at a well. Our new room was the middle one in a row of three.

The sun was just on the rise as we returned to pack up our belongings. Cockerels everywhere were crowing and pigs were snuffling around in the vegetation, gobbling greedily those early morning shits. As we approached the building we were staying in, we saw stuff strewn everywhere outside—clothing, books, bags, toothbrushes. It didn't take us long to realise it was ours. Not only had the door to our room been smashed open, our neighbours on each side had been locked in their rooms from the outside and were yelling to be let out. This freaked Dan out even more and it made me uncomfortable too. It was strange even for Indian thieves, who are usually a lot sneakier and far less crude.

We had nothing of worth amongst our possessions. The only thing I had left of any value was my camera, which was locked safely away with the family we rented the room from. The wannabe thieves must have been disappointed. After letting our neighbours out, we packed up quickly and made our way to the bus. I was finally leaving. My relief was tinged with sadness, not only because I was leaving without helping my dear friend Marta, but because I had learnt so much here. I would be eternally grateful for the gift of Goa. I had grown from an immature young woman into a 'warrioress', unafraid of the dark because she now knew the power of her own light. My body was fitter than it had ever been, exercised to perfection from playing hacky sack and all the nights spent dancing.

Tears rolled down my face as the bus pulled out, taking me away from one of the most amazing times of my life and on to my next adventure.

We were going to Pune, and I was excited. It had been the home of Osho up until his death in 1990. Now I realise Osho comes from a rather shady past. He was formerly known as Bhagwan Shree Rajneesh and was well known for his large collection of Rolls Royces.

While I was certainly curious about the intrigues of his Californian commune and the scandals that erupted, particularly in the '70s and '80s, after reading one of his books I simply had to set that all aside. For me his teachings resonated with truth, and I felt certain that the energy of his ashram would be a much-needed balm after the thumping, base-chakra thud of Goa.

At Pune we finally negotiated its madness, with its frantic traffic and polluted streets, and found ourselves a room to rent in the vicinity of the ashram. It was a cane shack on top of a shower block and the only way up was by a ladder. I felt worn out after the bus ride from Goa that had been so bumpy my kidneys were still weeping with pain. But I had to go and see the ashram; nothing would hold me back.

The road that led to the ashram was lined with stalls selling burgundy robes and dresses, the colours worn by sannyasins, the disciples of Osho. I bought myself a beautiful long embroidered dress and Dan got himself a kurta and some pants, which we changed into. I had never felt more ready for anything.

When we finally arrived at the ashram door, I felt as if I was at the gates of heaven. I was overflowing with joy to be there, so it was natural that I then felt slightly rejected when, in a business-like way, we were given a list of requirements that had to be fulfilled before we would be *allowed* to enter.

The first was an AIDS test! I struggled to get my head around that. It obviously meant that people with AIDS were unwelcome, and I couldn't help beginning to feel that the focus of this ashram was off-kilter for me. My mind flashed back to my experiences with sannyasins in Australia. I had met many back home and had several as friends. While I often enjoyed their company, I did find some of them a little arrogant.

They would say things like, 'You can always tell who isn't a sannyasin by their energy.' I had no doubt that was true, but while they saw themselves as being open and free, their energy to me often felt as if it was stuck in the region of their groin and had yet to blossom into the heart. And yet when I read Osho's words, the effect on my energy was totally different to that of the sannyasins I knew. I had been curious to visit the ashram because I wanted to understand how we got such different truths, and energies, from the same words.

I had one sannyasin friend I really respected and I bumped into him while I was in Pune. We had talked many times in Australia about freedom of sexual expression. I saw him take new lovers regularly, but it was never without a toll. Even though those women were sannyasins themselves, it caused a lot of grief.

It wasn't until many years later that he shared with me the results of three months spent in orgies with a large group of sannyasins who wanted to experience complete sexual freedom. By the end of that time all the women had suffered. Most broke down emotionally or found themselves in a very fragile state of mind, while one even committed suicide. This experience had drastically altered his attitude to sexual freedom.

My attraction to this ashram had been because of the change in consciousness I'd experienced through its teachings. The journey Osho led me on took me always to my heart, but the gates of his ashram, for me, did not radiate from that space— and that was hugely disappointing. But, we had come too far to give up! We went and got our AIDS tests, getting in queue with the hundred or so others awaiting their results, some nervously I'm sure.

Twenty-four hours later, with negative test results, we braved reception again. But, in my excitement, I'd forgotten to scroll down the list of entry requirements. We were told we now needed passport photos, and it was pointed out that my stolen passport was a problem. If I wanted to come in, I would have to go to Bombay and get a replacement from my embassy, the British Embassy.

Well, never one to be put off, I departed that night, catching the train to Bombay. I left Dan to work through the rest of the requirements. It took me three days, and all I could get in that time was a letter from the British Embassy clarifying who I was and stating that my passport application was being processed and my new passport would be ready in a couple of weeks. It was an official document, with a photo of me and I was certain they couldn't find fault with it.

It was such a relief to be back, even Pune seemed relatively sane after three days in the mayhem of Bombay. As I walked through the garden that led to our room, I was astonished to see that our room had completely disappeared! There was absolutely no sign of it. The shower block was still there, but there was nothing to suggest a cane hut had once stood on its roof. Had I imagined it? Maybe it was another shower block … I wandered around the gardens looking for our hut when a German woman I'd briefly met before I'd left for Bombay found me.

'Something has happened,' she said and quickly added reassuringly, 'but Dan's okay. He is at the doctors now. Your hut has burnt down; there was an electrical fault. Dan got out okay but dripping plastic from the roof fell on his back and burnt him.'

I was speechless and the full impact of what this meant did not hit me for a while. I finally tracked Dan down; he was miserable. His back had been cleaned up, but it was causing him a lot of pain. He couldn't even bear the weight of his shirt on it. I hadn't thought about my belongings until Dan told me they were all gone. The only possession of value I had left— the thing I had carried throughout my epic journey so far as if it were the Holy Grail—my beloved camera and about twenty rolls of shot film that captured all the splashes of splendour along the way, was gone.

I was gutted!

I couldn't help feeling the irony of finally getting my passport, only to lose everything else. The owners of the room gave us another room, free of charge, but were unprepared to offer anything else. I got the feeling they would have been happier if we'd left. They were uncomfortable with Dan sitting in the sun with his exposed back covered in burns. It was rather unsightly and not a great advertisement for them. They avoided us like the plague, which made it hard to stay within the confines of their hotel complex; yet we couldn't leave. There was no way Dan could sit on a bus.

Apart from my official British Embassy letter, everything we had acquired for entry into the ashram had been burnt. I felt incredibly low. I decided to go and speak with the gatekeepers in reception again. I showed them my official embassy document, which they said was not sufficient— only a passport would do.

As I spoke to them I had tears rolling down my face. 'Our AIDS test results have been lost in a fire and Dan has been badly burnt.'

All I needed in that moment was a hug, some kind and loving support. But in a clipped and cold voice the person at reception said, 'Your ego is obviously blocking you from getting in.'

I couldn't believe it. It took every ounce of my strength to stop myself from collapsing in a sobbing mess on the ground. I was worn out. I felt as if I'd already climbed a mountain to achieve acceptance into Osho's ashram and I still wasn't good enough.

'It's really convenient for you to place everything on me,' I cried. 'It frees you up totally from having to take any responsibility yourself. It doesn't take much to offer someone support, a hug, a cup of tea!'

I can't even begin to account for the logic that finally led them to give us a two-day pass into the ashram. Were all the reasons for which we had been excluded so far void because it was only two days? I don't know but there was no excitement left when the pearly gates finally opened—all my enthusiasm had gone. I could not connect with the place at all. I failed to comprehend how Osho's teachings could have been so misconstrued. The way we were treated at reception was only the tip of the iceberg of the strange and confusing interpretations and applications of Osho's words that I was to see in this ashram.

Osho's words had awakened a truth in me that I did not find within its walls. As newbies we were given the guided tour, and we soon realised how ridiculous it was to try asking any questions.

'Why are all the buildings painted black?' Answer: Because Osho requested it on such-and-such a date.

Every question I asked was answered with the same reply. Only the date was different. 'Because Osho said

...' 'Because Osho requested it.' No explanations as to the deeper reasons why. And I like to ask WHY! Why had I learnt from Osho to be my own master and to not blindly follow others like sheep? I could not fathom the place.

Once inside, Dan had taken his shirt off again. It was the only way his back would heal, and the only way to lessen the pain. But you could tell by the dirty looks we got that it was considered inappropriate— here in the land of sexual freedom. Life within the ashram was scrupulously clean and there were signs up everywhere reminding people to wash their hands. This was not a place for weeping sores, but Dan always liked to push the boundaries, and so did I, and quite frankly, I had moved beyond caring.

When Osho was alive, he would give regular discourses in the main hall. His big throne of a chair still sat up the front. I had no idea what to expect as we sat in the audience in front of this throne, waiting in anticipation with hundreds of others. Nothing could have prepared me.

A movie screen dropped down in front of his chair and everyone around us started chanting, 'Osho, Osho, Osho.' I love my sannyasin friends but I found this downright weird! I can only think that Osho must be having the biggest belly laugh wherever he is, or maybe he is bawling his eyes out that they got it all so very wrong. His teachings transcend our limitations; they shouldn't turn us into ants, wearing the same uniform, signing up for a new name that comes in the post, keeping us trapped within the thick walls of our limitations. His teachings can be practised by freethinking, rule-breaking and slightly unpredictable individuals like myself.

I did hear an interesting story later on my travels. A friend of a friend, whom I'd met once and vividly remembered because of his dynamic presence, visited the ashram. Just as everyone was settling in the main hall, all ready for the next DVD of a previous Osho discourse, Tom felt an overwhelming desire to sit in Osho's chair, which he did. Talk about a rebel. Several sannyasins, alarmed by this deviation from the norm, bustled over and asked him to get out, which he wasn't quite ready to do. Tom said they hovered around him not knowing what to do. They didn't want to openly use force to remove him, but they were flustered. This was breaking the rules and completely out of the norm, something they hadn't experienced, and they didn't know how to deal with it.

I reckon the Osho that I loved would have applauded this; he would have jumped up and down with excitement that someone had finally got it and broken free. Hallelujah!

There is no doubt that Osho's ashram was a sublimely beautiful place to be, and I am certain that many courses transformed people's lives for the better. There were many layers to the experience of the place and while I'm aware that mine barely tapped the surface, it was not energetically welcoming to me, and that simply told me it was not my path. The questions that I had hoped would be answered, remained, and if anything, I was left with more. How can one person teach free thought and free expression and have so many followers? It was something I couldn't understand.

It was about this time that Dan got some unexpected news. His girlfriend, who was looking after our home, was pregnant. He looked hesitant when he told me. I think we both felt a little sad, but it was very fleeting. We recognised that there was no going back; our relationship as we knew it was over. I cried a little, but I didn't want Dan back. He was much better as a friend than a lover, and I didn't envy his new partner. I couldn't see that her path with him would be any less treacherous, and she would have a baby to deal with too.

I told Dan to give her my congratulations and tell her to relax; I was more than willing to share my lovely home. It was naïve of me. I didn't think things through at the time, and I wasn't aware of how threatened Sheila felt by me. I simply thought I could create my own space in the sleep-out, give Dan and Sheila the house, and maybe have the best of everything—Dan as a friend and a sister to live and share with too. Of course nothing was to work out that way.

Why was I still with Dan? In many ways we were very similar. We jogged along together like an old married couple. There was a certain element of comfort in being with him. He was funny and always did crazy things that made me laugh. We'd shared many adventures together, from our three-week holiday in Portugal where we travelled from England all the way through Europe, hiding in trains—in the baggage holders, the food hatches, the toilets, under seats—sometimes for over eight hours, until finally we reached the silver coast ... to hitchhiking around New Zealand and staying with all sorts of quirky and wonderful people.

The wounds I'd experienced in the past with him had faded since my time in Goa. I didn't have the same expectations of him, and I didn't care who he loved. That changed the whole essence of what we shared.

Dan was the epitome of a Gemini carrying the knowledge of good and the knowledge of evil, and he swung like a pendulum between the two. When in his good side, he was a charismatic leader, wise and full of fun, gathering people together to meditate and chant or making up instant songs about someone he'd just met and playing them on his guitar. But there had been times I'd seen him as the devil in disguise. While many adored him for his light, in the past he would save his dark side for me. There were times he could be cold and menacing and cruel, and other times he was a lost little boy or a greedy and spoilt one that wanted everything his own way.

But he didn't have the same power over me anymore. I had flown my cage and I didn't give the petulant little boy any energy, so I didn't see him. We were getting on well, though I have to admit to feeling some frustration at times. Well, okay, rather a lot!

For the last five months I'd been totally going with my flow, and now I was stuck in Pune in a place I didn't feel welcome. Every time the owners of the guest house we were staying in saw us they would feel guilty and either run the opposite way or ignore us. We couldn't even get them to serve us a drink! It was stiflingly sticky and hot. I was so over the entire ashram thing, but I couldn't leave because of Dan's burns on his back—and I wanted to leave so badly.

I wasn't just feeling like leaving; I *knew* where I had to go—Pushkar. In fact, I began to obsess about going to

Pushkar; I couldn't stop thinking about it. Every moment I was held back from going was torture, like an awful itch you can't scratch. I paced back and forth with frustration, asking poor Dan hourly if his back felt ready for travel.

'We have to go to Pushkar,' I said, raving like a madwoman. I was *in love* with the word 'Pushkar'. I kept saying it over and over again, certain that Dan would be just as thrilled and excited by it as me, which of course he wasn't.

'Dan, listen, P-U-S-H-K-A-R,' I whispered again. 'Can you hear it calling?'

Dan just shook his head, looking puzzled by my obsession.

It was five long arduous days before we made it to the bus, and I was dizzy with joy. I was finally in my flow again. Pushkar. It whispered my name with every beat of my heart. I felt waves of energy surging through me, joy bubbling like a brook inside. Now, the reason for this gushing of energy, this Niagara Falls of a charge, I kept to myself. You see, I'm pretty slow sometimes at putting two and two together, but finally I had gotten it. I knew why I was so excited at the prospect of Pushkar. But I couldn't share this precious knowing with Dan, not yet anyway. I knew, and I shivered in anticipation.

Tui was there and he was calling me.

Eight
The Space Beyond Asking

You won't believe this, but after all that bottled-up excitement at the thought of seeing Tui, when I did finally see him, I pretended I hadn't seen him at all—I walked past looking the other way!

Dan and I had been in Pushkar long enough to rent a room and take a cold bucket shower at the well. Afterwards, I ran out into the busy street feeling like a fish caught on a line, being reeled in. Dan followed along behind me. There was nothing I could do, I couldn't fight it. The force of it was much too strong. Wherever Tui was, he felt close.

There was a carnival filling up the narrow street and bustling up the sides. This was no quaint little procession in an English country town. Imagine the percussive beat of hundreds of men drumming, an entourage of old trucks revving, hooting and blowing smoke, driving down a street that was barely wide enough, carrying giant, gaudy effigies of gods and goddesses garlanded with flowers, with eunuchs standing like guardians of the gods, haughty and disdainful. There were men singing, an endless procession of white, prancing horses and finally, as an afterthought, one smoky old truck with a piano on the back and a full load of men drumming and singing temple songs.

It was a spectacle that swept me up and left me standing breathless, waiting for the dust to settle again. When it did, I saw him. He was walking towards me, taller than everyone else. He always stood above the crowd. I felt vulnerable, I felt scared. I had Dan with me; how would that look? After all the time I'd spent dreaming of this moment, I carried on as if I hadn't seen him, but I knew he had seen me. I could feel him struggling to break free of the rip he was in, to turn and come up behind me, softly calling my name.

When I turned around, he was looking at me with the cheekiest grin, and as he waggled his finger at me, he said, 'I've been here for two weeks, and every day I've been calling out, Kye come to Pushkar, Kye come to Pushkar.'

It was strange introducing Dan, trying to make it clear to Tui that we were only travelling as friends. It was strange feeling romantic towards someone else with Dan there, and I knew it must have been challenging for Dan. Tui had helped me break the tangled, rusty chain that bound me to him.

I spent that first night with Tui in a space of so much love, it was only the day after that I found myself stuck in the middle of two men, and while Tui wasn't being difficult, Dan was. He could be really belligerent and superior if he wanted to be, and he did not like Tui. Of course he didn't like him. I should have predicted that.

When Tui asked me to get a room with him, I leapt at the offer. It was just what we needed—time on our own. We found a small and clean white-washed room on the first floor. I arrived with my bag just when a huge fight broke out between some men in the courtyards below. I'd only spent three weeks with Tui previously in Australia, so I was still getting to know him. We had honeymooned together, that was all. I had no idea what he was up to when he suddenly ran from the room. Then I heard the loudest, ear-piercing scream. When I looked out of the window, it was Tui and he was standing in the middle of the mob with everyone staring at him, mouths hanging open in astonishment. He had broken up the fight with a big scream, and then he sent the troublemakers home. Peace in the courtyard was restored.

In the time I'd been in India, I'd experienced many occasions when groups of men had begun socialising civilly, only to see it end up in a brawl. Each weekend families had gathered in front of my old hut in Goa for a picnic. The women would prepare the food while the men played cricket. It had gotten to the stage where we Westerners who lived on the beach would say with a wink to one another, 'Won't be long before they have their first blue.' Without fail, one of the men would get upset at another then his friends would crowd around him. Then they would go and talk to the man he was upset with, who had his friends backing him up, then two men in the same group would get upset with each other and they would begin to fight while others tried to hold them back. There were constant groups of men breaking off from each other and changing sides. They were like children and it appeared that the picnic was not a success unless they'd had a mini riot.

It was hard to know if there was stuff festering below the surface that burst out each time the family gathered or was it just too much testosterone? There were very few outlets for a young man's sexuality because women were kept hidden away until they were married.

Whatever the reason, I had total admiration for Tui's novel and expressive way of dealing with it. When he came back into the room, I was laughing. I had only just arrived when he had run from the room, and was yet to unpack. I expected Tui to be happy to see me. But instead I suddenly found he was really distant and was looking at me in such a way that I felt like I was a pile of dirty washing. It was as if he really didn't want me there. I was confused.

He invited me; I thought it was what he wanted.

I didn't say much. I just sat there for a while, trying to get a grip on what was happening. It was undeniable that there had been an incredibly strong, magnetic pull between us, so what was going on? It just seemed to have disappeared. Suddenly Tui said he was going out and he would meet me later at the café. Then he walked out. We had been together less than two days and it seemed I had already been delegated to the realm of the mundane.

I have come to realise in my life that every single time I have expectations, something completely different happens. Always. I have no idea where the beautiful love that had enveloped us when we spent those first few weeks together had gone, or what went wrong, but it had just fizzled out.

Well, after everything I'd gone through, after all I'd learnt about honour and love, there was no way I was going to accept this situation. I picked up my bag and left our little room. I had no idea where I was going, but as I strode out of Tui's room I felt that once again I had reconnected with my flow. How easy it was to lose it! I walked out into the narrow streets, radiant from being on my own again. When I came to a sign for a room to rent, I knocked on the door and was guided to the most magical room I had ever seen. Dried flowers hung from the ceiling and on one wall was a huge pencil drawing of Shiva. The detail in it was exquisite. The whitewashed floor was covered in sacred symbols and two beautifully arched windows looked out onto a flowered terrace where some monkeys played. I had landed in my own little temple.

Once again I'd been brave enough to trust and life had looked after me. But it only seemed to do it when I valued myself before everyone else. I was the centre of my own universe, and when I radiated from that space, the sacredness of life opened up. I'd spent the last few days trying to keep Dan happy and trying to fathom Tui, all of which had really pulled me down.

The truth was there would be no happily-ever-after with Dan, not as lovers and not as friends, at least not for a long time yet. There was too much crap wedged between us for me to ever feel the flow with him. It was like trying to make a nice fresh pot of tea with a well-used bag—all the flavour had gone. I had compromised myself when I'd let him back in, and maybe that's why Tui had turned away. But who knows? Perhaps he thought I'd been weak. Without the ability to speak and express ourselves honestly with another, I'd only be guessing. The bottom line was the reason didn't matter. It was my choice if I wanted to be the best that I could be in each moment. I didn't need to fill my head with ifs and buts and whys.

Was I happy? Did I feel joy? These are not selfish things to get in touch with; if anything, it's selfish not to. I can only give the best of who I am when I am the best I can be.

Goa had given me a priceless gift: the chance to unhinge myself from normal reality, with its stresses and strains that often force us to think and plan ahead, or mull over what's already been. I had experienced for myself the constant miracles that can occur when we live truly in each moment.

Everything I had learnt up until this time had shown me the value of 'ask and you shall receive', and while there are many influences that can make that simple philosophy inactive, from low self-esteem to living dishonourably, what I had experienced now went way beyond that. I had experienced the space beyond asking. When we live in the now, there is nothing to ask for, everything is already there. To ask for something is projecting a future need and detaching ourselves from the sacred flow of the now.

As I walked through the streets of Pushkar I passed several holy men robed in apricot carrying big red tridents. The pungent aroma of two huge, black billy goats mingled with the incense that wafted from the offerings left around the holy lake. I felt I had grown; I stood taller, bigger and shone brighter. I felt like a sacred chalice filled to overflowing. Even the people walking in front of me turned around to have a look, and those that were walking towards me parted to let me through. I was aware of everything.

I passed the sacred lake in the centre of town. There were many touts pestering tourists to sign up for some package deal—a dunk in the town's holy water followed by a camel ride through the desert—or maybe it was the other way around. But even they left me alone. There were dogs and donkeys and raucous monkeys that cavorted from roof to roof and swung down to earth to tease the dogs or grab a mouthful of food from some unsuspecting tourist sitting outside a café.

As I walked to meet Tui at the café—as arranged before I left—I had never felt more blissed out in my life. Every cell in my body was beaming. In the distance I could see a man coming towards me who looked as if he'd rowed ashore in a dugout canoe from some tropical island. Long hair, muscled and brown—he was beautiful. Did he have a garland of frangipanis around his neck, or did I just imagine that? When he saw me coming towards him he began to exclaim,

'WOW, WOW and WOW.'

When I got closer, he took my hand, bowed and said, 'You look so incredibly beautiful.' And I felt it. But the beauty that emanated from me was so much more than mere me, and I'm certain he recognised that. Our brief interlude on the streets of Pushkar was not lustful; it was a recognition of the Sacred within us both, within us all. We bowed in honour of each other, and then we passed on. I never saw this man again. Our meeting had been brief, yet glorious.

To have walked through the streets of Pushkar in such a holy and reverential way and to then land in the company of someone—Tui at the café—who didn't even notice me and seemed intent on focusing all his energy elsewhere, was just weird! When I told Tui that I'd left, it was only then he focused on me. He looked shocked.

'Why?'

Why? I didn't know what to make of this man; he had blown from hot to cold, without a single weather warning and he seemed unaware or unwilling to admit what he was doing. I wasn't one for games.

That night I sat on the steps at the edge of Pushkar's holy lake, watching all the lights of the town reflected in its waters. The bathing pilgrims had lit candles and made offerings of flowers that were floating like little boats in the water. I felt far away from the trials and tribulations of Tui and Dan. I felt at peace and wondered lightly what was next.

One evening, during my stay in Pushkar, I met a holy man who told me he was known as Hanuman Baba. He was tall and vibrant, very intelligent and spoke six languages fluently. There were four of us sitting in a circle with him. I could sense that he wanted to chat with me, but there was an Indian man sitting beside him who wouldn't stop talking and none of us could get a word in. I began to chat with an Irish man who told me he was about to visit Pune and he asked me if I'd been there. I answered a little vaguely at first, as my experience hadn't been the best, though I knew that what hadn't worked for me may for him. He sensed my reluctance to talk and urged me on. While I didn't share my personal experiences, I did share my confusion. I began to tell him how I couldn't make sense of what I'd seen. Osho teaches freedom and yet he has created all these followers.

All of a sudden Hanuman Baba broke away from the man that was still talking to him. Obviously he'd been listening to what I had to say.

'I was a disciple of Osho for twenty-two years,' he said.

Oh shit, now I've offended him. I asked him why he wasn't anymore.

'Because of everything you said,' he replied.

I was surprised, though pleasantly, I admit. I had felt so alone in my confusion about the ashram.

'How did it come to be like this?' I asked him.

'Because Osho never looked behind. He lived his life in each moment and didn't look back to see what people did with his words—and really it doesn't matter. When words are spoken in truth, they trigger a soul's journey to consciousness. While some don't need to be followers, others are doing exactly what they need to in order to wake up.'

'So the ashram is the perfect place for people to wake up, even if it's going in the opposite way to what Osho taught?' I asked.

'Exactly,' he replied.

This made sense to me and I liked it. It made me think of a meditation I'd done recently. I had found myself faced with two different paths up the mountain. One meandered around its edges. It was the sort of path you could saunter along, with no big challenges. You got to the top eventually, albeit somewhat slowly. While it was certainly beautiful, it didn't interest me at all. The path that captivated me was a short, steep, perilous climb that took me straight to the top. I certainly valued the directness of its route, but it was the challenge that excited me the most.

'There are so many different ways to reach the same place,' said Hanuman Baba. 'And what we seek outside of ourselves, always lies within! It took me twenty-two years before I recognised that the love I felt from Osho was simply the reflection of the love within me. I am Love and when I awakened to that divine truth I no longer needed to be a disciple; I had become my own master.'

I am Love, his words rang true in my heart and soul— it all resonated.

After some time, the Irish man left and Hanuman Baba settled himself down to sleep. He stretched out in the dirt, so totally free that nothing, not even a hard surface, came between him and a good night's sleep. The dark settled in comfortably around me like a loving blanket, and I sat mesmerised for a long time by the lights that still danced on the holy lake. On the edge of the lake sat a giant bull with huge, thrusting horns, chomping his cud rhythmically and staring, like me, into the reverie of the night. And as he chomped, I whispered to the night, I am Love, I am Love, I am Love, and I could feel my spirit soar.

The streets of Pushkar were snoring and farting as I crept nervously home to my temple room, wishing I'd done so when it was still light. All the tiny, open-fronted shops that lined the narrow streets had people sleeping in them. Life was being lived naked and bare. At one point, a man wearing baggy white underpants, scratching at his crotch, came running out in front of me and urinated like a dog pissing on a post. I don't think he'd even woken up; he didn't see me. I was so relieved when I finally arrived home safely to my little temple of a room and snuggled down to sleep.

I was enjoying being by myself again. Dan was still around and we planned to travel to the mountains together for a final few weeks before flying to England. He was spending a lot of time with a lovely young woman who asked me once why he blew so hot and cold. She couldn't make him out. It seemed that both my men, Dan and Tui, had the same tendency; maybe they were more similar than I thought.

I spent some time with Tui, which always left me feeling sombre. I had no idea why the magnetic pull between us had been so potent. I still felt it, but it was always with an awareness to let go of expectations. Whenever I connected with Tui, he was vague, distracted and slightly depressed, though I did wonder if that was because he shut himself down around me. He seemed different with other people. He was leaving India in a few days and I couldn't bullshit with him anymore. I was fed up with tiptoeing around this man, wondering what was going on.

'What the fuck's going on, Tui? What is our connection? I feel so drawn towards you, but when we meet there is nothing.'

Tui, whom I had loved for his truth, the honest way he lived, told me he had put me in a box and was afraid to open it!

'Give me a call,' he said, 'when you arrive in the UK.' Then he turned his back on me and left. I felt such sadness as I watched him walk away. I thought I felt okay about Tui leaving as our time together in Pushkar had been so disjointed, he no longer held that precious place in my heart. But I grieved for the loss of what we'd shared. And then I did something so stupid, and I don't know how it happened ...

I no longer even felt attracted to Dan, and I can't remember the moment when I opened up the door and let all the hell and suffering I thought I'd freed myself from, back in. But I did it; I fell right back into the arms of Dan.

I'd thought I was beyond it, that my own metamorphosis had been so total that nothing could lure me back to Dan's web again. I had been wrong. Being with him again, even as friends, strengthened the tiny thread that still connected us. I hadn't made the big cut, so our connection together grew again.

It was so easy for him to chip away at my confidence once again and to fill me with self-doubt. Why hadn't I expected it? He'd done it so many times to me before! Why didn't I just walk away? I asked myself the same thing over and over again. I could make the excuse that all my money was in travellers' cheques in *his* name but that doesn't carry any weight. I'd lived for the last five months without his money.

Once, I did run away from him. I grabbed my bag and jumped on the nearest leaving bus with only enough money to pay the fare, but by the time I'd fled, my wings had already been crushed and I didn't manifest the miracles I'd experienced in Goa. I spent two weeks camping in someone's tipi, crying my eyes out, and feeling so ashamed that I'd let Dan back in. I felt desperate and completely alone. When I bumped into Dan unexpectedly several weeks later, I was almost relieved to see him.

The last few weeks of India wore me down. I felt desperate to leave, to find some calm haven where I could quietly reassess. I kept dreaming of my good friend Jane who lived in a cottage in the Peak District of England, the only place in the country of my birth that still feels like home, even though I only spent four years there a long time ago. Whenever I returned to England, I stayed with Jane in her tiny cottage, and each night I would roll out a mattress in her front room by the open fire. I clung to that image of me by the fire, lying on the hearth of a friendship that felt sturdy as a rock, absorbing the last six months of evolutionary growth while I once again tried to strengthen my defences against Dan who was going to be in the UK at exactly the same time as me.

I could never have anticipated the way my life was about to take off in another, completely unexpected direction, but this time I would travel into the dark and hidden secrets of my past.

Nine

Skeletons Jump Out of Their Closet

It's really a tribute to the depth of my love that one of the first people I visited in England was a friend from Goa. He now resided in a rather squalid London squat. 'Show us yer tits, girls' was dribbled down the lounge room wall in red paint, and you could barely open the back door because of all the rubbish. It totally offended my delicate Libran sense of beauty; but I simply adored my friend.

I've not mentioned him before. Quite honestly, unravelling the various strands and layers of intimacy that made up Goa is still beyond me. Suffice to say, the love Smithy and I shared was not physical, yet it was tender and gentle. When I think of it, I see prisms of intense rainbow light dancing around a room as sunlight hits a crystal dangling in the window. There have been few men I have loved with the same heartfelt innocence I felt for Smithy.

He had a bald scalp covered in a tattoo of a cobweb, rings in his nose and a heavily inked body. He looked like every mother's worst nightmare, and yet as soon as he opened his mouth to speak, everyone, even reticent mums, were lulled and wooed by his gentle Welsh accent and his kind and caring ways, and would do anything for him.

When we were in Goa, we just used to hang out together. He'd pick me up on his Enfield motorbike that he'd hired for the Goa season and we'd blatt out to some café or visit some town. Somewhere in the day we would always find ourselves sitting, often on some rubbishy bit of street with the mangy dogs and pigs snuffling in the gutters and we would sit for hours and hours, not uttering a word, completely absorbed by the life that was unfolding around us.

I had just arrived in London from India and was staying at a flat with a couple of friends I had met in Australia—Kate and Shaggy. Dan had already returned to his family in Sheffield and I was enjoying the breathing space. I was still castigating myself for letting him back in. I felt like I'd lost everything I'd learnt in Goa. It should have been such a simple thing to cut him loose and yet it wasn't; he had hooked into me, just like he had before.

I'd only been back in the country a few days when I decided to catch a train over to see Smithy. There were several people visiting, and in the wrack and ruin of this squalid squat I had a conversation that totally impacted my life. We were talking about our parents and I made the comment that I had never met my biological father. I remember a Kiwi woman looking me straight in the eyes and asking, 'Do you know how to find him?'

'I know the area in London where he used to live,' I replied. When she answered, she spoke to the core of my being—every hair on my body stood up.

'Well, find him,' she said. 'If you don't, you will always wonder.'

'I will,' I replied, and I meant it. I had not a single doubt.

I was still so absorbed in that conversation, that later that day, when I caught the train back to my friend's flat, I failed to get off at their stop. I was not familiar with London, so it came as a complete surprise to discover the next station was Lewisham. I couldn't believe it. It was the suburb I knew my father had lived in when I was born. When I arrived back at my friend's house, I grabbed the phone book and lo and behold, there was my father's surname. I was suddenly taken back to the day when I first discovered he existed.

I don't believe in accidents and I know first-hand the nature of skeletons. They will jump out of their closet, or in my case the attic, at the first opportunity they get. Secrets don't like to be hidden; they fester away in the dark until someone opens up a window, just a crack. Then they erupt. The last thing I ever expected from my middle-class family, with its middle-class life, was a turgid secret, especially about me.

I was sixteen years old. It was a wet day and I'd been trying to amuse myself indoors. My parents were out and for some reason I was drawn to the attic, a place I was never allowed to visit. Boxes were piled high. I climbed on top and found a smaller box, which I opened. It was full of love letters from my dad to my mum. I could not believe what I was reading. My parents had travelled to the furthest point from love since those tender words were written.

The first letter told me I was illegitimate. I remember breathing a huge sigh of relief. My parents were human after all! The next letter shocked me to my core. In it was my dad saying he really felt as if I was his natural child! I had spent all my years, until the age of sixteen, completely unaware that the man who brought me up, who was on my birth certificate, was not my biological father. Again, my first response was of overwhelming relief. Suddenly, the struggle I'd had with this man made sense. I had never resonated with him; the current between us had always felt wrong. I could never understand him; many things he said made absolutely no sense to me.

'When I was in the air force,' he'd rant, 'we'd have to polish coal to learn discipline.' I would stare at him in disbelief that people could do something so stupid. He tried to run his family like a military unit. There was no talking back, no insubordination and no gushes of childlike passion. It was elbows off the table, don't speak unless you're spoken to and we all had to be in bed by 7pm, just before he got home from work. He treated me no differently to his natural children, my three younger brothers and my little sister—he expressed no delight in any of us. Just as he'd been unemotionally unavailable to me, he was also with them.

In truth, he was a damaged man who found showing love impossible. He played all sorts of emotional games, and when Mum wasn't around, he would often taunt me. When I'd react, he'd send me to my room. I was fifteen years old and I would sit on my bed spitting with fury, trying to calm myself, rocking from side to side while he opened and shut my bedroom door again and again and again; however long it took for me to crack. My mother always returned home from work to a war zone. Broken pot plants lay smashed against walls, tables were upturned and there was broken glass everywhere. Whatever I could throw or wreck, I would.

It took me a long time to forgive my dad. My parents' long overdue separation occurred soon after the secret was out, and for years I had nothing to do with him. Even so, he regularly wrote me letters. I read them many times and kept them carefully stored away. He felt safe loving from a distance, and all the things he'd been unable to say poured out in his written words. 'When people ask me how many children I have,' he wrote, 'I always say five, with a daughter at each end. I'm equally proud of all of them.' I read those letters for years before I finally agreed to see him.

When I had found out he was not my biological father, the last thing I'd wanted was to find another dad, even if it was my 'real' dad. At the time my mother had struggled to speak about it. At the end of the fifties, carrying an illegitimate child was not something to be proud of. The only information she gave me about my father was his name and the area he had lived in. It wasn't much, but it was all I needed to find him now.

So seventeen years had passed and here I was— standing with the phone book, staring at my real father's name. I sat down, stunned. He was a phone call away. When I told Kate and Shaggy what was going on, they were incredibly supportive. I'd met Kate when she was travelling around Australia. She'd come into my life as a friend of Dan's and I'd offered her some work sewing. She was from Liverpool and spoke it as it was; she didn't hold back.

'I think the world of Dan,' she'd said, 'but he's really fuckin' you about, Kye. What the hell are you doing with him? You're bloody beautiful, girl; you deserve better than that.' Those words had been like a lifeline to me. I'd been drowning in a house full of people and only Kate threw me a rope. We were so different; Kate loved to party and was happy in the midst of a crowd while I preferred nature and being alone. Even so, we were friends. I was so grateful for her presence that day. Just as she had encouraged me to ditch Dan, she encouraged me to make the call.

I felt sick as I dialled the number. It rang for only a few tones before being answered by an elderly lady. I told her who I was looking for and she replied that he was her son. When I explained who I was, she started crying.

'We have been waiting for you to turn up,' she wept. 'Your father will be so delighted.' In numbed astonishment I gave her my number. She said she would ring my father right away and then call me back. As I put the phone down I was completely unable to integrate the miracle that was unfolding.

They had been waiting for me to turn up?

Five minutes later, the phone rang. As I picked it up I felt so nervous. It was my father—Phillip. What did he say? I haven't a clue. I listened in a daze. I had not expected all the emotion I felt. I'd thought I'd be checking him out in the same way I would visit a garage sale—if there was nothing I wanted, I'd leave. Story over.

When I put the phone down, I was overwhelmed with joy. 'He sounds amazing.' I told Kate. I was dizzy and breathless. I could see Kate's worried face. She was trying to calm me; she didn't want me to build him up from a five-minute phone call only to be disappointed.

'Let's just try and take it a step at a time,' she said cautiously, and perhaps wisely.

The following day he rang at 11am and asked me what I was doing for lunch. I wanted to lie—I felt terrified. It was all happening much too fast, but there was nothing I could do to stop this flow. It was me who had opened the door.

'A taxi is coming to pick you up at noon. I'm taking you for lunch. See you then.'

I didn't even ask him where we were going. How should I dress? I was in a panic. All I had were my well-worn but much loved rags from India, and on my feet were some shredded canvas pumps, and Kate was out. It was Shaggy who came to the rescue. He took me by the hand, led me into his and Kate's bedroom and began selecting clothes of Kate's for me to wear. He chose some black pants and a matching shirt and left me to change. When he came back in, he looked me up and down and began shaking his head when he came to my well-worn pumps.

'They're going to have to go,' he said. 'You won't get in a restaurant wearing them.' I reluctantly took them off and exchanged them for some black boots. I looked smart, but I didn't feel like me.

'Do you need money? I have some if you do,' Shaggy asked me, as kind as he always was, when we heard the taxi beep outside. I shook my head and reached out to give him a hug. I felt so grateful to him and Kate for everything they'd done. Not only had Kate thrown me a rope when I needed it most, once when I'd been feeling so shaken by something I'd seen, Shaggy—a big bear of a man— had sat cradling me in his arms like a baby, rocking me from side to side. I loved them both so dearly and had no idea how our lives were already so entwined.

The taxi pulled up outside a small Spanish restaurant. I was shown to a table at the back where my father rose to greet me. I recognised him immediately. I am my father's daughter and here was my reflection.

We both stood gawping at one another, relieved that there was no need for excuses and a hurried escape.

We didn't eat our lunch. We merely toyed with it on the plate and got drunk on several bottles of champagne. When we finally left the dark and womb-like restaurant and landed in the dazzling light of the day, my father cleared the narrow sidewalk of passers- by, telling them he had just met his daughter for the first time and he wanted to dance for her. Even two traffic wardens, feeling our joy, stepped to one side as he jigged down the street like an Irish leprechaun. I was enthralled by this man. My father!

He then drove me around to meet the rest of my family—his wife Jill and my brothers Josh and Toby and, youngest of all, my sister Clare, all in their early twenties. They were born within three years of each other and were all friendly and welcoming.

At first they'd looked at me a little strangely, sensing that something wasn't quite right—so they told me a day later when I arrived wearing the clothes I'd had from India. I'd finally unveiled the real me and we'd all breathed a sigh of relief and laughed. It was the real me that fitted in ! They hadn't been able to figure me out before. Even though I had looked smart, I had worn a vintage, beaded tribal necklace I'd bartered from a gypsy in India, and it had led them to believe, I wasn't quite who I appeared to be. I didn't mean to try to hide who I was. I told them that it was because I didn't know where I was going to eat. And that was partly true, but it went deeper than that; I hadn't yet learnt that I was perfect just the way I was. I didn't need to change for anyone. The door I had opened was guiding me to that gentle place of acceptance.

Until then, I had felt as if I'd lost everything I'd gained in Goa. I was struggling in so many ways. But the reality was that I'd been given many tools that I had yet to fully integrate into my life. We can't build strong foundations for ourselves on pain, and pain doesn't disappear just because we ignore it. I wasn't even aware until I met Philip that I had such deep wounds. But a long time ago, just before I split up with Dan, just before I got on that plane to India, I had been feeling so desperate and alone and had prayed for my unhappy life to change. In that moment, a beautiful Ulysses butterfly had fluttered so close to my face and I knew I had set my own healing in motion, and every step I took would lead me to that place of wholeness. I just hadn't expected the steps to be so big!

How interconnected we all are! Later that night, Philip and Jill took me to a pub to see my new brothers, Josh and Toby, play in a band. I'd invited Kate and Shaggy to come too, and in the intermission Toby came over and before I'd had a chance to introduce him, he said, 'How you going, Kate? Good to see you, Shaggy.' Unbeknown to all of us they had known my brother all along!

When I asked Jill if it was weird with me turning up, she replied, 'We've all been waiting for you. Philip has always said, she will turn up one day, I know she will.'

I had spent most of my life not knowing that Philip even existed and yet here was a family that had kept a place for me in their hearts. What a difference their love would have made to me as a child. How I would have walked taller, trusted in myself more and believed I was worthy if I'd known that somewhere out there my real father waited with his heart wide open, knowing I'd finally come.

There was a lot I needed to come to terms with, but there was even more I didn't know about myself. When Philip tossed me a folder of photos to look at and said, 'Here's the rest of your family,' I was utterly gobsmacked. 'That's your great grandfather,' he said when he saw me gawping at a faded picture of an African man wearing a suit. 'He came from Ghana, from the Fante tribe, and was a church minister here.'

I had been brought up so white and middle-class. Black people had simply not existed. I kept looking at Philip, thinking he'd tell me he was joking, but he didn't. This was my bloodline, my heritage. The man in the picture was part of me, and yet it was all too overwhelming for me to absorb.

'And here's your great grandmother,' Philip said, handing me a picture of a woman wearing the tiniest lacy corset. It was 1901 and she had next to nothing on, her entire legs showing. A big flamboyant hat sat tilted on the back of her head and she leant pertly on a cane. 'She was a Jewish actress and this was her on the stage.'

'And she married an African church minister?' I asked, astonished.

No wonder I had always been a black sheep, a rule breaker and a rebel! A weight began to lift from me. I had spent so many years working on healing my pain, yet until I met Philip, I had not noticed that my relationship with Dan mirrored the one I'd had with my dad, Ron.

I knew at the core of his being that Ron, who had brought me up, was loving and kind. I had seen that in the stack of letters he'd written me, never giving up when I didn't reply, and even though I'd met up with a father who, if I could have handpicked one out of thousands of applicants, I couldn't have made a better choice, I still felt loyal to Ron. For better or worse, he had been my dad and I couldn't simply replace him. I went to see him shortly after and told him I'd met Philip and that whatever happened, he would always be my dad. Nothing could ever take that away. He didn't say anything; he still couldn't find a way to express what he felt, but tears rolled down his face. I knew this was as big for him as it was for me.

Philip did not get Dan. 'He has a girlfriend who is pregnant living in your house? What the hell are you doing with him?' They were questions I had asked myself over and over again. I wanted to break free of him, but it felt like escaping from quicksand; the more I struggled, the faster I went down.

Once Dan and I had been walking through the streets of London and he said something so incredibly cruel to me I had burst into tears and run away. All I wanted in that moment was to talk with Tui. When I finally found a phone box and rang him, the first thing he said was '

What's happening to you? I felt overwhelmed with grief five minutes ago and I knew something was wrong.' The connection between us was still this intense, magnetic pull, which felt all- consuming until we actually met. On the phone he was the loving Tui I knew. He felt safe then, but when I had tried a couple of times to reconnect with him, each time we met, the bright, beautiful, soulful man who had caressed me with his words and loved me like a treasure had gone. He was only safe expressing how he felt from a distance. It suddenly hit me how like Ron he was.

I'd been living a very nomadic life since arriving back in the UK, staying a few nights with Kate and Shaggy, a week with Philip and Jill, then back for a night at Smithy's, but I didn't finally relax until I arrived at Jane's. A four-hour bus trip north of London and I was finally in the Peak District, home.

I could walk from Jane's cottage following public right-of-ways that cut through fields of clover and dandelions, wound alongside the river, edged with comfrey and fragrant meadowsweet, then climbed up onto the purple-heathered moor to one of my favourite stone circles, the Nine Ladies.

Sometimes I'd visit and the stones would feel restful and calming and I would leave feeling energised and fresh, but I was often drawn to them when there was an eeriness about them and then it would be me that gave to them.

On my previous visit to the UK, on the autumn equinox, when day and night were in perfect balance, just before the sun set, Jane and I had visited the stone circle, certain there would be other like-minded souls gathered to honour the next phase in the wheel of life; the passing from summer to autumn. We had started walking up the track that led to the circle with such eagerness but as we got closer our mood changed. We could hear the voices of many people and there was nothing celebratory about them, in fact they sounded angry. We had crept the final yards and hidden in the darkness of the trees, watching.

Several large fires were burning within the circle and they were surrounded by people who were very drunk. There was even a huge gypsy truck backed up to one of the stones, which must have been driven through fences because there was no vehicle access to this hallowed ground. One person was yelling out 'fuck the government' then others began to shout in agreement. On the edge of the circle someone was trying to hack the branches from a live oak as they staggered drunkenly. Normally, neither Jane nor I would have hesitated at telling them to stop, but it would have been like lighting a match and throwing it into a hay barn, and we didn't want the marauding rabble to even know we were there. We slunk away from our beloved stone circle, tears rolling down our faces, holding each other's arms like a couple of old dears, unable to comprehend the lack of respect these people had shown.

When we went up a few days later we met a woman who described herself as a seventh generation witch who'd birthed seven children and she was doing a cleansing ceremony to soothe the circle. Together the three of us worked energetically to restore balance.

There were numerous other stone circles in the Peak District and many of them were within walking distance from Jane's house. The one I loved most of all was hidden away in a pinewood. Six little stones in a circle that were always strewn with oak leaves and corn dollies, seeds and grains, flowers and the nubs of candles.

I loved being at Jane's, not only because I adored my stoic rebel of a friend who once shocked the socks of me with her giant painting of her vagina that dominated her lounge room wall and this was at a time when one didnt even mention the word vagina, let alone do self portraits, but because I loved the landscape and felt at home in that part of the country. There was always such a cosy familiarity being at Jane's.

The first time I ever saw her I longed to be her friend. She was a local girl, brought up on a farm, and yet unlike other farm girls, she hitchhiked everywhere, wearing skirts that were really short when no one else in the rural backwaters did, and she had a crop of brilliant red, spiky hair. We finally connected at a Friends' of the Earth group. It had been bitterly cold and at the end of the night Jane and I went into the hall to reclaim our coats. We were putting on our boots and rugging up, getting ready to brave the cold night air, when we turned to face each other and both began laughing hysterically. We were mirror images, each wearing woollen berets and gabardine Macintoshes. Our friendship grew from there. It was Jane I rang after speaking with Philip for the first time; it was Jane who gave me a safe haven so I could piece together my fragmented self. I couldn't have done it without her!

Yes, meeting Philip had been wonderful; but it brought everything up—including stuff I didn't even know was there. There were times I felt ecstatically happy. I couldn't believe my life had transformed in this way; yet at other times, I felt raw with sorrow. However much I tried to deny her, inside of me was a wounded little girl who felt broken-hearted that this love from her father had come so late. In the midst of joy I would find my bottom lip trembling and my tears would overflow. I didn't feel at ease with this pain. It made me vulnerable, and that was a place I didn't like to be. Whenever I had kept this tough exterior around me, I had felt in control. But now even that was crumbling under the loving gaze of my father. He thought I was beautiful. He called me an angel, and when he saw my tears he told me there were times he could roar like a lion, but when he needed to, he could also cry like a baby.

I could see many aspects of myself so clearly now, though I still struggled to comprehend how Dan had entangled me again. Why wasn't it easy to leave him?

Why was I once again hoping and praying we'd work out? The reality of our relationship was a mess. Nothing good ever came from our love and now there was someone else in the equation who wanted me gone: Sheila. Dan had just received a letter from Sheila who, despite my offering her the shelter of my home, told him that nothing she was doing there was for me; it was all for him. For once Dan had actually felt protective of me, but now I had become the other woman!

On some level I could feel Philip's rock-like presence in my life, rewiring everything from within, reaching out a strong arm for me to grab hold of, reassuring me I was worth a whole lot more. It was becoming so clear that every time I stepped away from Dan, my life rolled along incredibly well.

One morning Dan and I had gone out looking for a car to buy together. I only had two hundred pounds and I didn't think I could buy a reliable car for that. On the surface it made sense to pool my resources with Dan, but straight away with that decision I'd fallen into fear, let go of all I'd learnt in India and compromised myself.

Dan and I had scanned the morning's papers and been to look at several cars, but none felt right. On top of that we'd had a fight in the street and I ran and caught the bus to Jane's, leaving him to return home to his gran's in Sheffield.

The paper we'd scoured that morning was still sitting on the table when I got in and I picked it up to have another look. I immediately noticed an advertisement for a car we'd somehow missed. A vintage Triumph Herald with six months' registration for only one hundred and fifty pounds. Anyone interested had to phone after 4pm. It was 3.55pm. I had five minutes to wait. I held my breath as I rang the number, praying it would still be available to buy. It sounded perfect; I could afford it. *Oh, please God, let it be mine.*

Jane drove me there, and as soon as I got out of the car and saw it sitting on the street, I knew with every fibre of my being, in my blood and my bones that this little car was mine. The owner was so sweet. He asked me what I wanted it for. When I explained that I was home for six months and wanted a car so I could visit family at different ends of the country more easily, he said, 'Look, love, I don't advise you buy it. I would hate you to break down. The clutch needs work and could go at any time.'

I thought about it for a second and replied, 'It feels really good to me and I'm going to go with that.' I was delighted

I had manifested my own car without needing Dan. I was over the moon.

I hadn't intended for several weeks to pass by before I went to visit my mother and sister whom I hadn't seen for two years. Life had just unfolded in such unexpected ways since my return, and I'd needed some time to absorb meeting up with Philip before I told Mum. Mum is pretty open about most things, and although I knew there would be wounds exposed because Philip was someone we'd never talked about, I didn't see it as being a major drama and I was certain we would work it out.

When I'd first come to Australia, I'd met up with Mum's oldest and closest friend whom she hadn't seen for many years. 'When you were born,' she'd told me, 'everyone was against your mother. Her family all wanted her to abort you, but she wouldn't listen. She left home and came to stay with me. Your mother is one of the strongest and bravest people I know.'

I hadn't known any of this. I'd seen my mother get so crushed by the man she had married, the man who had fallen in love with her and offered to be a father to me. We can't heal our pain with closed doors, and I knew that as much as my life was transforming, Mum's could too. Bringing everything out into the open, blasting it all with the light of day, could only be healing for us all.

It was Christmas Eve when I set off for the long drive to Wales. My gorgeous little Triumph Herald ran like a dream, and as I headed for the motorway, putting on the windscreen wipers as the rain began to fall, I felt well and truly united once again with my flow.

I had no idea what the next few days would bring. All I knew was that I was being looked after and I could cope with anything.

Ten

My Knight Came on a Tractor

I was approaching the small Welsh town of Brecon when I saw the roadblocks. It had been raining heavily the whole trip and I was shocked to hear floods had blocked the road ahead. A kind policeman told me there was a small country lane I could try, which cut around the town and went up over the hills. I was keen to arrive and deeply relieved there was another route.

I drove successfully through one flooded section of the detour and then the narrow country lane, with its hawthorn hedges on each side, twisted and turned up and over the hillside then meandered down into a flooded dip. The light was fading and I felt worried I'd be stuck in the middle of nowhere. I couldn't see any other option than to drive through. I took off, holding my breath and praying I'd make it, but the car stalled midway and, despite endless attempts, wouldn't start again. I was sitting in a flood, it was almost dark and I hadn't the faintest idea what to do.

It would have been easy to fall into panic and fear, but I felt the lessons of India taking control. I reminded myself that the only times life let me down was when I was letting down myself. What happens within is what happens outside, and there is no escape from this. Life gives to us when we give to ourselves, and I was taking only little tentative steps to do that, but enough to know I was looked after. I knew help would come.

My knight came on a tractor. He was big burly farmer with a jovial face who told me he was taking some bales of hay to his horses down the road. 'I'll only be fifteen minutes, love,' he said. 'If you're still here when I return, you can come home with me.' I wasn't exactly eased by this proposition. I knew I had nothing to fear per se, but I was so disappointed that I wouldn't be arriving at Mum's that night. I kept trying to start the car. The battery grew weaker and weaker, and by the time he got back, it was flat.

My knight was driving an old Landrover this time. He climbed out, waded through the flood towards me, hitched a tow rope to the front of my little angel car and towed us both up onto the verge. He didn't live far away. A big old stone farmhouse looked deceptively dark and cold from the outside. But as he opened the front door to guide me in, the warmth and love that burst from that room was almost overwhelming. It was such a contrast to the bitterly cold and wet night. His home was festive and full of love, with the family gathered together for Christmas—sons and daughters, aunts and uncles and grandparents too. Even after all these years, I can't write about it without the tears welling up. People raced to relieve me of my wet clothes, a bath was run and a glass of hot punch put in my hands. The spirit of Christmas was alive and well in this home, but I suspect it would have been the same welcome every night of the year.

After a hot bath, I spent a night sharing with this family who made a place for me by the fire as if I was one of them. In the morning I woke up to breakfast. The farmer had been up early to check on my car; unbeknown to me he'd had the battery charging overnight. He drove me back out to my car and then followed me in his for twenty miles to make sure I didn't break down. Then he tooted his horn, gave me a wave and returned to the warmth of his own hearth. I give blessings always for that man and his family.

It had been challenging making the long drive along roads that were hectic compared to the ones in Australia, and not only that, driving a car that I'd been told by the owner would probably break down. But I'd listened to what felt right for me, honoured myself and life had stepped in to help when I'd needed it.

It was Christmas day and I was so excited to soon be seeing my sister Marti and my mum. Growing up with parents in an unhappy marriage had been a challenge for all us kids, but the one aspect of our life at that time that pulled me through was my mother's love for the animals. She rescued every forlorn and needy critter that came her way. There were baby hedgehogs and squirrels being kept warm in the airing cupboard that she would wake me up to feed in the middle of the night. We'd creep softly through a slumbering house with warmed bottles for the babes. Once, she rescued all these cruelly treated ponies that we told Dad belonged to someone else. He was always complaining about the animals in the house and would have had a heart attack if he'd known we owned even more. It was Mum who filtered money out of her tightly controlled housekeeping to feed them.

They had been rescued from a farmer with bloodshot, saggy eyes who seemed to have a tribe of deformed children and kept all his horses in a yard littered with rusty sharp-edged junk and tangles of barbed wire. My best friend Carole and I rode his horses, and if we'd known about sexual predators we might have understood why he kept trying, unsuccessfully, to grope us.

When his yard filled up with skeletal yearlings, I begged Mum to buy a chestnut with a flaxen mane and tail that I'd fallen in love with. Eventually, my grandparents combined several years of birthday presents and bought it for me. When we came to load it, two other ponies walked up the gangplank and wouldn't get off the truck. I don't actually remember anyone trying to get them off. My mother was incensed as the little Shetland pony had whiplash marks across its back and the grey Welsh mountain pony was timid and thin.

'I'm going to make that bastard pay for his cruelty,' I heard my mother mutter. When the farmer rang up for his money for the two additional ponies, my middle-class mother, in her twin set and pearls, swore blind she'd paid! And when he took Mum to court, it was Mum who won.

We hadn't only rescued ponies from this farmer. We'd rescued a greyhound with a broken leg, left to die on a bitterly cold night while locked in a ramshackle shed, and a hairless guinea pig covered in sores. Several times a week, always when it was dark, my mother would drive my Dad's pride and joy gold Cortina down the tiny country lanes and park so we were hidden in the trees. Then we'd climb a fence, walk across a field, jump over a small creek, and head towards the farmer's hay barn. We'd drag bales of hay back to the car that Mum had carefully lined with plastic, so Dad wouldn't find out what she was doing. He prized his Cortina above us all. It took several trips before the car was full. My arms would be aching from the strain, but just like Mum, I wanted this farmer to pay, and I loved the irony of his own hay feeding the ponies he'd starved.

I hadn't seen Mum or my young sister Marti for two years. I wanted to feel my way back in gently, not arrive with a sledgehammer, but there was no way I could soften the impact of what I had to say. The words tumbled out and landed like stones around us.

Nothing can heal in the dark, and for the first time in my life fresh air was blowing and all the windows were wide open. It wasn't easy for Mum; it bought up a lot of emotion. I understood the reasons why she'd hidden the truth from me, but I wish I had been told. My world would have made a whole lot more sense if I'd understood why I didn't fit.

Back in the sixties, people didn't realise the implications of keeping children in the dark about who their real parents were. The simple fact is it's impossible to build a relationship of trust on a lie, however well meaning. I didn't fully understand then how those untruths had manifested in my life as a deeply sensitive child or how the pains in my legs at I'd grown up with, which no one had been able to diagnose, were connected. That awareness was to come later.

I had healed a lot since I'd discovered I had a different father. I knew the importance of forgiveness and I had come to see from my own actions that we all mess up. We are all children learning, we make mistakes and that's how we grow. When we reach that understanding, we can release a whole lot of pain.

I was glad my sister Marti was there while I shared my news. She was barely fifteen, though wise and earthed like an ancient tree. She was happy for me, and as we sat around the table talking I could see Mum getting visible lighter. The following morning, Mum told me she'd just had her first good sleep in thirty-three years, since the day I was born. The power of truth!

It wasn't easy for me embracing all these new aspects of myself that had been denied me for so long. I kept shaking my head in astonishment that I came from African and Jewish ancestors. The Fante tribe, me! It seemed obvious to me now, from Philip's looks, that he wasn't totally white. His skin was dark, and he had tightly curled hair. Yet I felt as if I had no right to claim this part of myself. I was aware of it, but it only existed as a concept outside of myself—it just hadn't sunk in. There was also something else I struggled with—being loved. It seems ridiculous, doesn't it? For years I had dreamt of having a father who loved me, and miraculously, I'd manifested one. But as much as I leapt for joy at this unexpected fortune, there were times I wanted to run. Being loved scared the hell out of me, and I kept finding myself reacting from past pain.

On one occasion I had just spent a few days with Philip and Jill. As I got into my car for the long drive north back to Jane's, Philip had said 'Give us a ring when you arrive.' I was literally bubbling over with fury as I drove away. *I'm thirty-three years old! I've managed all these years without him and now he wants me to ring him when I arrive!* It was ridiculous, yet I loved it that he cared.

It was winter and I had to drive across a moor near Manchester on a long stretch of isolated road. I didn't pass another car for hours. There was a howling wind and it was raining so heavily I was hunched over the steering wheel, driving so slowly, struggling to see the road. It was much too bleak a place to stop.

My little treasure of a car had run like a dream. I'd been up and down England without anything going wrong. I had been right to trust my gut; she was the perfect car for me. She was even a willing conspirator to wake me up.

As I was driving back to Jane's, across that grey and lonely moor, the exhaust came apart. Despite the howling wind, the noise was deafening. I had no waterproof clothing and had to slide under the car, water running down my neck, soaking all my clothes while I struggled to wire the exhaust back on. My fingers were so icily cold they were numb.

It fell off five more times on the trip home and I got under the car and tried to reconnect it each time! I was shaking with cold, crying my eyes out, feeling so damn sorry for myself. My vintage car had no heater and over and over again, as I shivered, unaware of what I was even saying, I was repeating, like a mantra, 'I'm glad I have a dad who loves me, I'm glad I have a dad who loves me.'

Was life looking after me then?

Most certainly it was. All my sharp edges were being whittled away, and I had to find my vulnerability before

I could finally stop fighting the beauty and love that was transforming my life. I didn't need to analyse all the times I had felt unworthy as a child.

I just needed to let go.

Eleven

Facing our Shadows

After being in England for almost six months, I had a very powerful dream that I knew was giving me guidance... *a beautiful man leading three humped beasts, which I assume are llamas, walks towards me and says, 'I will be waiting for you; you'll know where to find me' and then he disappears.*

I find myself at the top of a pinnacle, hundreds of feet high, surrounded by water, and I'm being told to jump. I feel scared, but there is no other way to get down, so I do. When I come up out of the water, a surfboard pops up beside me, so I lie on it and paddle along. Next a huge shark comes out of the water, mouth open and teeth bared, and he knocks me off my board. I fall into the water and sink down; when I resurface there is a boat beside me. I climb in. I can see a small tropical island not far away, and I begin to row to the shore. When I arrive, I'm drawn to a small track that disappears into the rainforest and I follow it. It leads me to a scene as if from a fairy tale. A beautiful waterfall cascades into a pool of crystal clear water. Lying on the ground sleeping is the man who came to me with the three humped beasts. He is surrounded by animals, all at ease in his presence. He opens his eyes and when he sees me beckons me to come to his outstretched arms.

I didn't know who the man was in the dream. I looked up the symbology of llamas, but nothing made sense. However, I could relate the rest of the dream to what was happening in my life. I was aching to go home. I had been away almost a year, and while it had been one of the most amazing times of my life, it had also been one of the most gruelling. I needed space and time to mellow into whoever I was now, but going home—to Dan's partner who was about to give birth and had made it very clear I wasn't welcome in my own home—was not enticing.

I knew the dream was telling me I had no choice but to return home. Yes, I would face challenges, but I was, and would be, looked after. I finally demanded that Dan return and find Sheila her own place to live. He was only gone a week when a friend told me of a weekend workshop retreat in Wales. I knew I had to go.

Shonteeha was a shaman, a bridge between the visible and the spirit worlds, a healer who channelled wise beings and the fairy folk. A small group of us were gathered together in her tipi for this retreat.

There was my part Cherokee friend, Camille, whose normal reality included bizarre psychic phenomena happening all around her, like tap dancing ghosts, angels with ukuleles, as well as crazy coloured lobsters that walk up walls. There were also four men, so well groomed and squeaky clean they could have passed for Mormon missionaries. They told us how they always reincarnated on Earth together and each lifetime they progressed further in their understanding of the Tree of Life. Their psychic abilities were quite phenomenal. One of the exercises we did was holding different rocks and tuning in to where they originated. Each of these men had been so explicit in their descriptions, all validated by Shonteeha. They had seen the country, the snow, the birds and trees that grew around the rocks, and the mountains and the valleys. I'm sure if we'd had GPS technology back then, they would have given the coordinates too.

The workshop had started off a little erratically. As a shaman, Shonteeha lived a very disciplined life and had requested that all participants leave their tobacco behind. When one of the men was caught hiding out the back having a fag, it had a disruptive influence. Even though no smoking had been a condition of attendance, when he returned after being caught, he was resentful and we could all feel it.

As well as that, Camille, who is pretty straightforward and says what she thinks, had a question for Shonteeha, which I felt was too personal and I hoped she wouldn't ask it. We were all certainly curious about Shonteeha. She was very tall with broad shoulders, and while she didn't emanate a masculine energy, it wasn't entirely feminine either. I felt that however intriguing Shonteeha's story was it was really quite irrelevant unless she chose to share it.

As we sat in the tipi together everyone felt disconnected, it suddenly hit me that we all had a responsibility to be present and give the best of ourselves. How could one person carry the responsibility for those who were unwilling to honour or even reach beyond their own limitations to be there? I had been as bad as everyone else. I had been sitting in judgement, criticising the workshop for being a failure when it had barely begun.

When I changed my attitude and saw that I was as responsible for its success as I was its failure, everything began to change. It may not have changed for everyone, but it did for me. I could feel my heart opening up and the energy in the tipi blossom like a flower. In this remarkable space Shonteeha told us she would like to share her story.

She had been born a man and been guided by Spirit to undergo a sex change, which she did. Every aspect of her transformation was communicated to her well before the time, including the surgeon and the day the surgery would occur. Even though it was still several years into the future, it was all accurately predicted. She told us this was her sacrifice and choice she willingly embraced so she could align her energy with a being she channelled called White Buffalo Calf Woman, a Wakan (holy woman) who brought the peace pipe to the American Indians and taught them seven rituals that would unite their people. After, as she walked off into the desert, she turned into a white buffalo calf and galloped away. Shonteeha told us that White Buffalo Calf woman only communicated through her when there was a pure heart connection. When she came through, I felt incredibly honoured and overwhelmed with love at her message of peace.

I had never met anyone like Shonteeha and have not since. Tucked away on her farm in the Welsh Hills, every aspect of her life was divinely guided. Spirit even taught her a language she spoke fluently but had been unable to identify until many years later when she visited the American Indians and discovered it was fifteenth century Dakato, the Indian language when it was in its purest form.

Shonteeha had warned us about Florence the Fairy who often popped up at inappropriate places like the checkout at the supermarket, with her high-pitched voice and excitable ways and it was Florence who turned up the second morning as we sat together in the tipi. That cheeky little fairy knew exactly which button of mine to press. She looked me directly in the eyes and said, 'You have a cockatoo on your shoulder. Why don't you take it home?' That was all it took. I nodded, biting my lip as I tried to hold back a sorrow that threatened to engulf me, and failed. Shonteeha gently led me out into the garden where we sat in the watery sunlight of a wintry welsh day. There was no need for words. She sat silent yet comforting as I cried myself out. 'I feel so confused,' I finally sobbed.

'After lunch, we'll meditate together and see what guidance we can get for you,' she said, reassuringly.

As we returned to her cottage, she stopped to pick a strawberry, the only one left of the season. She gently removed the leaves and the bits where the insects had munched and offered it to me. It was an act of such tenderness. That little strawberry, stripped of all its imperfections yet with still so much to give, cast a light in my gloom and I began to smile.

Later, sitting together in meditation, I was totally unprepared for the depth of counsel I received. 'It's only when we face our pain, it has a chance to heal,' Shonteeha said. 'If you don't return and deal with what's happening in your life, it will always be with you.' I knew she meant the situation with Dan, Sheila and the baby.

'You will need strength and courage to get through the time ahead, but the trees are there to help you; don't forget the trees.' Shonteeha told me many things and all the advice was so explicit. She even warned whom to avoid when I was menstruating. 'Do not go near them at this sacred time as you are then at your most vulnerable and they will turn your energy against you.'

In the weeks ahead, every single thing she had told me, as well as the guidance I'd received in the dream with the amazing man with the three humped beasts, came to pass.

I flew home when I heard that Dan had found somewhere for Sheila to live. He'd reassured me that it was me he wanted to be with, not her, but Shonteeha's words of warning before I left were ringing in my ears. 'If you return to him, he will do the same to you again.' She had also told me of a new relationship that was coming into my life, 'If you resist it,' she had said, 'life will show you.' I didn't really know what she meant by that, but I sure would find out!

It wasn't easy to return and face the situation. I had booked a flight for three weeks after the baby's birth. These things are not random. Everything that happens to us can catalyse awakening if we are open.

I had only been home ten minutes when Dan received a call telling him Sheila had gone into labour! I stood in my home that had been uncared for since I'd left. Black mould grew up the kitchen walls and all my gear that had been carefully packed away had been pilfered. I was home, but I didn't feel it. The community of friends I'd had when I'd left were now all part of Sheila's pregnancy, and it was me who stood alone. I felt so angry. I had been so willing to share what I had and now I stood on the edge through no fault of my own. For three days I fumed. I didn't know what to do with my rage. I didn't sleep. I paced up and down, never feeling more alone in my life.

Eventually I splattered my anger onto a canvas and found a release for my huge gaping wound. At the end of three days, painting finished and burnt ceremonially, I knew I didn't need to hang on to that space! I felt calm, renewed and able to cope.

One of my first friends to come and visit was Nikki, a gorgeous Greek nature goddess with black, curly hair that fell past her bum. One day when I came into the garden, I found she had climbed into a tree and was yelling excitedly to me, 'Kye, look at the trees, look at the trees.' I was surrounded by beautiful trees— twisted and ancient frangipanis, a giant umbrella tree that was a haven for parrots, coconut palms, an old dame of a lemon tree and all the silver gum trees that over the six years I had lived there had trebled in size. In Nikki's excitement I could hear the words of Shonteeha reminding me the trees were there to give me strength, and I felt reassured.

Less than a week later, as I reached out in the darkness to make peace, I found myself standing with my gift—a box of shopping—on someone's doorstep— Sheila's. We both needed to face each other, and yet my entry to that house was barred and I was turned away. I left feeling weak and dejected until I got home and realised I had begun to menstruate. I had almost thrown myself into the lion's den.

My connection to Shonteeha always felt strong, even long after I'd left the Welsh hills she lived in, but finally home, back on my own hill, it didn't take me long to weaken. Dan had mastered the art of contriteness, and gullible me—always flayed by his tears and wooed by his declarations of love—believed him. I ignored Shonteeha's wise council. I threw myself back into the arms of this demon love and pretended we could build our own Taj Mahal on sand. When I got a letter from Shonteeha, I didn't want to open it. I did not want to face the truth.

Wrapped up in a piece of silk was a feather with the message, 'I send you this eagle feather for strength; my advice remains the same.'

It's not necessary for me to list all the cruel and jagged little steps that led to our final demise. Let it be enough that Shonteeha was right! Even so, every experience in my life I have learnt to treasure, including the journey I shared with Dan. He flew back to England several months later, on his own, and I am grateful to him. We can never blame. By doing so, we give away our power and acknowledge ourselves for being much less than we actually are. I was not a victim, and from my relationship with him I learnt lessons that changed my life forever and opened me up to love.

Facing our shadows is much harder than running from our pain, but the thing is, all the time we run, we will never be free.

When Sheila was finally ready to see me, it wasn't easy for me, but I took those first little fearful steps, which grew into big, bold strides. The reality is never as bad as we imagine and facing our fears is only difficult the first time we do it. Dan was not there to give her the support she needed and the friends she'd made were fed up with her dramas and left her alone. I was the only one helping her. It was me that drove her to hospital when she thought she had mastitis, chopped open a pile of fresh coconuts and emptied the juice into a jug so she had plenty to drink, and me who did her shopping. I was blown away at how easily all my anguish over the situation dissolved. I found it easy to be giving and kind. Their baby was beautiful, and while I still had a lot of pain to let go of around betrayal, at least with this situation, I was finally free.

When Sheila moved away within a month of giving birth, Shonteeha was proved right once again—'She will not be able to handle your energy and she will leave.'

If I had thought life was now going to get simple then, I was wrong. I had summoned the powers of change and I had asked to be shown the way to live a life I loved. This would not come until I'd fully let go of all my fears around trust. Just when I thought I had entered the calm, my life began to heat up and in more ways than one!

Twelve
The Lovers

I lived in a ramshackle dame of a house perched on top of a seventy acre peninsular with a view of the ocean from three sides. She sat in a circle of the oldest frangipanis trees I had ever seen, which grew so twisted and gnarled yet still continued to birth. I adored my home. She was an old Queenslander, built up on stilts, and you could barely see her. She peeped out from a cascade of magenta bougainvillea, coconut palms and a huge umbrella tree where the lorikeets would gather and make such a din I couldn't hear myself talk on the phone.

On one side grew a mango tree as big as an oak, and every wet season when the mangoes were ripe, they'd crash onto the tin roof. I had gotten so used to them falling, but anyone who came for a visit would jump out of their skin. From the sun room window I could pick bush lemons straight from the tree, and every day at 8.30 am precisely the Quicksilver catamaran from Cairns to Port Douglas would cruise past, way out on that tropical blue sea.

I loved my home with an intensity I had never experienced elsewhere and never have since, but it went beyond the house. My connection with this hill was so strong, we were entwined. And that was why, despite my troubles with Dan, I had never left.

I had found this magical haven after going to a healing workshop and telling everyone I was looking for somewhere to live. When someone told me I would never find anywhere nice to live with my three dogs, I'd thought about it for a moment then turfed that thought out. It was ridiculous. Was I destined to always manifest less than the best because I loved animals? No! I knew the universe looks after those who are brave enough to love. Less than a week later, I had manifested my dream place to live and people asked me how I did it. While everyone else's rents went up, mine only went down, until, a year after taking on the place and paying a sizeable rent during that time, I was offered the place for free.

For the first time since I'd lived there, I was free to enjoy my home. Dan and all his party-going friends had gone. I had a couple of women I'd met at the market, musicians that were travelling around Australia, staying with me. I also invited Jemma, for a couple of weeks before she left for India. I had only just met her. I knew she was splitting up with her partner and having a hard time and to help her out I told her she could stay with me until her flight left. That way she didn't have to pay the huge rent where she had been living and could save more money for her trip. I hadn't met her partner, Gill, but I knew she was breaking up with him. So I was surprised when she arrived at my house with him and all her stuff. I wasn't sure if she had misunderstood my invitation and was moving in with Gill. I was really enjoying some female energy and didn't want any guys staying.

It's true I was defensive. The last few months of being with Dan had ploughed fresh wounds and I was so over men. I didn't want to know them, and even though Gill seemed gentle and kind, I anxiously paced around, trying to work out how to ask him to leave without sounding as anal as I felt.

When I glanced out my window and saw him watering my wilting paw paw trees, I softened just a little. He could visit, but that was all. At lunchtime, when he went into the kitchen and cooked up a sweet potato curry with freshly made coconut cream that he had climbed my coconut tree to get, I softened a little more. How could I not? Well, he could stay the night, but that's all!

He turned up again in the final days before Jemma left for India. She was only a few years younger than me and was upset they were splitting up. 'He's beautiful,' I said, 'but he's young. You're going in different directions; just let him go.'

One night Gill and I found ourselves sitting at the kitchen table while everyone else was out. I soon lost that stilted uncomfortable feeling I'd had with him— he was so easy to talk to. We sat sharing stories, unaware of how time was slipping by. It was the early hours of the morning when we were jolted out of our ease and flow by Jemma arriving home, bristling and sharp as if she'd uncovered some dirty secret, when all we'd done was talk.

I was shocked by Jemma's attitude. There was no doubt Gill was gorgeous and incredibly sexy, but he was much younger than me. I'd only just got rid of a relationship that had been like trying to extract myself from glue. I was adamant; I was not looking for another, especially not with a lovable pup! Though ... I was intrigued by our connection. We got on so well. When I pulled a tarot card to see what our connection was and got the Lovers card, I thought it had to be wrong. It had to be!

It was months before I saw him again. He lived several hundred kilometres away in the rainforest and only came to town occasionally. The next time he did, he called in. I was so aware of his presence; every part of me was drawn to him, but I tried to ignore it. I spoke with everyone else but him. I found him so attractive; I couldn't even look at him. I was behaving like a kid! Later in the day, when a group of us climbed down the steep track to the beach for a swim, Gill came too.

I dived into the sea in the same place I did every day and hit my head on a rock. When I came out of the water, blood running down my face, it was Gill who was there to comfort me. I was completely naked— we all swam nude in those days—and I felt really vulnerable, sitting on the sand like a child as Gill tended my wound.

The next time I put up resistance a really strange thing happened. Gill had finally persuaded me to visit him at the community where he lived up north. But as soon as I arrived everything started to go wrong. I felt overwhelmed by the intensity of the rainforest—it was almost suffocating. There was a dark moon, and as night settled around us I couldn't see even a step in front of me. I was helplessly clinging to Gill, being guided around as if I was blind. When he led me through the forest to his tipi, the night went from bad to worse. I woke up, sleepy, needing to pee and unwilling to disturb Gill. So I crept silently out into the rainforest to relieve myself. It was only as I tried to return to the tipi that I realised I was lost. Nothing stood out in the dark. I crept through the forest, naked, getting scratched by vicious barbed vines that hung like tentacles, all the time praying to somehow miraculously bump back into the tipi. I was desperately trying not to call Gill and hanging onto my last vestige of pride as I wandered further and further away. By the time I'd humbled myself enough to call for help, I had to yell at the top of my voice and his answer came from a long way away. He came and helped me back to the tipi.

When I woke up in the morning, I had five ticks latched onto my eyelid and my face was enormously swollen. I looked like a gargoyle and felt terrible. We had planned the following day to hike into a deserted rainforest beach and camp for a few days with a couple of other friends. When Gill pulled out at the last moment, I felt gutted, though I wasn't surprised. Our night together had been an absolute disaster.

I returned to the community three days later after a miserable trip. It had rained the whole time, forcing us to huddle under dripping tarps, craving cigarettes we didn't have. My expectations of a reunion with Gill were not high, so I was surprised and delighted when he invited me and a few others to sail his small catamaran through the mangroves out to the beach.

I felt an intense awareness of Gill's presence. The rips and flows in my own body kept me in touch with where he was, what he was doing and when he came close. But we didn't speak. We didn't even look at one another; we acted as if the other did not exist.

Arriving at the beach, I left my clothes on the sand and went for a swim. It was a tranquil, tropical day and the blue sky was completely clear and the ocean as still as glass, not even a ripple; I lazed around in the water, dreamily watching two friends getting smaller and smaller as they walked up the deserted beach, fringed with the rainforest. I had drifted into another world, and it was a few moments before it registered that what I was now looking at was smoke. By the time what was happening, and its implications, clicked, it was much too late to stop it. My clothes, mysteriously, had caught fire and burnt to cinders. Nothing was salvageable; sitting on top of the pile was my plastic cigarette lighter, still intact with just a corner slightly melted. I had not been smoking nor lit a fire.

I was naked once again. The others heard me laughing and came over to see what had happened. We stood around the blackened pile that had been my clothes, trying to work out a logical explanation, but could come up with none. I spent the next few hours ritualising the change I could feel within. Naked as a babe and covered in sand, I dragged driftwood, tangles of seaweed, even bleached old thongs I found washed up on the beach, to the site of my clothes and made a grave, decorated with shells to my past. It was symbolic; I knew the fire had been a doorway to yet more change.

Then I had to work out how to get back with no clothes! I had noticed earlier an old apricot blanket hanging from a tree. If I tore it in half, I could make a sarong-style skirt with a top held together at the sides with a couple of twigs. And that is what I was attired in as we climbed back in the boat for the journey back. It was appropriate. I felt like an Indian Baba in apricot robes and I had no idea the blanket belonged to Gill!

That night we lit a fire and everyone was dancing out under the stars. I felt different. I'd let go and gotten back in touch with the magic and mystery of my own life. I don't know how it happened, what steps occurred to lead me to what happened next, but I found myself standing, wrapped in Gill's arms. As we stood looking up at the slither of new moon, I began to feel that everything might just be alright.

How do I even begin to share the magic of that night? My beautiful man, holding my hand as he led me through the forest, our bare feet, silent and soft on the thick green moss that covered the path where the trees grew so thick, they kept out the sun. I had never felt so beautiful and as we wound deeper into the forest we both gasped in awe when we saw trillions of tiny lights carpeting the forest floor, spreading in every direction. It was the luminous fungi that grew in clusters from the trunks of all the trees, glowing in the darkness, lit up like fairies' lanterns. We crouched in the dark for a long time, enraptured by the lights of the fungi that had chosen this night, our night to garland the forest. My body was glistening from a sheen of sweat from the heat of the tropical night. I couldn't speak a word; my heart was beating so loudly it sounded like a tribal drum. Every cell of my body was tingling with the anticipation of stepping into Gill's arms.

When we arrived at the tipi I sat on the mattress covered in sheepskins as Gill built up the kindling and lit a small fire in the hearth. We didn't need it for warmth, that was for sure, but the forest had cast a dampness on the tipi that would be soothed by the flames. I felt so nervous and vulnerable and yet awakened on such a deep level, I was breathing slowly, savouring each breath, completely wrapped up and enfolded by the sweet intensity of the night and my love for this man. I had thought we were over and that nothing would recover the clumsiness of our previous night. I was wrong.

Gill sat down beside me, the light of the fire was dancing on his face, in his hair, flickering up the canvas sides of the tipi as well as in my heart. I am sure I heard the forest breath a huge sigh of relief when Gill pulled me towards him and kissed me. The anticipation had been so intense, our earth and all its sentient beings felt it and we all breathed in and sighed as one. I had not loved like this before, not with anyone, but I didn't need to learn, the force that was guiding me was stretching itself out inside of me, reaching out into the long slumbering gorges of my soul, my secret places, the caves where I had hidden, never feeling safe to bare all in love, before.

There was no separation that night. We two were one. Where he began and I ended was no longer clear. Together we stepped beyond the mortal world and made love in the stars, and it wasn't until much later, when we lay wrapped up in each other's arms, that he'd reached over and, tenderly stroking my face, told me the whole time we had been making love, he'd heard angels sing!

I slept like a blissed-out Fairy Queen that night and in the morning, just as the sun had begun to dapple the day with its light, I got up and gathered my things. My lift home was leaving at first light and I hadn't wanted to wake my slumbering love, hadn't wanted words to shatter the treasure of our night with their clumsiness, so I crept out to catch it, without saying goodbye.

Weeks passed before I saw him again. I was surprised at that. I had thought he would eagerly pack his bag and rush with the speed of the wind just to be by my side, but he didn't. Everyday I looked down my driveway in the hope I'd see him. Why didn't he come? I felt absolutely wretched. Had I imagined what we'd shared to be more than it was? As the days passed and my hopes of seeing him waned, I began to think so.

When he finally came he did so casually as if it was the morning after our night together, telling me how he'd been clearing the orchards and mulching up the rambutan and rolinia trees where he lived. He was loving and clearly happy to see me, but my insecurities clung to all the things he didn't say. He offered no words of love or even reassurance that he'd missed me. In all the uncertainty I had created, my happiness had done a dive, whereas his hadn't missed a beat. Whilst I had been building up my fears, reinforcing resistance and convincing myself that loving Gill was a silly idea, he had been happily gardening! I felt so needy and I didn't like it. I felt much too vulnerable, I was still struggling to trust and running away seemed easier than facing my fears. I convinced myself the last thing I needed was another man in my life, especially one as attractive as Gill. Every time we went out I would see women looking at him. He was like an ad for Levi jeans with his perfectly muscled body, his beautiful face and pale blue eyes but it was more than that. It was almost a Pan-like quality he exuded, he was so anchored in his body, so connected with the earth and I could see it wasn't just me that found his masculine energy arousing.

I edged around him, unable to express what was going on for me or even feel safe enough to do so. I was shut up hiding once again. My love was perfect yet he'd come too soon, much too soon.

I'd only been living on my own a few weeks. I still felt fragile and broken and I was still bone thin. I wanted to plump myself up and lay spread-eagled on the giant rock that shelved out over the Coral Sea and never lost the heat of the sun, listening to the splash of the ocean as it rucked and swayed on the rocky coastline below. I felt like I needed days and weeks, empty time stretching ahead, to soak up the early morning sun on my face and hear the circling calls of the sea eagles that soared in the cloudless sky. I needed gentle, soft people whose steps didn't make a din and gentle moments to fill in the cracks that all my trust had tumbled into and been lost—but I didn't need love, not yet.

But being with Gill again was like balm for my soul. I wanted to run away but my heart wouldn't let me. I loved every minute of being with him. The first night he was back he told me to grab a swag and a billy and some water for our tea, we were going to sleep on the beach. When I looked surprised at the lack of provisions he reassured me he had everything else. He only carried a little bag so everything else couldn't be much. It took us five minutes to climb down the steep track to the beach. We unrolled our swags in the still warm sand and I began to gather driftwood for our fire, whilst Gill cast in a line to catch some fish. The ocean favoured Gill. He often walked her shore and had told me of the time when he'd seen something splashing out in the ocean that warned him some creature was in trouble. When he swam out he found a big old sea turtle stuck in one of the shark nets that edged the tourist beach. Without Gill's help it would have drowned. He untangled it, swam it back to shore to check it was uninjured and when he saw it was, swam it back out, safely beyond the shark nets before letting it go.

It didn't take him long to catch a couple of flathead for our tea and I was surprised to see him give thanks for them. 'I always honour those that nurture me,' he told me.

I had never been connected to the source of my food before. It had always come from the shops and I found Gill's way of feeding himself very honest. I'd seen him climb coconut trees and chop down a bunch of green nuts for us to drink, and he often had mangos and bananas with him that he'd found growing wild. I had puzzled over how he would cook the fish, but I would never have guessed. He made a rack out of green twigs; four sticks with V's in the top, stuck in the sand formed the frame with other sticks laid across making a flat surface. 'Hopefully the fish is cooked before the green sticks catch fire,' he'd said, laughing at my astonishment at yet another of his bush skills.

I found being with Gill so soothing. I craved his silent and soft sanctuary, yet I still resisted, still tried to hold myself back from love. I had wild passionate moments with him where all my joy would leak out and then, feeling vulnerable, I'd immerse myself in fear. Fear that he would leave, fear that I would repeat what I'd had with Dan, fear he would betray me and fear that I wasn't worthy of his love. I'd hear Gill so often say, 'Just follow me and you'll be okay,' and there was always such a deep resounding truth in those words, even if they were said lightly just to guide and reassure.

Finally, after he'd been staying for a few days, I told him it was over. Total insanity on my part, I agree. I couldn't make sense of myself so I couldn't make sense of anything I was doing. I was in agony, yet when I saw the tears roll down his face, I walked away. I couldn't trust myself to even look at him. My heart was breaking, but I couldn't take any more pain. I sat at the kitchen table long after Gill had gone to bed. I was utterly miserable. After everything I'd experienced, all that I'd learnt about trust and the power of love, I was huddled up inside myself like a knot, and I wanted to die.

Suddenly and completely unexpectedly, some words burst from my mouth. There had been no conscious thought behind them. I spoke as if I was giving a command: 'I wish to die a death that is so complete I am never as I was before.'

If I could have foreseen the impact of those words, would I have spoken them? I would have to say, YES, but in the nineteen years that have passed since, I have never even whispered them again. My life was about to change drastically—once again. As I slipped into bed beside Gill, tears were streaming down my face and I lay in the dark for a long time before I fell asleep.

On the surface it was a night like any other. The build up to the wet season had begun and it was stiflingly hot and humid. The moist air was palpably thick with the scent of frangipani and ripe mangoes, mingled with salt from the ocean that slapped and tickled on the rocks below, resonating with the constant drone of cicadas and the croaks of green tree frogs that lived like lords in our shower.

The only weird thing that happened that night that I should have picked up earlier was the peculiar way my dogs behaved. They had howled for over an hour and wouldn't shut up when I yelled. I had never heard them howl before, it was eerie and mournful, but it was also very strange. If someone arrived, they barked. They always let me know someone was there and for the events of that night to occur someone had to have been there, prowling around in the dark. So what made my dogs howl instead of bark?

I drifted fitfully off to sleep and then suddenly woke with a jolt, like a drowning woman scrambling madly for wakefulness. Three rocks crashed down on our roof, one after another. Gill sat bolt upright in bed beside me, one hand on me warning me to be still. We sat listening in the dark, danger splicing the night like a bloodied knife. It was only seconds, long, fraught, anxious seconds, before we heard an unmistakable sound, a sound that still all these years later can cause a wave of panic to surge through me.

In the fast-fuelled charge of the night, there was no time to think. No time to consider the possibility that whoever had thrown those rocks might still be there. Did they hide in the darkness watching, licking their lips in pleasure when they saw us running naked into the madness, yelling and screaming to Nick, our only neighbour in the studio next door to ring the fire brigade? Trying to connect hoses to put out a fire that's burning so fast there's nothing you can do but back off, move away ... and let go—again.

My dogs, Foxy and Wunjo, were by my side, but I couldn't find Sprout, my rescued street dog who knew every rubbish bin within a two kilometre radius and had an army of people that regularly fed him, thinking as I had, that they were the only ones. I had tried to tame my little street urchin of a dog, but he was wild and free and didn't need me—and secretly, I never wanted him to change. He was often out, doing his own thing. But I was certain that this night I'd seen him snuggled up sleeping on the settee, just before I'd gone to bed.

I ran frantically around a house that was engulfed in flames and seconds away from caving in, screaming out his name. Outside the kitchen two huge propane gas bottles were releasing, sending jets of flames into the black smudge of sky. Fridges and stoves, hopes and dreams, all crashed and tumbled and exploded. I screamed out for Sprout until my mouth was so dry I couldn't speak. I was sick with despair with an ache in my belly that was about to rip me open when Sprout leapt out of the flaming doorway like a circus dog and ran towards us, humbly wagging his tail, as if he'd done wrong. As I knelt down on the ground and held my precious little mate tight, I felt this unexpected happiness—just like in Goa when my bag was gone.

I was in the midst of what most would see as a crisis and yet in the four potent minutes, which was all it took to completely extinguish my home, I'd had an epiphany—again. I had just lost my lovely weathered, wooden home, full of all my stuff. She had sat like an old matriarch on the highest tip of the hill, growing frail with age; but she had not been a happy place for me. It was hard to grasp it had all gone. If I could have imagined this scenario a year before, a month before or even the previous week, I would have guarded that house like a hungry lion. Yet as I stood with Gill and my three dogs safely at the bottom of the garden, away from my car that we'd been unable to move and was now filling up with smoke, the plastic edging on the rear vision mirrors dripping like melted wax, I was overwhelmed with *relief*.

The phoenix definitely rose for me that night. The flames were so huge the gossip that swirled and eddied through the suburbs below spoke of a plane that had crashed into the hill. It took that savage, brutal night for me to stop fucking up my life, and in some crazy misshapen way my prayers had finally been answered.

I'd been afraid of getting hurt again. *Well, grow up Kye. Are you going to run away from one of the most beautiful things in your life because you're too scared to love? Not anymore.*

Gill had his arms wrapped around me, holding me close, whispering into my ear that he loved me and never wanted to hurt me and even though my past was going up in flames, in the volatility of the night all that mattered was the love I felt for this man. I could finally surrender to our love! Shonteeha had been so right when she'd told me that if I resisted this love, life would show me. It had!

I was jarred from the absolutely inexplicable serenity I'd felt by the sounds of sirens getting closer, awakening us to the fact that help, even if it was too late, was on its way. We raced to find something to cover our nudity. A garbage bag, a hessian sack and an oil rag! It was all we had.

The roof of the house had caved in by the time the fire engine arrived. They told me later it had only taken them four minutes to respond to our call, but by the speed in which the flames had engulfed my home, we had known from the first moment this was not a battle we could win. The police tried to take a statement from me as I watched my house burn down. Bland, monotone questions that were completely out of place and lacked any sensitivity. 'Name? Address? What time did you go to bed?'

'I don't know. I don't have a clock or a watch. About forty minutes ago?' I was rocking from side to side with the energy of the fire.

'Would it have been 10.30pm?'

'I don't know, I don't have a watch.' I was getting exasperated.

'Were you smoking?'

'No, I wasn't fucking smoking. My life is burning here and you're asking me all these stupid questions.' I had tears rolling down my face. They backed off.

'Okay, just come down to the station and make a statement in the next couple of days.'

After everyone had left—the firemen, police, TV channels, electricity board, gas board and all the onlookers that had been drawn from the sleeping suburbs below to watch the fire—we returned to the only building that now stood, the sleep-out. We huddled up to each other, too terrified to sleep. The dogs howled again like wolves all through the night into the acrid, still smoking sky. It was hot and humid, yet I felt chilled to my bones. I wanted to be somewhere else, someplace that felt safe, but the night felt so full of menace, we were both too afraid to move. It felt like a demon, darker than anything I'd ever experienced, was charging around the embers of my home as if it had had its head chopped off.

In the first rays of morning light we crept from the sleep-out, sloshing through a marmalade of mangos, cooked by the fire, to get to the bus that was way down the garden, parked there while someone was away. We lived in that, cowering in the shadows of whatever was burning itself off in the smouldering remains of my home. A few days later, we woke up early at sunrise and found the air translucent and calm. The darkness and pain had all gone.

The next morning, I rang the church that owned the house and the hill it was on. I was pretty sure they'd know by now what had happened, but there was something persistent, a nagging voice inside that kept urging me over and over again to phone them and tell them I had more than a little reason to feel suspicious about the fire.

'We were woken up by rocks hitting our roof. Someone burnt the house down,' I told the development officer for the church, the ex-colonel I'd always dealt with.

'We were always worried about that house. One of the light switches didn't have a cover on it,' he replied gruffly, seemingly from a vast distance, ignoring my previous comment completely.

'But we were woken up by rocks hitting our roof!'

'We've been advised there were no suspicious circumstances. If you wish to make a complaint, you will have to go to the police.'

I put the phone down. My mind was in turmoil. *Been advised there were no suspicious circumstances! No one had even taken a statement from me and what switch didn't have a cover on it? I know that's not true.* I'm so cautious of electricity. I pay attention to things like this, and only three weeks before I'd had an electrician in fixing a few things I was concerned about. A switch without a cover on it would have been a priority. *Why did he say this, why did he lie? And when had he been to the house?* It had been over a year since I'd seen him, and then we'd spoken in the garden. He definitely hadn't come in.

Gill stayed in the bus while I went to the police station. I wish I'd had a tape recorder. I was told I was imagining the rocks and nothing I said was taken seriously. There was no police investigation, no detectives sifting through the ashes to find the cause of the fire. We were there for three weeks after the house burnt down and the only person who came was from the church. I'd been caretaking the house for six years and any hope of help, a tea bag, some donated clothes—even an 'Are you okay? Is there anything we can do?'—was dashed. He came only to check out the damage for the insurance and was unwilling to engage in any conversation with us.

I didn't have the answers. I had lots of loose ends that didn't lead anywhere and didn't make any sense and no time to dwell on any of it. My life was moving fast in a totally unexpected direction. I was in love and happier than I had ever been. I had loved my home and felt a connection with the hill that ran so deep it pulsed through my veins, and yet leaving gave me no sense of loss. I had come out of the fire with nothing. Everything I'd accumulated in my life up to this point was gone and there wasn't a single tear of regret. Many people had their own memories and connections with my old matriarch of a home and felt her loss deeply. I comforted others as they sobbed in my arms, but all I could feel was joy. I was certain we would find a new home easily. I had no doubts about that. Somewhere special had to be waiting for us, somewhere I'd connect and entwine with, like I had my precious hill.

My friend Kaz invited us to stay while we looked for somewhere to live. As I gathered up my only bag for the three-day trip ahead, I couldn't help chuckling at the cosmic joke being played on me. Gill had come into my life uncluttered, carrying everything he owned in a little green bag. I'd laughed when I'd first seen that bag. *This guy's not going far in life*, I thought to myself dismissively! Now here I was throwing my own little green bag in the back of the van with his.

If I thought my fears were all behind me, I was wrong. I was so caught up in the fairy tale of our love that I was blind to its weak spots, the places I'd slip through the ice. I had no idea, as we drove off in our newly purchased transit van that was already blowing smoke, laughing and happy under a sky that was brightest blue, that life still had something very important to teach me, something vital that would soothe my harrowed past and be a guiding light in all my lost moments to come.

But if I'd known this lesson was coming, I might have been tempted to run.

Thirteen

Rainbow Man

Even though I loved spending time with my dark skinned, soft-as-velvet friend Kaz, I'd always had an uneasy relationship with her home. In many I loved it, but I could never stay there long. It was a beautiful property with a huge, rambling, wooden home on a creek that sat in a deep-sided valley. But it lost the sun mid-afternoon and for the rest of the day was in shadow. I often felt claustrophobic, as if I was trapped in a jar. I needed more light. I'd always lived up high, not in the damp and the mould with its big black leeches. But it wasn't just that.

Kaz's home was so full of visitors, so to have a bit of space for ourselves, Gill and I camped in our van in a corner of the garden. I would have been happy with that, but when a woman at the house started flirting really openly with Gill, old fears began to choke me; I felt insecure and desperate for us to go. It took six weeks to find a home. I was so relieved, though even that was to be short-lived. It was a small cabin so high up the mountain range that for days at a time it was in the clouds. It was surrounded by the severed trunks of ancient trees. When I walked amongst them, my belly ached as if it had been split open, and I felt a sorrow that made me want to howl. I was always turning quickly because I would feel someone behind me. Was that the face of a frightened child peeping from behind that tree? Was that an old man, ochre painted with a spear? Once when I was sitting cross- legged on the top of a giant stump, stilling myself so that I could hear the voices of the spirits that haunted these woods, a group of spirit women came to me, clutching their bellies and wailing. I knew it wasn't just the trees that had been slaughtered here, it was whole tribes.

Our cabin was a tiny box with a step-in kitchen. On the rare clear days, we could see the ocean, fifty kilometres away. The rest of the time, we lived in cloudy, dripping grey. Our only visitor was a huge python that should have been hibernating but instead slept curled up on the frosted tufts of grass outside. Every time we found him, we built a warm home around him to protect him from the cold, but the following day he'd always be gone and we'd find him, later, in some other unsuitable place, coiled up having a snooze.

On the days we did brave the cold and dripping clouds, we could walk through the forest to the very top of a waterfall that plunged hundreds of metres straight down the mountain to the pools below. Or we would walk just down our track to a crystal clear pool where we always stopped and bathed when we were returning home from town.

On the clear days we lived in a majestic enchanted beauty, but when the clouds rolled in, it was even more oppressive than Kaz's beautiful home in the valley. We were always struggling to either get out or back in. It rained nearly non-stop and the upwards road that wove around the edge of the cliff turned to slippery clay when wet. One skid and you could plummet to your death. I dreaded the days we'd get stuck out because then we would have to stay at Kaz's and the flirtations would continue right in front of me. Gill didn't say much. He certainly didn't flirt back, but my new confidence in life was feeling fragile.

Several other women were trampling their way to Gill, heedless of our relationship. On one occasion we gave someone a lift home. I had no idea they shared a house with one of these women. She saw our distinctive red van coming down the track and was there to meet us. She had a top on that was completely undone in the front and nothing on underneath. She stood on the driver's side by Gill, her arms on the roof of the car, her breasts hanging out for us all to see.

I thought I'd let go of so much hurt from my past with Dan, but this behaviour was breaking open old wounds. This was nothing new to me, and I had never understood women betraying women for the attention of a man. It's a line I won't cross and after six years of it I felt sick in my guts at the prospect of more.

Another woman, Bonnie, always seemed to be in town when we were. She wore long, hippy dresses and she would come rustling over, bangles jangling, and start flirting with Gill. I would be standing on the street like a loose end. I couldn't believe how many women were prepared to stomp over the top of me to get what they wanted. There are some things I've clung to, no matter how deep into darkness I've fallen—truth, honour, being able to look one another in the eyes, walk tall. I have never been a pushy person like this. If things come my way, they come because they're mine. *If I have to fight to keep my man, I am going to lose.*

I didn't know how Gill was being affected by his seducers. When we got home, we were far enough away from it all in the land of the clouds for me to feel disconnected, at least temporarily, from the predators below. We never talked about it, and I was foolish not to because his absence of words did not mean that everything was okay.

When the engine finally blew on our transit van, which had chugged its way exhaustingly up and down that mountain, time and time again and we were unable to get home, we ended up staying at Kaz's. She was away and for once the house was empty of visitors. It was just us. We had only been there a few days when one evening, as I was sitting in the lounge, I looked up and got the shock of my life. Standing in front of me was an enormous eight foot tall being emanating intense rainbow light that was as real and solid as everything else in the room. I wish I had been more courteous, but my first response was 'Fucking hell!'— exclaimed so loudly that Gill came running to see what was wrong. My 'Rainbow Man' disappeared. After I'd explained to Gill what had happened, I found myself apologising to thin air, hopeful he would hear me, praying he would return again and promising to be more welcoming if he did. I had no idea what his appearance signified. So many inexplicable events had occurred since I met Gill that I could no longer doubt that we had something very special to do together. It was only a matter of time before that was to be unveiled.

A few days later, I began to feel a little strange. As if my body was continually filling with light, more and more. The feeling just kept building in intensity, making me so dizzy I had to lay down. I was so disconnected from my physical body. Right away I knew what was happening. My rainbow visitor had returned and was aligning his energy with mine. It was only a short visit, but over the next week or two, he came many times. Gill and I soon worked out that it really helped me to stay earthed if Gill lay on top of me, which he did.

Each time Rainbow Man came he would stay a little longer, always leaving just before the crucial point when to dally meant I would fry. His energy would build up inside me with such velocity and always, just at that point when I thought I couldn't take anymore, he'd be gone. I had no idea what this angelic being wanted to communicate with me, and it didn't matter. When we merged, it was bliss.

I thought life was finally coming good for me, so it came as a huge shock when walking back up to the house after a swim in the creek, relaxed and happy, not for a single moment expecting the worst, Gill met me in the doorway. I knew straight away something was terribly wrong, by the look on his face. When he spoke, his words hit me like an avalanche and almost buried me alive. While I'd been swimming, he had packed his bag, ready to leave. There was no explanation and nothing he had said that morning had prepared me for this. He walked out of the door, out of my life, as if nothing we'd shared had meant a thing to him.

Why hadn't I felt this was going to happen? Why hadn't I picked up on it? Why, why, why? It was a cruel and heartless break in trust, and to not even give me the time to tell me why. He'd thrown a bomb and raced to safety so that he didn't have to deal with the blast.

I don't know how I got through that day and the long night. Kaz's house was a hard and lonely place to be. Many years ago a family had drowned there when the river had been in flood; sometimes that sadness enveloped the house like a fog. As night settled, there were nooks and hollows even the lights didn't reach— dark shadowy places that ached and groaned and wept.

I didn't sleep. I lay tucked up into myself, weeping with pain, not knowing how I could ever trust myself to love again. How can I love when I can't tell what's real? It hurt that he'd left, oh my God it hurt. But most of all, what writhed and shat inside me was that I hadn't sensed a thing. Not a bloody thing! Was I so disconnected from reality? Was I so wound up in myself that I'd been unable to see who Gill really was? Or was it that Gill lived so encapsulated in himself, unable to show or share feelings, unable to create even a surface ripple in the veneer of nice? I didn't fucking know. Six years of suffering in a dysfunctional relationship of lies and manipulation, six violent years, had not cracked me open like this.

When sunlight finally hit the valley, I fled the house, determined to find Gill, desperate to understand. I didn't know where to look. I was haggard with grief; all I could think was to hitch into town. It took me two hours and I struggled to converse with the kind people who gave me lifts. I didn't see their faces. I didn't care that my eyes were swollen and red; I was consumed with the need to see Gill. I was desperate to know why.

I found him within the first five minutes. He was getting out of the car of the woman that had hunted him like prey and offered her breasts like bait. It was obvious what had happened that night. When she saw me, she casually outstretched her arms along the car, her back to it and gave me a look of such gloating venom. Like a vampire she was feeding off my pain. When I called out to Gill, he was aloof. I was drowning and he didn't care. It was as if the intimacy we'd shared had never been and there was no way back to our love.

There was no solace in anything for me. I was raw with pain, and just when I thought life couldn't get any worse. It did. My dear dog Foxy, who had been by my side through all my years of shit, died. She'd been unwell all day. I rang a vet who wouldn't see me without cash up front, which I didn't have. I pleaded, but his heart was chiselled from stone. All I could do was nurse Foxy and pray for the best. By late evening I realised she had the symptoms of a paralysis tick. Her back legs were failing and she was having difficulty breathing. A few hours later she died in my arms. All the lights went out. The darkness was everywhere. I howled in pain. My little Foxy, my innocent and loving friend, was gone.

I was so relieved when Kaz arrived home. She has a presence as serene as moonlight as she wrapped her love around me like a cape. I clung to her, crying for a long time. The pain inside went so deep I was in fear of being swallowed by it. Without Kaz I would have. She had two young children to look after, her own emotional upheavals to deal with, yet she still gave. Sorrow can be selfish; I know mine was. Yet she allowed me to be, and all these years later, when the memories of pain and betrayal have faded, I still well up inside at the gift she gave me, that gentle place to heal, that watery haven where my tears could flow freely.

I stayed in her tipi at the bottom of the garden on the edge of the swimming hole where, if you were silent enough, you could see the platypus play. I loved that space and spent a lot of time on my own. At night I would light the fire and play my guitar. I'm only a three-chord wonder, but I would sing with such depth that I touched magical places in myself I'd never been before. Singing was my release and gave me an anchor to face and heal my wounds. When I thought of Gill, I couldn't make sense of anything. All I could focus on was me and the moment, nothing else. Even so, a tarot card kept forcing me to think of him. It was the nine of cups from the Mythic Tarot deck, the reunion of Eros and Psyche. Their love has undergone many trials and tribulations, but they are reunited and stand together, stronger for the challenges, able to see each other in their own true light. Aphrodite stands beside them and gives them her blessing. I didn't even have to pull it; it had a mind of its own and would literally spring out of the deck whenever I picked the cards up and plop on the table or the floor. For a long time I cherished that card as a silent hope.

The day I heard Gill had moved in with Bonnie, I ran to the toilet and was violently sick. I hung over the toilet bowl, thinking it would never end, the strong taste of bile bitter in my mouth. When I went to town, I often saw them together. I felt tiny and vulnerable, walking down the street alone, hurting so badly, trying to look bright and brave when our orbits circled close.

One afternoon I was sitting with mutual friends at a pub overlooking the beach when they joined us. It was the first time we had all been this close and I didn't feel comfortable. There was no way I could sit chatting superficially, pretending I didn't feel stifled by all the things I couldn't say to Gill and wanted to. It could have all been so much easier; even with the pain, if we'd talked. There was nothing soft or caring for me in being around him and I was not honouring myself if I stayed.

I got up to leave and was just on my way out when I bumped into Bonnie. She was standing on her own as if she was waiting for someone. The jostle of the pub was like the drone of bees around us. The salty slap of the ocean was in the air. I don't know why I thought I could create a bridge with her. Nothing she had done had ever shown me that I could, but I was tired of the quagmire of emotion that sucked me into a bog every time I saw them. It didn't just come from me, I could feel that.

'I just wanted to say,' I stuttered nervously, 'whatever's happening with you and Gill, all the best.' As I was speaking she looked around the pub with a bored look on her face, completely disinterested in what I had to say. I'd dug down so deep for those words and they were met as if they were the irritating buzz of a mosquito. I thought it had mattered, but it hadn't. This was the moment when I woke up and fucking got it. I would not give or share myself with people who didn't give a shit about me, again.

This was a turning point in my life, but even, so I kept having one particular dream. My grandfather died over a decade ago. I absolutely adored him. He was the man I looked up to and he was the only man that was there for me as a child. Singing old Peggie Lee songs, he'd waltz me around the room as I perched on the tops of his polished leather shoes. He was the nurturer of my childhood dreams and the bard who made up fantastic stories that would transform my plain old Nan into a cat burglar who walked upside down on ceilings. When she was out of earshot, he'd pull me and my brothers close and tell us in whispers how the police had finally caught her. Then swearing us to secrecy, he would enthral us with torrid tales of Nan's last stint in jail.

Since his death, he has appeared in my dreams three times. Each time has been at a transitory moment in my life where he shared an insight that only the passing of time showed me was true. Here he was once again....

I'm sitting in an audience at a village hall. I don't know what's happening, but I see Gill come onto the stage and I scream out his name. He comes to the front of the stage and says to me, 'Wait for me, I'm coming. I've just got some things to do.' I sit back down. The lights are turned off and it is pitch black, so I can't see a thing. I feel shaky, not knowing what to expect. When the lights came on again, I see my grandfather walking towards me. 'He's just got some things to work out with his heart,' he told me. 'Don't worry, he'll be back.'

For a long time I clung to that dream and the message inherent in the nine of cups card, feeling Gill and I would eventually get back together. But it was that day at the pub when I finally and irrevocably let go. It was madness to even want Gill back in my life.

I still hurt. I still struggled to make sense of what had happened and still wanted to know why. But the ache inside began to diminish. I no longer pushed it away from me or tried to disown it like an amputated limb; instead, I nestled it to me and I soothed it.

I know the path through sorrow. I know what it's like when you're fumbling alone in the dark and everything you touch hurts. I know the darkness that even the warmth of the sun doesn't reach. I didn't think I'd ever find my way out, but I did, and I found a light within myself I didn't know existed. I came out the other end feeling more beautiful than I had ever done, and for the first time in my life, my wellbeing was in safe hands—mine.

News of Gill and Bonnie still smoked and billowed through the valley on blustery days. I'd heard they were in love, so it came as a surprise when Kaz told me she'd seen Gill get on a bus heading back to the tropics. 'He'll only be gone for a few weeks,' I was told. 'He's left all his stuff with Bonnie and is coming back.'

'I really felt he was missing you,' Kaz told me. I thought she was mad and I told her so, even though I knew she often saw what wasn't plain to see and Kaz was known for her prophetic dreams. There was much I hadn't known about Gill, but what I did know was that he gave no value to stuff. All he owned and needed he'd taken with him. It was the way he was, with that little green canvas bag. What he'd left behind were all the wooden bowls he'd carved from burls, last remnants of an old forest he'd found when we'd been together, and the beautiful stool he'd made me from an old tree stump that in a fit of anger I'd insisted he take back when we cleared out the house in the clouds. All these things that were created when we did love together were at Bonnie's now.

It was nothing to do with Gill when, a few weeks later, I returned to the tropics myself. I was homesick. That was all, and 'my' hill was calling. I rang Gerry, my old neighbour who lived in the studio behind my once-was house. 'Come, Kye. You can use all the facilities here, the sleep-out's still there.' I loved Gerry. She was an earth mother with grown-up kids and exuded warmth I often wanted to snuggle into. I didn't have to be told twice.

I managed to buy an old Holden for six hundred dollars. Finally, I had a car and my independence. Kaz had been amazing. She had let me be in my grief for as long as was needed, with no pressure. I hugged that goddess hard, tears running down my face with gratitude. I started up the car, no smoke with this one. I had a couple of backpackers from England coming for the ride, willing to share fuel costs and help drive. My two dogs, Wunjo and Sprouty, sat on the back seat, wagging their tails, just as keen as me to return home.

With a last wave of goodbye, I set off on the long journey home. Fuelling my quest to head north was the burning desire to be back on my magical hill, back to the only place that felt like home. I didn't have a crystal ball. I couldn't see my future and I had no idea that the force that was taking me home was the same force that would lead me to discover truths I wouldn't be too sure I was happy to know.

Fourteen

Cane Knife

I felt that familiar surge of energy as I drove up the winding track that led to the peak of my hill. It was a place of such intensity and drew to it light and darkness. Just before I had come to live there someone had been murdered there, and once during one of my times away overseas, a young woman had been raped. It was hard to imagine such heinous acts in a place of such beauty, but the forces of good and evil had been battling over its possession for a long.

This seventy acre peninsula had originally been gifted to the church to use for under-privileged kids. The old lady who had owned it had already built chalets that overlooked the bay for the children to stay in, and they had been enjoying holidays on the beach for years. The house I lived in on top of the hill was the only part the church didn't own ... at first. It had been left to the old lady's long-time companion for her lifetime. On her death it would return to the church, who would then own the lot. The companion, an eccentric old lady, rented her house to me for a year before she accepted a settlement from the church for her lease. The church became the new owner of the house and was happy for me, and the tenants in the other three houses that were scattered around the hill, to stay rent-free as long as we maintained the properties ourselves, as caretakers. Not only was I living in paradise, I was doing it for free!

The church assured us that if ever we had to leave, we would be given at least a year's notice. It would take that long for any development proposal to go through. The church was keen to sell. It was a developer's dream, a magical, beachfront property. Stuff the kids. Stuff the dreams of old ladies; as soon as their benefactor died, they bulldozed all the chalets she'd built just for the children.

People had been fighting to save the hill for years. A well-known TV programme had even run a story on it. It had been fought out in the courts, and even though the church had been given the green light to develop, another force more potent than money, one that didn't follow the dictates of man scorched anyone that tried to destroy the dream.

One development company had paid their deposit a long time ago, about the time I had just moved into the house. At that time it was up for sale for sixteen million. They came onto the hill with their bulldozers and chainsaws and devastated an area of pristine beauty. I cried all day, hearing the agony of trees being felled.

When everyone had left, I walked out to the edge of the garden and looked down on the hell they'd created. I was yelling out inside, *What can I do? Tell me what I can do.* An answer came immediately. It was crystal clear: LOVE them. It was as if the hill had spoken to me herself. To those less versed in the power of love, this would seem crazy. But I did it. I stood there sending everything love— the bulldozers, the men, the fallen trees. Everything.

They came back the following day with truckloads of car tyres that they used to set fire to the green trees. Black smoke from burning rubber billowed out for days. I rebelled against sending love. I was so angry, but eventually I calmed my thoughts and I did it. The following morning no one came. Days passed and still no developers. Weeks passed. Finally, I heard the company had gone broke. Over the next six years I saw this happen many times.

My friend and neighbour Jen, who lived in a cute wooden house on the edge of the cliff with spectacular views out over the ocean, was an avid and vocal campaigner to save the hill. She owned her property and was not beholden to the church in any way. She fought them in court, she handed out petitions, and being a journalist, she got the story of the hill a lot of press coverage. In her twenty years of living there she had been a constant witness to the hill's undeniable power to repulse anyone that tried to develop it. Was this the spirit of an unhappy lady that haunted the place where she'd cherished her dream? We often thought that, but we also knew the hill was seamed with quartz crystal and was a powerful place in its own right.

Jen and I would often go to the huge rock that shelved out breathtakingly over the ocean. If we were lucky, the dolphins would be swimming below. And if we were really lucky, we might get a glimpse of the giant manta rays that swam in the deep blue waters. We would sit on the rock and visualise love, like rays of sunlight beaming from the hill.

I was overjoyed to be back. The garden had turned into a jungle. Gerry's intention to care for it had been sabotaged when she'd broken her arm.

'That garden just didn't want me there,' she had told me on the phone. 'The energy needed time to settle after the fire.' I'm sure it was no coincidence the hill attracted people sensitive to its currents and flows. Gerry told me that one morning she'd felt the urge to walk through the garden. A single while lily was flowering right in the soot and the ash where the house had been. Now it was a mass of young tomato plants. They covered the ground like grass. As I walked towards the sleep-out, I was puzzling over how they'd got there.

The sleep-out was a small room, ten foot square, tin roofed with a small veranda out the front. There was

nothing fancy about it, and it could have done with
a coat of paint. After six months living away, I was
expecting it to be a mess. As far as I knew it had been
empty since I'd left, so I was surprised to see the veranda
swept and the whole place looking cared for. Someone
was obviously living there. I called out. No one was
home, so I peeped through the window. It was so tidy
with tea towels with pretty pictures pinned to the walls
and a bed neatly made. I was puzzling over who'd moved
in when I heard footsteps behind me.

'Hey, Kye. You're back.' It was Cane Knife, looking
bashful, a sheepish grin on his face, unsure about the
delicacies of human interactions. Did we hug? Shake
hands? He was never comfortable with all that, but I
knew he was pleased to see me.

'I'm moving out, Kye. I was only looking after it for you,'
he said, apologetically. This cared-for home was alien
to what I knew of Cane Knife. He'd lived on the hill
almost the whole time I had. I'd originally invited him
to camp for a couple of days when he had nowhere to
live. Despite my promptings he'd never left. He'd made
a shelter out of black plastic on our magnificent rock
where Jen and I meditated. It became a mess, littered
with his rubbish. In fits of rage I often pulled his shelter
down when he was out, but the next day, there it would
be, blowing tattily in the wind again just to annoy me.

I didn't realise until many years later how lost I would have been without that man. His rubbish was a paltry price to pay for what he gave to me. He was my rock. He was steady and kind, but most of all, when everyone was against me and my back was full of spears, he loved me like a treasure.

The local pub was only a short walk away, and the nudist beach just a steep climb down from my home. Occasionally, those venues attracted wandering, predatory men. It was Cane Knife who would do a last check of my home before he went to bed, making sure I was safe when he knew I was staying in the house on my own, and it was Cane Knife that woke up in the middle of the night to find a strange man sitting on his bed and his first thought was to run like hell to me, to make sure I hadn't been harmed. And it was always Cane Knife's tattered little camp I'd run to when I was so choked up with pain I couldn't speak. I didn't need to be anything with Cane knife. I was perfectly fine just the way I was, even when I was mad! We had our fights, always dramatic and theatrical. He would call me a witch and I'd call him a wanker, but always five minutes later we'd meet on the track that wove through the long grass and connected our homes, both as willing as each other to bury the hatchet and admit we'd been wrong. Though he did confess to me with a chuckle I wasn't wrong about the name I called him!

He was a wild-looking character and most people found him very gruff. Six foot five, thin like a matchstick, with a shaven head. If you met him in a dark lane you'd freak. Once Gill and I gave him a lift into town when we passed a man on the footpath being attacked by dogs. Cane Knife leapt out of the car to help this man, who, when he saw this wild-looking fella running towards him yelling at the top of his voice to frighten the dogs away, started to punch Cane Knife thinking he was being attacked. He'd had the desired effect. The dogs took off running for their lives, but Gill and I had to get out of the car and rescue Cane Knife from being beaten up.

He didn't fit into society and experienced life from a tangent I'd not known before. He was so different from anyone else I knew, he could have come from another planet. I asked him once if he had. 'It's funny you should say that,' he replied, earnestly. 'When Mum was pregnant with me, she saw a flying saucer. I remember asking Dad where I came from once. He pointed to the stars and said, That's where you come from, son.'

One night we were sitting on the rock watching the full moon rise up out of the ocean. The sea sparkled silver in its light. It was undeniably beautiful. 'It's just a dead planet,' Cane Knife said in a droll voice. 'I don't know what all the fuss is about.' He didn't get moved by the grandeur of planetary events, but he did little things with such sensitivity. Every birthday without fail he would give me a gift. It was always wrapped and something beautiful. A glass swan candle holder, a pretty cup (probably nicked, but I wasn't going to ask). I was always touched by his gifts. He became like a brother to me and people often couldn't equate the Cane Knife I'd come to love with the one that loped about the streets of town. There was no way I was going to kick him out of the sleep-out.

'I can't believe how beautiful you've made it look. You stay here. I can build a camp in the garden. I'd prefer to do that.' I could see him hesitating. This wild-looking, middle-aged man was a gentleman. 'It's yours, okay,' I added decisively.

He looked chuffed. 'I've never had a real home before,' he said, chuckling to himself.

Cane Knife lived more or less on fruit. Every morning he would come down to my camp, which was made of black plastic, no less, and share his food. We would sit under the mango tree overlooking the ocean and eat—a ripe papaya freshly picked with lemon juice squeezed over it, a bag of purple mangosteens, a coconut on the cusp of sprouting.

'The coconut is at its most potent just before it sprouts,' he told me. 'That's when you get maximum goodness. As soon as that little green shoot begins to sprout, the energy in the coconut is going out.' He would make me hold and smell every piece of fruit we ate. It was a ritual of appreciation, but it also taught me how to buy fruit when it's at its best.

Within a few days of being back, I'd rung the church to inform them of my return. I had had an arrangement to care-take. The sleep-out was still there and I was sharing facilities with Gerry and her husband Clem. They couldn't really object, but even so, I'd thought carefully about what I was going to say—I didn't leave them any room to say no. I spoke briskly.

'The garden was an absolute mess. The grass was so long, it was a fire hazard. But no need to worry, I've cleaned the place up. I had to evict a couple of squatters (a half-truth). I can't see there being any future problems now I'm back.' There was a pause when I'd finished then a terse 'Thank you' before the phone was put down. That was all they said. I was relieved the call was over, but I felt uneasy.

As I went back to mulching my papayas and planting more basil, I couldn't help feeling that something was wrong. I kept trying to convince myself it was my imagination. It was a beautiful day; the sea eagles glided lazily in a pristine blue sky, the ocean was still like glass and bees buzzed around the giant blooms of the pink hibiscus. Everything looked perfect in paradise, yet I felt weighed down with apprehension and I hadn't the faintest idea why.

Fifteen

Sacred Love

I'd only been back a week when Gill came walking through the jungle of my garden. I had convinced myself I was over him, but who was I trying to kid? My heart did the wildest lurch. Seeing each other took us both by surprise.

'I didn't realise you were back,' he said.

'Yeah well, I knew you'd come back, but I thought you were heading south again.'

'I never planned to,' he replied. I didn't say anything, it wasn't my business. But I knew someone's heart would be breaking and I was glad that this time it wasn't mine. It felt as if a lifetime had passed since we'd shared love, yet it was only a few months ago. When I had first met him, I thought he was too young. What had I expected?

He was walking around the shelter I'd built for myself. Black plastic strung from some trees with my bed underneath. I'd lain in bed a few nights already, listening to the wind buffeting it around, hoping it would still be there in the morning.

'You know the first bit of weather we get, you'll get soaked. The rain's going to pour straight in. I'll fix it up if you like.'

'Go for it,' I replied, though I felt really weird. I was not feeling comfortable at all. *How do I just sit here and be polite, chit chat, pretend nothing has happened? I can't do it.*

I watched him disappear barefoot into the tall guinea grass with his machete. Two or three steps and he was gone. Only the tips of the flower heads parting and rustling betrayed his direction. It wasn't long before I heard the sound of chopping and I knew he'd found a sapling that was long enough and straight enough to serve as the crossbeam for my new home.

In so many ways Gill reminded me of me. I walked everywhere barefoot on my hill and often cut through ten-foot tall guinea grass to explore secret places that no one else had ever been because the well-trodden paths didn't go there. I knew there were deadly spiders and snakes, but I didn't fear them. It had never occurred to me that they would harm me, and they never had.

Over the years I had lived on the hill, I had only ever taken one friend with me into the guinea grass to explore. I had run on ahead excitedly as we made our way downhill. I knew when I ran I always tripped, but the grass made a soft mattress for me to fall in and falling was fun. When my friend didn't catch me up, I had to find my way back to him. He was frozen with fear; unable to take another step, certain that something hidden in the grass was about to get him. His world was the ocean where he swam like a dolphin, unafraid of the creatures of the deep while fearful me rarely left the shallows. Gill was the only person I had ever met who was comfortable in my world, and I didn't want to think about the implications of that. I couldn't be vulnerable again. I wouldn't!

For the next hour or so we rebuilt my camp. Gill had cut two posts for the uprights, each with a V at the top, their ends buried in the earth. The long crossbeam ran across the centre of my camp and sat one on each end inside the V's of the upright posts. The huge square of heavy duty black plastic went over the cross beam and was secured on each corner by stakes that Gill had knocked into the ground. It was perfect. Inside I'd made a platform out of old crates that I had my mattress on.

To most people I was living like a vagrant, but I absolutely loved the simplicity of my life. Lying in bed looking out at the ocean, feeling the soft breeze on my face. Smelling the jasmine that grew tangled in the mango tree. It was paradise for me.

I opened up a papaya and offered Gill some. I was full of mixed emotion. This man had hurt me so deeply and I thought I'd dealt with it all, but I hadn't. Unexpectedly,

I felt angry and let down and mad. I wanted to smash this polite veneer, to scream in rage at him for what he'd done, and yet crazy me didn't want him to go. I DIDN'T WANT HIM TO GO. I knew the moment was fast approaching when he would get up and walk out of my life once again. Just a little taste had left me aching for the soft and gentle haven of what we'd once had.

We sat hunched up in an explosive silence, the papaya covered in flies, and I didn't care. From the knot of words caught in my throat, all I could untangle was, 'What the fuck's going on? You haven't given me the time of day since you walked out. So what the fuck's going on?' I expected him to pick up his bag and flee, duty done, camp built, karma restored, but he didn't. He did the exact opposite; he got up, walked towards me, sat down on the ground in front of me and looked me in the eyes. I dropped my head; I did not want him to see my tears and I could not trust myself to honour all I'd learnt without him. He gently reached out and lifted up my chin, and when I looked into his eyes expecting pity, I was surprised instead to see pain.

'Kye,' he whispered, 'I was overwhelmed; everything happened so fast.'

'You could have told me. You could have damn well taken the bloody time to tell me!' I cried.

'I couldn't make sense of it myself.' His anguish was palpable. 'I only realised what I'd lost when it was too late.'

I sat there stunned and speechless. Nothing had prepared me for this. I couldn't believe what he was saying. Kaz had been right after all. Silent tears slid down my face. *I have dreamt of this so many times, but now you're too late, you're much too late. Why didn't you realise sooner?*

It was a long time before I spoke, and when I did it was in a whisper. 'I still love you, Gill, but I love myself more now. You trampled all over the love we shared.' He was always so at ease in his body, yet now he sat, arms wrapped around himself, hunched in pain. My anger had gone. What had I been thinking? He had been much too young for me and I had expected way too much. I was overwhelmed with compassion and reached over to give him a hug. As I wrapped my arms around him I could feel all the sorrow of all the women he'd loved. They had woven their pain into his.

'You're so wrapped up in women's tears; you haven't got room for me anymore,' I said, laughing gently.

'I'm feeling crowded just giving you a hug.' I kissed him lightly on his forehead. 'Just relax. I'm going for a walk. I'll be back soon.'

I called my dogs and headed for the steep path that cut down the side of the cliff to the beach. I had to get away; I couldn't trust myself if I stayed. After everything I'd been through, I couldn't lose me again. I sat for a long time on a rock, listening to the slap of the waves, the soft drone of a speedboat on the ocean. Sprouty and my scruffy wolfhound Wunjo sat perfectly still like guardians, one on each side of me. I sat there until I could feel the strength of my own light again; I needed every part of me to stay strong. It would be too easy to succumb to this man again.

When I got back to camp, Gill was looking so pale and said he didn't feel well. When I felt his head he was burning up. I helped him to his feet and led him over to my bed. For the next three days I nursed him. I cooled him down with wet clothes when he was hot, I held his head up so he could drink. At night I slept beside him. I'd had to plunder the absolute depths of myself to resist this man and life wasn't making it easy for me.

On the third night, I was laying in bed beside Gill. The tips of our fingers were touching and I was about to drift off to sleep when I began to feel a presence that hadn't visited me for a long time. When Gill had left, Rainbow Man had too. I had been deserted by them both. But now, in this moment in my simple camp, nothing else existed but the light that was flooding my being with an ease that hadn't been there before— beauty and love were penetrating me to my core. I moved through joy into a space of ecstasy. I had never felt such bliss. Nothing was spoken, but I began to hear words inside my head and I began the only communication I'd ever had in pure thought.

'You and Gill have walked through the darkness and each of your experiences has prepared you to be together in a conscious way.' My response came in a wave of pure emotion—utter, joyful relief—that washed through me, bathing me in the radiance of its light. Tears were rolling down my face in thankfulness. I then felt a powerful surge of sheer unadulterated joy as I acknowledged what I had always known— Gill and I were destined to be together. I felt as if I was the waves crashing on the shore, and the ocean itself.

'You have learnt that love for yourself begins within. No one can give you what you are unable to give yourself. For the first time in your life you are ready for Sacred Love. Gill's journey has been different. The intensity of your connection with him brought up his own fear that he was losing himself. He struggled with his loss of sexual freedom and it was only when he reclaimed it, he realised that what he'd gained was far less than the depths he'd shared with you. It was a huge awakening for him and opened up his heart. He can now walk beside you as your equal.'

All through our separation life had been trying to tell me we'd get back together, through the dream about my grandfather and that wily nine of cups card, and while in the beginning I'd clung to those messages and hoped, I'd reached a point when any self-respecting goddess could only acknowledge it was irrevocably over. Without letting go of Gill completely, I would never have reached that point of loving me. My journey through my darkness had challenged me, but it had been so full of gifts. It seems incredible to me now that so often we run from our pain. We put our heads under our pillows and pretend it doesn't exist. I know I've done that too, but I can honestly say it's only when we face our shadows that our life is able to transform.

The loving voice continued. 'You have both come to learn that your sexuality is sacred. Each time you make love with someone, you connect your energy with theirs and absorb into your own energy field, not only the karmic load of the person you have merged with but all the men and women that merged sexually with them, and all the men and women that merged with them and on and on. You are no longer dealing with your own stuff; you've now got everyone else's as well.'

I was communicating with a being of such benevolence, of such compassion, such love. I felt absolutely safe and my tears flowed in open-hearted thankfulness. If there were parts of me that had not yet been reached by the radiance and love of this angelic being, they were now. Windows everywhere had been flung open and light was streaming in.

And with this light came awareness. I knew why, when I'd given Gill a hug I'd felt crowded out by other women. He was still connected energetically with the women he'd loved since he'd left me.

But most of all and this was such a huge relief. It explained the tangled web I had been woven into when I lived with Dan. He had been so promiscuous and never truthful, and I had existed so drained of energy, that I hadn't even got the strength to crawl to the front door and leave, let alone fight my way out. There was even a time I became so weak I almost died. I was bound up like a fly caught in a spider's web.

'So how do we avoid this and how do we separate energetically from previous partners?' I asked. There was so much I wanted to ask him.

'The answer to every question,' he went on, responding to my thirst to know more, 'is always LOVE. Love yourself and honour your body; it is your temple. So you ask how you can separate energetically? The divine evolvement of any relationship that ends in pain and betrayal is to recognise the lessons it was trying to teach you. When you attract relationships like this, it is because you are learning to love yourself and to honour the divine being you are. You have already discovered that if you don't, no one else will. Each step, however painful at the time that took you to this place of awareness, is a gift. When you recognise what an incredible life-changing gift this is, you will move beyond pain and anger and transform the energetic connection between you with gratitude and love. Then it will no longer have the power to drain you.'

'I understand what you are saying,' I replied. 'On one level I do feel gratitude for my old partner and everything I've learnt through being with him. But there are still times when unexpectedly something triggers a surge of anger towards him.'

'And this man you are with now will help you heal. Love will help you transform your pain.' I could hear his laughter, like more waves of bliss. It reminded me of the chortles of the Dalai Lama who often sees the humour in the decay. You have already seen the power of love create powerful transformations in other aspects of your own life and love is the key to every door that won't open.'

'Do I have the right to ask Gill to be monogamous?' I asked.

'Your sexuality is sacred. You *must* honour that.'

For a long time when I lived with Dan, I had grappled with the concept of monogamy. Was this tying someone down? A part of me thought we should be free to love, even though for me monogamy felt more natural. I had often thought you could pour water through a bowl that's full of holes and see it leak out in lots of small dribbles, or you could direct it into one powerful force. I wanted to try that. I wanted to experience a focused relationship where two people channelled their energy into that powerful force. I was certain you could create miracles with a love like that.

'It's Gill's choice,' Rainbow Man answered. 'He has free will to decide if monogamy is what he wants to experience with you.'

All through our communication the intensity of the light had been building to such a velocity, I knew I couldn't take much more. But Rainbow Man had something final to say.

'You and Gill have something very special to birth together. You must both be committed to your relationship and to working out any problems that arise. You will anchor a new awareness on this earth and everything you have both experienced is preparing you for this.'

My ecstasy was beginning to hurt; I couldn't hold any more light. I was on the edge of being fried, and as much as I wanted to hold onto the bliss, I felt Rainbow Man move away. He knew my limits better than I did.

The whole time, without being aware of it, I had been softly tracing a spiral with my fingertip in the palm of Gill's outstretched hand and when Rainbow Man left, he woke up with a jolt.

'Don't stop,' he cried. 'That was amazing.'

'It wasn't me, Gill.' I began to tell him what Rainbow Man had said. He looked incredulous the whole time. When I'd finished, he leaned over towards me and tilted my head so he could look into my eyes.

'It's what I want, Kye. I want to be with you. I want us to be monogamous and I want to create with you whatever it is that life wants us to do. I'm here. We can work this out.'

I was ecstatic. I felt sheer and utter relief and joy, oh so much joy. Since our separation I had tried to see myself loving someone else, but I couldn't. Whenever I saw the face of my love it had always been Gill. I could finally let go. I didn't have to fight my feelings for this man anymore.

I had never experienced anything like this before—talking with an angel—or met anyone who had. I certainly went through some insecurity the following day, doubting what had happened. *Have I gone mad, lost the plot? Did it really happen? Talking angels? You can't make up ecstasy like that Kye, you'd imagine it all the bloody time if you could!*

It didn't help when Gill and I went to a party the following night. I was still glowing from my communication with Rainbow Man and in my excitement had said to a room full of people, 'You'll never guess what happened to me last night!' I went on to tell them how I'd talked with a rainbow-emanating angel. Not one person responded. Everyone stood sipping their gin and tonics, looking uncomfortable. There was this huge silence until someone eventually changed the subject and said something safe. Off everyone went, chatting away again as if I hadn't said a thing. No one had even been curious about my experience! It was a massive lesson for me to be very discriminatory about whom I shared the intimacies of my life with. Even so, it hadn't given me much confidence in my own sanity.

The following day I decided to ring Kaz. She knew me. I'm sure she would vouch I wasn't mad!

'Congratulations,' she said knowingly, as soon as she heard my voice. Before I'd told her *anything*!

'What do you mean?'

'You and Gill getting back together.' 'How the hell do you know?'

'I had a dream!' This was all getting a bit too cosmic, even for me. She continued. 'Last night, I dreamt I was at a big party. Everyone was dancing and suddenly I heard the phone ring. I answered it and it was Gill telling me you were back together. He said he would look after you and he really wanted to make it work. I yelled out to everyone, "Kye and Gill are together again," and everyone started cheering.'

'I rang you up for a bit of sanity, Kaz, but I'm not sure you're any help,' I said, jokingly, and I began to tell her everything that had happened. She was delighted I had finally had a conversation with Rainbow Man. She had often teased me about the manner I had welcomed my rainbow angel when he had first appeared to me in her lounge room.

'And you know I don't like to say I told you so', she said, laughingly, 'but I did try and tell you Gill was missing you! I'm so happy for you Kye!' Kaz's words meant so much to me. I knew she hadn't held Gill in high esteem when he had walked out and left me but for my sake my dearest friend was prepared to give him another chance.

I had only just put the phone down when a car pulled up. It was some old friends, Ollie and Sue, with their children Billy and Bloss. We hadn't seen them since the house had burnt down. About a year before that they'd lived in my garden in a tipi and had cared and loved my home as I did. That was the first time I had felt supported living there. They were equally horrified at the endless stream of people Dan bought home. People who used everything we had and gave nothing in return. When the various visitors staying in my home overwhelmed me, I often found peace in their tipi. I missed their gentle way of living when they left. They had bought land north of the Daintree and seldom came to town. But when they did, they always called in. They had known Gill a lot longer than I had and I wasn't even sure if they'd heard about my relationship with him. I knew we had lots of catching up to do, but I was totally unprepared for what Sue had to say.

'Oh my God, I can't believe you're here. I've wanted to see you two for so long!' There was so much emotion in her voice, and relief too, as if she'd been travelling down a long and hard road alone and she'd finally arrived. 'I didn't know where to find you. I had no idea where you'd gone after the house burnt down.'

'It was a wild time, Sue, everything happened so fast.' I replied, not for one second thinking she had something important to tell me.

'The whole thing is very suspicious,' she answered, shaking her head. 'I knew you had no idea what had happened. I forgot even to tell Josh. It didn't occur to me it was important until I heard the house had burnt down.'

'What are you talking about, Sue?' A chill was running up my spine. 'What on earth are you talking about?'

'We called in here to see you when your brother Josh was looking after the place. He told us you had flown to Byron for a Beltane celebration with Gill.'

I'd forgotten all about that. Kaz held an annual Beltane party and she sent me an air ticket to fly down. I'd only just met Gill and we pitched in together to buy his ticket. My gentle, new brother Josh had been staying with us for several months, on holiday from England, and I'd left him looking after the place. He'd continued his travels just a few days after our return and within the week the house had burnt down.

So Sue had known we were together, but I was completely in the dark as to where our conversation was going, yet keen to hear what she had to say. She was someone I respected, who had often given me really sound advice. All her friends valued her judgement. She was quick to see what wasn't clear to most and always first to come up with the solution to any problem, even though she generally didn't take the credit. She would see the solution and guide the rest of us there with the questions she asked, waiting patiently for the penny to drop! She was practical and wise, could cope with anything, never got in a flap and had her feet so firmly anchored on the earth. I was *desperate* to hear what she had to say. 'Tell me,' I said, hunched and expectant.

We ended up staying here a couple of nights. On the last morning we were here, two men from the church turned up. They weren't exactly rude, but they *were* pushy. I'd had to stand with my arm across the back door to prevent them from coming in.

'You're kidding me,' I said, 'Josh didn't mention anything when we got back.'

'He was out walking,' Sue answered. 'He didn't see them and I forgot to tell him.'

I couldn't believe it. Alarm bells were starting to ring. 'Oh my God, Sue, what did they say?'

'They said the electrics looked really dangerous.' She sat gazing at me with her big, brown eyes, waiting for me to absorb what she'd said. I sat speechless. I had not expected this. For sure I'd pondered over the rocks that hit our roof and woke us the night of the fire, but so much had happened recently, I'd barely had time to breathe. I finally looked at her, heavy with the implications of what she'd said, and as she caught my eyes I could see her gently nodding, a sympathetic look on her face. She had given me another dot and she could see I'd finally begun to join them.

'I even know the date they came,' she went on. 'After they left we drove into town and bought a paper. It had a big article about the hill saying it had just been sold for development. I've got it here.' She pulled the paper out of her bag. 'It was the thirteenth of November,' she said, pointing to the date on the paper. I'd just missed them; Gill and I had flown home on the fourteenth.

The church people were here only ten days before the house burnt down, making comments about the electrics from the porch of the back door. The only thing visible would have been one light switch. Was I reading too much into this? I felt worried. Could they really have been involved in the fire? Surely not. Then why had they made a false statement to me about a light switch without a cover? I'd often puzzled over that. If I trusted anyone's judgement, it was Sue's. If she felt something was suspicious, I was very alarmed.

I should have seen the next move coming, but I didn't.

Sixteen

Garden of Eden

Life certainly wasn't dull. In the space of a few days I'd been reunited with Gill, spoken with an angel and pondered the intrigues of arson. My world had done an unexpected flip and I was delighted. Rainbow Man's words had opened the door to loving Gill again and I was so happy. Yet having Gill back brought up hurt I'd thought had gone. Trust had been broken, there was no denying that. But I also had to look at the part I'd played in our demise. I'd nurtured so many fears and they'd all borne fruit. I'd been holding on to my past, worrying about the future and I had failed to enjoy what we had.

It had taken an angel to reunite us, but it was up to us to nurture and cherish what we now had. To talk about the past when it came up, but also to let it go. We had both changed, and for the better. There was a new maturity about Gill, a strength I hadn't seen before. He wasn't afraid of the shadows and he was much more willing to talk. I had so much more confidence in myself. I felt lighter, brighter and guided by a certainty I'd always felt but been afraid to trust. There *was* something on this planet I had to do, and at the grand old age of thirty-four, I'd finally been given a sign.

I treasured every moment of being back on my hill and living simply in our bush camp. I couldn't remember a time when I'd been happier. I didn't need the noise of people; I didn't need their parties or their loud music or their predatory ways. I loved silence and being on my own, and Cane Knife and Gill, both nature spirits like me, were nurtured in the same way.

I was settling into a truly blissful existence when Rainbow Man came again. This time it was in a dream. I had woken from a very deep sleep, but my memories of the night were crystal clear. Rainbow Man had shown me several events that were to come and given me a warning that he told me was relevant right now. That warning was repeating itself like a mantra in my thoughts.

'You have to leave the hill now, Kye. It's not safe for you anymore.' I lay for a long time trying to figure out what he'd meant. It had been less than a fortnight since Sue had told me of the visit from the church just before my home burnt down. I knew there were puzzles that didn't make sense, but I couldn't see where following them was going to get me. On the rare occasion I had opened up to tell someone about it, I only had to look in their eyes to see they thought I was mad. It just seemed wiser to let it go. So when Rainbow Man gave me the warning, I automatically assumed it was due to a natural calamity rather than a predatory threat.

Still sleepy, I threw something on and headed to the garden where I could hear Gill chopping open a coconut with his machete. Being back with Gill was a score on every level. I loved drinking green coconuts, and for the first time ever I was with someone who could actually climb the tree and get them. Climbing up the trunk was a feat of strength and agility, and I was always a little nervous watching my love, barefoot and without a rope, shimmy up the tree. The hardest part he told me was climbing into the fronds at the top. They naturally break off from the main trunk, so he had to be certain the one he used to lever himself up was totally secure. Then if it wasn't spiders, it was the green ants, and they always swarmed. He'd usually manage to chop out the coconuts before the ants got too bad, but they'd be in his shorts, biting his face, chomping into every bit of his body. Yet at the top of a tree, where to fall could mean death, his only choice was to stay centred and calm, which was how he was anyway. He was always incredibly serene.

That morning, my little patch of paradise felt perfect. Everything sparkled in the morning light and the ocean was so still I knew that if I took the five-minute walk to the rock, I'd see dolphins. I was pleased to see the rainbow lorikeets were beginning to feed again in the umbrella tree. It had been badly burnt by the fire and was only just beginning to recover. As I slurped on a refreshing green coconut, I told Gill all about the dream.

'I can't understand why I'm not safe here; the words were so clear, Gill.'

'Maybe it's warning of a cyclone or something like that,' he suggested.

'Yeah, that was my first thought,' I replied. Cyclones were part of living in the tropics. I'd never experienced a direct hit, but I'd sheltered from one that devastated the coast fifty kilometres away. Even on the outer fringes we'd experienced 170 kilometre winds. The tops of the coconut trees had bowed to the ground and twenty foot waves crashed on a beach that didn't usually get them because of the reef.

I was still pondering on the dream when we heard Gerry call out. There was a well-worn track through the buffel grass that led to her gorgeous little studio with its huge windows, which nestled into one side of the hill, with a fabulous view of the ocean. She looked really solemn.

'I'm sorry to have to be the messenger,' she said heavily,

'but I've got some bad news.' Once again I didn't have the faintest idea what to expect. People were telling me all sorts of things these days and most of it was well beyond my normal realms of reality. But the look on Gerry's face warned me it wasn't going to be good.

'We've all been given a month's notice to get out. The church just phoned and told me.'

I could not speak. I had not expected that. I was shaking my head in absolute disbelief. 'But they said they'd give us a year's notice,' I finally stuttered. 'They promised they wouldn't do this.'

Gerry shrugged her shoulders. 'I know,' she said wearily. Gerry always exuded calmness and seemed to flow without attachment to the ebbs and flows of life, but I could see tears rolling down her face. She loved the hill as much as me.

I sat on the earth for a long time after she left, stunned at the news. I'd only been back a month and in that time, with Gill's help, I had transformed the garden. We'd mulched up all the papayas and planted lots more vegetables and herbs. I could not believe we had to go. I could not have received more devastating news.

'It's weird when you wake up from a dream where you're being told it's not safe for you and within an hour you're given notice to leave,' Gill said, shaking his head. 'That's got to be more than a coincidence!'

I felt that too, but I couldn't shake off this overwhelming feeling that my return to the hill had been responsible for all the other caretakers, like me, having to leave, and I couldn't stop thinking about my conversation with Sue.

'Am I being blind here, Gill?' I was hesitant to give words to what I was feeling; I didn't want to go there. 'Is it the church I'm not safe from?'

'I don't know Kye. All I know is that if they were involved in the fire, the things that didn't make any sense suddenly do. There are some pretty powerful forces working in our life right now, so let's trust in that.'

I felt so heavy as we walked down to the sleep-out to find Cane Knife and tell him the news. I didn't think he'd be happy. He loved his home, but he took the news stoically.

'That's okay, Kye. Don't worry about me. Mango season will soon be here. I might go and camp on the beach for a while.' Mango trees grew wild all around us, and just up the coast they lined the roadside that led to the beach. Cane Knife often spent the season there. Every morning the ground would be covered with mangos, fallen in the night. There was stiff competition. If you wanted to get the best ones, the ones that had landed in the leafy mulch below the trees and weren't bruised; you had to be there at first light.

I hadn't felt it as keenly when I'd left the hill after the house burnt down, but this was truly the end of an era. How could I possibly find somewhere to live that I loved as much as this?

The colonel, the development officer I'd always dealt with from the church, arrived two days later. I had no idea if he'd been one of the men who had visited my home ten days before it burnt down. He certainly fitted the description. There were no devout emanations coming from this huge man. He was condescending and rude. The first time I had met him, he had come to the hill with the Bishop. They'd gotten out of the back of a chauffeur-driven black limousine with tinted windows. If you didn't know they were from the church, you might have mistaken them for mafia. Over the years I'd maintained a polite relationship with the colonel, but I didn't like him. He never gave out warmth. There was nothing friendly or soft, and he had the generosity of a well-picked bone. Fortunately, his visits had been rare.

'You are to be out of here by 8.30 am on the thirty-first. Is that clear?' he barked. He hadn't even said hello. After all that had happened, the house fire, six years of caring for the place, he hadn't the graciousness to be polite. I ignored his rude hostility.

'Good morning,' I replied and gave him a bright smile. He ignored me and went on; he was used to trampling all over people. We were only fodder.

'The bulldozers will be coming up after that date to clear the site.'

'Bulldozing the gardens?' I feared to know, but I couldn't stop myself asking.

'We'll clear up this mess. The bulldozer will be coming straight through here.' He looked distastefully around him. He was standing in the Garden of Eden and he couldn't see a thing. The air was thick with frangipani and jasmine, and he stood right by the rose bush that was laden with ruby red blooms. I moved away so he didn't see the tear that slid down my cheek. This cold man would probably find joy in that. I was devastated they were going to destroy the garden; even without me it could survive.

'We'll be dozing all the houses too. We don't want any buildings left on the property,' he said, getting back into his car. He'd done what he came for, to spread his doom. I was inconsolable after he left. I'd thought my connection to the hill was so strong that not even money could part us, and I'd been wrong.

'Kye, remember your dream. You're being warned about something,' Gill spoke firmly. 'You've *got* to listen, Kye.'

I'd been hoping to have my last month soaking up the sanctuary of the hill. It didn't happen. As soon as the news was out that the church had evicted its caretakers, people swarmed all over the place. Our peace and solitude had gone. There were journalists, protesters and people who came just to have a look. The authority

I'd previously had to ask people to leave was now gone. There was nothing we could do but get our lives ready for our own departure.

We decided to go north to the community that Gill used to live in. There were reservations amongst members as to whether we could live there. Some residents didn't want any more dogs, but others wanted us there. Since most of the members that didn't want extra dogs were away for the wet season, we were told to come and see how it worked out. We needed a 4WD if we were going to live in the wilds of Cooktown. It was all dirt roads, which would be impassable when wet. We sold the Holden and bought a G60 Nissan Patrol with a soft top. It was a rust bucket, but we loved it.

Early on the morning of the thirty-first we'd been loading up our gear when Lukey, the old Labrador from next door, jumped in the back of our 4WD. I'd known Lukey six years. When his owner who was renting the studio moved out, he left Lukey for the next tenants to look after. Over the years there were many changes in tenants and they didn't always look after Lukey. Yet he was always so loyal to that house. One wet season he'd been kept outside with nowhere dry to sleep. I was so angry with the new people that had moved in. They told me they would get him a kennel, but they never did. Lukey had arthritis and I was really worried about him. One day it was raining so hard I went over to try to coax him home. He was sitting in a pool of water, looking so miserable. It broke my heart to see this honourable and lovely dog being treated like this. He followed me back like a little lost lamb. I towelled him dry and gave him a soft bed to lie on. But ten minutes later, ever loyal to home, he was off.

Several days passed before I saw him again, this time he came over himself. He stood whining piteously in my open doorway, wet, bedraggled and alone—and much too courteous to come in unless asked. I fed him, dried him and fussed over him so he wouldn't leave. But once again, he did. Over the years I became his solace, the place he would go to when he'd reached his lowest ebb.

When Gerry moved in, Lukey was loved and looked after for the first time. Finally someone adored him, but Gerry's dogs and Lukey didn't get on. After all those years of coaxing, Lukey had finally made up his mind; he was coming with me. He was now fourteen years old and he stank. It didn't matter how often you bathed him, he still stank, and he had a hacking cough. There was no doubting I loved this old dog and didn't want to leave him. But we were going somewhere that didn't even want two extra dogs. How could I turn up with three? I was in a dilemma. I called him and tried to get him out of the back of the car, but he just sat there wagging his tail, looking excited, all ready to go. When I looked over at Gill, he was laughing.

'Let him come, Kye. We'll work it out. It will be okay.'

I knew Gill was right. It would have been cold and heartless to do anything other than allow him to come, but I had to okay it with Gerry, and we didn't have much time. It was already 8.15 am and we had fifteen minutes left to vacate. I ran along the track to the studio. Gerry was closing up her house, ready to gather the dogs into the car. Closing the windows and locking the door as if somehow that would keep the home she loved safe. Both our lives at this moment were teary and sad. She gave a big sigh when I told her Lukey wouldn't get out of our car. Gerry really loved him, but she knew he wasn't having a good time with her dogs. Neither of us had any choice. Lukey was doing what he wanted to do; I knew Gerry would respect that.

'Bring Lukey back to see me, won't you?' Tears were rolling down her face. We were both being wrenched from a place we loved. We gave each other a hug that held so much warmth I wanted to stay in it forever. In that moment it seemed such a cruel fate that people who don't give a shit often have more power than those who do. I was wiping my own tears as I ran back to the car.

It was 8.40 am when we were finally loaded up and driving out—just as the colonel drove in. We stopped the car and I got out. I like to complete cycles in an honourable way, and even though I didn't like him I appreciated all the years I'd been blessed living on the hill and I wanted to say thank you. But I didn't have a chance to say anything.

'You know I could do you for trespassing.' He was cold and arrogant and spoke with venom. His words were so unexpected, they almost knocked me over. I was leaving and he could see that. I couldn't speak; I felt so shocked.

Every single word we utter has a consequence; there is nothing in life that we do that does not create an effect. I turned my back on him. I would not give him the dignity of a reply, and I would not sink to his ungracious level. But as I walked back to the car I felt as if I had been terribly wronged.

Without a backward glance we drove off into our new lives, Lukey panting happily in the back. Wunjo and Sprouty were hanging out the sides of our 4WD, oblivious to it all.

I was leaving my home. I thought it was for the last time, but unbeknown to me, and the colonel, the hill hadn't finished with me yet.

Seventeen
Ghosts of Old Ladies

In many ways the community was an idyllic place to live. There were numerous established tropical fruit trees, rolinias, jack fruit, bread fruit, blacksapotes, bananas, mangos, just to name a few. In half an hour, following tracks that wove through the rainforest and then through the mangroves, you'd arrive at a pristine, deserted beach that is pure white sand that stretched for miles. It was a tropical paradise, but as beautiful as it was, it never felt like my home.

We had erected our camp a few kilometres from the main communal area so we had space to relax with our dogs. They were right; there were far too many dogs and most of their owners had gone away for the wet season, leaving them to fend for themselves. On our first day, Gill returned from visiting one of the residents in the community with two tiny puppies, just a few days old. One was being eaten alive by maggots and the other, inbred, was born the size of a mouse in a litter of nine huge pig-hunting dogs. Her mother kept carrying her out into the rainforest to die.

We spent hours picking maggots out of Patchi, a brindle pup with huge, sorrowful eyes. I prayed so many times he would die. Even in India, I had never seen a dog in such a mess. He had deep wounds all over his back that were infested. We were a long way from help and the best we could do to make sure his wounds stayed clean was to dunk him in salty water. It was heart-breaking. He howled every time we did it, but it was all we could do.

We then bandaged his body, covering the wounds to keep them safe from further fly attacks. We tried to get him to feed from his mum, but she wouldn't take him. So we fed him through a finger of a rubber glove that we pierced a hole in and filled with milk. The following day we undid the bandages and took a look. I felt so sick when I saw the wounds were half full of maggots again. All the eggs we'd missed had hatched. If we didn't get on top of it, we'd have to put this little pup out of his misery, and I could not bear the thought of that.

On the third day I took off his bandages. Patchi looked at me with a worried expression on his face. After everything we'd done for this dear little pup, he still trusted us! I was so anxious and felt much too sick to look, so I passed him over to Gill. There was complete silence as Gill examined his wounds. 'What's happening, Gill?' I asked, fearing the worst.

'I'm still looking,' he replied. 'I can't see any maggots; it's looking good!' Finally I looked. The wounds were all clean and nothing was wriggling. I sat for half an hour watching, just to make sure. This little pup was over the worst.

Patchi's little sister, Chia, was so tiny she didn't have a chance of surviving on her own. She was a strange looking pup with a completely round head bereft of a nose, just two little pointy flaps of ears. She was a soft brindle colour, but hair only grew on her face and legs. She was bald on her body and tail. In the first few hours she was with us, we thought she'd died three times, and for the first month of her life she trembled and looked so frail, we expected each breath to be her last. Then one day she woke up with such ZING! She was here! And from that day forth she lived life with a passion and gusto that put everyone to shame. She milked the joy out of everything. Her nose finally appeared, but it would be three years before her hair grew, and when it did, it sprouted between her claws and tufted out of her ears. She looked part-possum and part-hyena. Once when we were in town, a child, on seeing Chia, grabbed hold of his mother's arms and exclaimed, slightly horrified, 'What is it?' She certainly was a strange looking dog, but Gill and I absolutely adored her.

There were some people around us that thought we should have knocked these pups on the head. 'Why don't you chuck 'em in the crab pots?' one guy said.

He laughed as if he'd cracked the funniest joke, and I couldn't help feeling that he was mocking us.

We now had five dogs and I couldn't have refused the arrival of any of them in my life! I did not like living in this community. It had been Gill's world before he met me and I'd given it my best. But I found our camp amongst the trees so gloomy. There were many people I knew and liked from this community, and some I'd known for years. But it had a very masculine energy and felt much too harsh for me. I was so homesick for my hill. I missed bright blue skies and looking out over the Coral Sea as the sun rose in the morning. I ached to run barefoot through the long grass, or to sit under the huge white ghost gum with its big, burly trunk that grew on the edge of the cliff and was home to a family of possums.

When Gill suggested we take a break and drive to town along the Crebbe track, a dirt road that runs from Bloomfield to Daintree, I couldn't wait to leave. We were going to call in and see the hill, and as much as I yearned to do that, I was also anxious about how it had fared with the bulldozers.

The Crebbe track was spectacular. It's only accessible by a 4WD. There were a few times I pleaded with the Nissan to keep going as it trudged up a hill that was so steep we were in danger of falling backwards. My knuckles were sweaty and white with tension as I gripped onto the hand rail, looking straight up at the sky, and only breathing again when we reached the top.

Once, when we stopped to see what was sparkling on the dirt track, we discovered quartz crystals washed out by some recent rain and we filled our pockets full. It was so hard to stop looking for them. We found some had tiny moss gardens inside and some were double tipped. Finally, with severe cricks in our necks from walking stooped for several hours, we prised ourselves away and continued our journey down the track.

That night we camped by a creek that ran through the rainforest from the mountain. It was as clear and sparkling as the crystals we'd found. Lukey loved the adventure his life had become and embraced everything with eagerness. We'd taken him off the dry dog food and were feeding him veggies and rice, and when he did eat meat it was raw. His cough had almost gone. He had looked as if he was on his last legs when he first joined us, but with all the fun he was having, and the healthy food, he'd regained his youth.

We unrolled our swags and built a fire. The dogs were all sleeping around us. That night as we sat talking about our life and where to go, unbeknown to us we were weaving a thread into our future.

'Let's get some horses,' Gill said, 'and just go. Take the dogs with us and what we need to live and walk away from everything. See where we end up. Trust enough in our life to let go.' His words were like spun gold in the firelight.

'And we could take seeds with us so that wherever we end up we can plant a garden,' I added, excitedly.

'And we could cut tracks through places where no one would ever find us!' We were so animated; we talked by firelight late into the night.

I'd been feeling so tossed around by life. I didn't know where my place was anymore. Maybe this was how I'd find it. We had no idea this was the first tiny seed planted of a dream which, when it did manifest, would be much bigger than either of us could ever have imagined.

We'd been invited to stay with Jen, but I couldn't resist doing a quick drive up to the top of the hill to see what had become of our garden. I was so relieved to find everything as we'd left it. The garden looked beautiful; the gardenias were all in bloom. The sleep-out was still standing. They hadn't bulldozed a thing.

We followed the track to Gerry and Clem's home. It was a different story here. Their lovely studio with its glass windows that looked out over the ocean had been destroyed. It was a pile of mangled tin and broken glass. The only intention the church had was to prevent anyone from living in it. Nothing had been recycled, the site had not been cleared, and to any conscious person it was a crime scene.

I felt so thankful my home had gone with majesty in the fire. There was no reason to have done this. The hill was not sold as reported in the paper; the sale had obviously fallen through. People could have lived in these homes for many years to come. I walked sadly back to the car. With all this destruction I did not want to stay long, but our car would not start. Gill is very mechanical; already I had become a little blasé about his ability to fix absolutely everything. I had already witnessed many car fixing miracles. Once I had even seen him create a new gasket for our exhaust when it blew in the middle of nowhere and the only thing he could find to fix it with was a coke can, which he cut up, wrapped with wire, covered in muffler putty and fitted back in the exhaust. When we had started up the car, she had purred so sweetly. We drove with that coke can gasket for almost six months until Gill decided to replace it—just in case, not because anything was wrong.

If Gill couldn't start our car this time, we were in trouble.

After endless attempts to get our Nissan going, I finally walked down to see Jen to let her know we were back and camped on the hill with the car. She promised to call her mechanic first thing in the morning. I wasn't relaxed staying on the hill. Jen told me the bulldozers had moved down to the two houses on the beach, but I had no idea if anyone from the church would turn up. They'd made their intentions pretty clear if they found me on the hill again.

The mechanic didn't arrive until mid-afternoon. Our battery was flat by this time, so he gave us a jump-start and the car started first go. He had a look under the bonnet, couldn't see anything wrong and off he went. I was so relieved. We packed up all our gear, put the dogs in the back and went to drive off. The car stalled and wouldn't start again. Nothing Gill did made any difference. I felt like screaming. I was so eager to be gone. The destruction on the hill had had a devastating effect energetically and even though everything was just as we'd left it, the place felt dark and mean.

When I had first come to live on the hill, I had dreamt there was a quartz crystal under the house, the size of a double-decker bus. I knew the hill was a potent place and amplified the energy that was on it, and although I hadn't known fully what was happening at the time, I could feel that when I was living there, my presence helped maintain a positive charge. I'm sure there were other elements too, as well as other people involved. But I was also very aware that not only did I feel the transformation I underwent, every time I was on the hill, others did too.

Even though I did nothing to outwardly portray that I was practising magical arts, I was often called a witch, and it was spat at me like a swear word and always by those who'd been less than honourable and could not handle a woman in her power. Not that I always was, there were many times I felt as if I was laying face down in the mud, but there were other times I seemed to be able to access a force that went way beyond mere me and I didn't have to practise any magic to connect with it.

In a rather undisciplined and spasmodic way I would often honour the cycles of life with ritual by creating a magical pouch, a prayer stick, a crystal bag, or string up a garland of frangipani flowers to wear in my hair as I celebrated the full moon or solstice, and I often sat drumming or meditating on the giant rock that shelved out over the Coral Sea. I honoured witches as the wise women and I certainly related to that aspect of myself, and whilst it was certainly never meant as a compliment, I took it that way. I understood why people saw me as a potent force on the hill.

The minute I stepped onto this land an aspect of myself amplified. I became bigger, I resonated more. There were times I spoke words of truth that sent shivers up the spine of those who heard them.

Once, in my early days on the hill when I'd been a smoker, Cane Knife had said to me, 'How come you speak such powerful words, yet you still smoke that poison?' It had horrified Cane Knife to see me smoke, and sometimes I'd even hide my tobacco when I'd see him coming, knowing he'd be so upset. Polluting your body and speaking truth were incompatible as far as Cane Knife went. Yet even he recognised the source of what I often said. The only way I can explain is that when I was on my hill, I felt as if I was finally plugged in to the right socket. Even so, I didn't want to stay there as it was. I couldn't stay there. The church had claimed it back. A few acts of destruction and their hill was purring darkly for them, once again.

I wanted to leave, but we had no choice. Our car would not start; we pulled everything out again and made up camp for another night. It took two days for the mechanic to get back to us. He did a few tests, twiddled a few leads and the car started. He took it for a test run and it drove perfectly. He left, we packed up again, got in the car to leave and it wouldn't start. It was hot and very humid; the water supply to the hill had been turned off. It was not a pleasant place to camp. This time I felt like screaming hysterically.

Once again we had to wait days for the mechanic's return. We could tell he was as keen to see the back end of us as we were to leave. He was rushed off his feet and had made a big effort to fit us in. He went over everything thoroughly and once again it started. We did a quick test drive before packing everything up. It went with success. As we reached the highway we were whooping with joy; we'd escaped. We made it ten kilometres down the road and were at the very start of the coast road that winds along the edge of the cliffs, a sheer drop to the ocean on one side, when we broke down. It's a treacherous road and in the midst of my frustration, I failed to see what a miracle it was we broke down just before we got there. A lone cyclist, already puffing from exertion, stopped and helped us push the car off the road. We were stranded outside the only pub, the last bastion of civilisation for over a hundred kilometres. I could see nothing fortuitous in this either. I was cursing. I felt so pissed off. I trudged over to the payphone to ring Jen, failing miserably to even be thankful that she was the only person in my life that always said when she knew I was coming to stay, 'Make sure you bring all your dogs.'

The car was parked in the full sun and Lukey would not get out. He was obsessed with the car. I felt so frustrated. He wouldn't listen to anything I said. When I tried to pull him by his collar towards the door, he locked his legs to create traction. Finally, Gill climbed in the back, picked him up and carried him out. We were sitting with our five dogs on the side of the road, feeling really down in the dumps when Jen pulled up.

'You're just meant to be on the hill right now,' she said brightly. 'It's the old lady. She's trying to talk to you.' Jen was convinced that the old lady who had originally gifted the hill to the church to use for under-privileged kids was not happy.

'Just go with the flow,' Jen said, making me snarl even louder. That news did not help my mood, and I found absolutely no consolation in the ghost of an old lady manipulating my life like this.

As we drove back along the route of our fleeting dash for freedom—Gill in our car being towed behind—I could hear a voice I didn't like, playing over and over like a stuck record.

'Let go, Kye, just let go. You know things always work out when you do.'

'I don't want to!'

'Come on now; you haven't got a choice. Just let go.'

I was still struggling with my fate when Jen dropped us off.

Eighteen
Tattooed Angels

We moved into the sleep-out. The first rains of the wet season hadn't fallen yet; when they did it would be torrential and we'd need shelter. Living in the humidity of the tropics in a one-room shack that we were not meant to be in, without a running water supply, was not my idea of fun. I was being eaten alive by mosquitoes and there were times I felt overwhelmed by frustration. Yet I knew there was something I had to do on the hill. It wouldn't happen while I battled, and I couldn't leave until it was done. I was in a corner and I had no choice but to let go.

I hadn't previously dwelt on the inconsistencies around my house fire, partly because with the few attempts I'd made to talk to people, no one had taken me seriously. Even the policeman I'd spoken with had mocked my claim. Even after I'd made my statement, not a thing had been done and nobody had been to investigate the fire.

There were some things even a vivid imagination couldn't explain. Gill and I had been woken that night by rocks hitting our roof, and they don't fall out of the sky.

We'd even climbed on the roof a few days after the fire and found them. Whoever had burnt the house down had not wanted our lives on their conscience as well, they had intended to wake us up.

The news report on TV the day after my home had burnt down began, 'An unoccupied house burnt to the ground.' I had actually rung them, wanting to know how they'd got their facts so wrong in such a short space of time. After all, Gill and I had been standing in the garden almost naked. They had even tried to film us and only left us alone when Gill told them to. Their response was that mistakes often happened!

Was it the ghost of an old lady keeping me stuck on the hill? I certainly felt she was one of the currents involved. A huge injustice had indeed been done. A kind and caring woman, who believed in the organisation she belonged to and had no reason to doubt that they would continue caring for the under- privileged kids that she had made a place for on her land, had been terribly wronged.

I had tried to ignore all the niggling aspects that surrounded the house fire, but I couldn't any longer. The hill and all its guardians wanted me to know the truth.

On one of our first days back, when I'd been struggling with the dark energy that had been unleashed on the hill, we'd walked down to visit Jen. When we returned, there was a car parked in the garden and we could see a man and a dog. There was something deeply disturbing about his presence. When he saw us, he held to his face a newspaper and tried to hide behind it, as if he believed that if he couldn't see us, we couldn't see him. He was swaying from side to side and appeared to be mentally unstable. He also had a savage dog that ran out at us and was snarling nastily. Gill had yelled at him to get his dog under control and picked up a big stick in case we needed it. He had called his dog back but been unwilling to communicate or even acknowledge we were there.

This was the power of the hill drawing all sorts of darkness to itself once that energy was activated. It didn't make me feel any better about being there, but neither of us wanted to leave our car. We eventually decided to move down to the rock where Cane Knife had camped for almost five years. It was far enough away to feel safe from this menacing man.

We had a beautiful night looking out over the ocean. The energy felt fresher there and I was feeling quite renewed. We had our swags on the ground and a small fire burning. I felt as if I was in a completely different reality from the dark stew up at the old house site—we had forgotten the man in the garden completely! Sounds strange, but we had.

We had even made love and were laying on our swags afterwards, cuddled up to one another, when we got the fright of our lives. All of a sudden the man from the garden leapt out of a bush really close to us and yelled something very strange that made no sense. It was terrifying and disturbing to think he had been watching us and that he'd crept so quietly down that even our dogs, who always let us know when people arrive, didn't hear him come.

My heart had leapt into my mouth. I was so shocked I almost stopped breathing. Then something really bizarre happened. A burst of electricity hit the earth beside us and then spread out over the top of us, blanketing us protectively in this blue current of energy. It simultaneously zapped the disturbed man who had crouched back down in his bush, absurdly pretending not to be there. When it hit him, he screamed and took off at a run.

Nothing had ever happened in my life previously, or since, to give me a clue as to that what just happened, what this current of energy was. Where had it come from? I couldn't answer this; I didn't know. But I certainly felt a lot safer being on the hill. I knew we were being looked after. When we returned to the garden in the morning, creeping up the path quietly in case he was still there, we were so relieved to see all traces of this man had gone and the energy was feeling clear again.

The next thing that happened seemed so serendipitous that I could no longer doubt what I was there for. Three weeks before the house had burnt down I'd paid an electrician to replace some wiring inside the house that looked unsafe. I had tried to locate him shortly after my return to the hill, just after Sue had told me about the visit from the church and what they'd said about the wiring. But I'd lost everything in the house fire and couldn't remember the name of his business. Every time I tried to find him I came to a dead end. I didn't need anyone to reassure me that there had been no light switches without a cover on them, like the church had told me when I rang them the day after the fire. I just wanted someone to back me up.

When that same electrician turned up unexpectedly in the garden and told me he had been wanting to contact me since he had heard the house had burnt down, but had no idea where I had moved to and only that day he had felt drawn to drive up the hill on a whim. He was as surprised to see me, as I him!

I let go to my fate. I surrendered. It didn't mean I wouldn't have future moans but for the time being at least, I recognised that life was guiding, not just me, but everyone else involved, to uncover *Something*.

'When you did the work on the house, do you remember a switch without a cover on it?' I asked him.

'I checked everything before I finished working on that house. There definitely wasn't a switch without a cover.'

He looked puzzled at the question. 'It would have been the first thing I noticed and the first job I fixed.'

That was all I needed to hear. The electrician had given me the validation to finally ask myself.

Why had the church lied?

There was one image that kept coming into my thoughts. A solitary man walking a black dog the day the house burnt down. I'd been out all day and was walking up the track in the late afternoon when I passed him. I'd felt uneasy about his presence. I hadn't seen him before and I was familiar with the people who walked their dogs on the hill. Even after we passed, I still felt uncomfortable. If I'd known that my house would burn down that night, I might have understood why.

When all the caretakers had been told to leave with only a month's notice, despite numerous assurances from the church that they would get at least a year, nothing was said directly, but I knew some felt my return had been to blame. The repercussions of moving back had simply not occurred to me. How could I have possibly conceived that it was my presence that was seen as undesirable on the hill? If I'd had an inkling of this I would have returned silently.

But even this seemed verging on the ridiculous. I still kept feeling I must be going a little crazy even thinking this, but if all the dots joined up it would appear that the church had been focused on removing me from the hill. Even though I was aware of the energetic repercussions of me being there, it didn't occur to me that the church would be. I didn't think they were that aware, but that I was beginning to see had been very naive of me.

My initial thought when I had begun to think of the reasons they would want me gone from the hill was that it was in response to the fire walks I'd hosted there. When I'd first agreed to have a fire walk, I'd had no idea how big the fire would be or how many people would see it. And I definitely wasn't aware of the judgements that would be hurled at me because of it. All three fire walks had been an incredible experience for everyone involved and had changed people's entire perception of reality.

Each event had begun around sunset with the building of a massive fire that a truck load of wood had been delivered for. When the wood was all in place, ready to be lit, the stack stood ten feet tall. When it was lit, the flames were so high they could be seen by everyone living in the suburbs below. It took hours for the wood to burn down to a bed of hot coals that were then raked into a pathway, ready for us all to walk over. Meanwhile, during the night, we would dance and drum and chant and build the energy to such a height before the first person leapt onto the embers and began walking across them.

Each time I had done the walk my experience was totally different. The first time I felt so fearful. Then when I stepped onto the coals and began walking through the six feet of red burning embers, I was so ecstatic that I didn't feel the heat that I danced across the fire several more times that night.

On the second fire walk, I had absolutely no fear. The first time had been such a breeze, I wasn't worried at all. I got the surprise of my life when I stepped onto the coals and my feet sunk up to my ankles in hot embers that felt like they were going to burn me. I focused on my breath and walked across, feeling the intensity of the heat, yet miraculously I didn't get burnt.

I had seen so many wonderful things happen each time we hosted an event. On the third occasion, a thin slither of a man, wringing out his hands in anxiety, had arrived a whole hour before it was due to start. He really wanted to take part but was so full of self- doubt, he wasn't even sure he should stay. We gave him so much encouragement. Seeing the delight on his face after he'd done it was something I will never forget. He wasn't the only one whose life changed for the better that night.

Only the year previously, I'd been made aware of a sermon in a local church about fire walking and the devil worship practised on the hill. This smacked a little of the Catholic church's so called "Holy Inquisition" and their persecution of all the wise people. As tragic as that was, I'd laughed when I heard about it. I had been unable to take it seriously. Devil worship—really? I couldn't believe they were talking about me! The woman who'd told me had stood up in the middle of the sermon and asked the minister what he knew about fire walks. It was apparent he knew nothing. Theresa, who at that time was a complete stranger to me, told him he ought to be more responsible before he condemned people and walked out. If this was the reason the church wanted me gone, why didn't they just give me notice? It would have been well within their rights to do so.

The power of the hill to repel development had always drawn attention. A well-known TV programme had visited me when I still lived in the house. One of the questions they'd asked was why everyone who tried to develop the hill got their fingers burnt. If I wanted to keep my home, I couldn't get involved and I wasn't exactly free to say what I felt. It's the hill's own magnetism, the haunting of an old lady that can't settle in her grave and a group of people that believe in the power of love. Did the church believe that what we were doing was making a difference? It's the only conclusion I can draw.

Jen often interviewed intriguing people from all walks of life. I got goose bumps when she told me of a disillusioned minister who wanted to speak out about corruption within the ranks of the very same church. I don't think anyone ever took the story on. Making accusations about powerful entities, be they people or organisations, is a dangerous world to enter, but the conversation Jen had at least led her to consider my suspicions.

'Did they burn the house down?' she asked the minister.

'I don't know if they did or not, but if they did, it would be one of the lesser things they've done,' he replied. 'They do what they have to, to get what they want.'

He was not talking about the minister of the local church; he was talking about the higher echelons, the people who control the money, the people at the top. Because I was the caretaker of a ramshackle house on a multi-million dollar property, that's who I dealt with.

I had little that would stand up in a court of law, yet the old lady kept urging me on. She certainly was not resting in peace. I had always felt she was a kindred spirit. I knew she'd loved animals and grew lots of vegetables. The hill still had remnants of the gardens she'd planted: the frangipanis twisted with age; the giant agave-like cactus that grew so tall it speared the blue sky; bromeliads crouched in the shade of the umbrella tree; and a magenta bougainvillea that had engulfed the house.

The pieces I was putting together were tiny fragments and life wasn't giving me many more. But I did have enough to join the dots, and when I did it didn't look good. There was no silence for me on the hill now. It whispered and coaxed me to see, and always bought me back to that little lie about a switch without a cover on it. If nothing had been said, I would never have entertained the thoughts I did, and those thoughts were making me worried. I don't always have dreams that are prophetic, but the ones that are stand out. I woke up from one such dream where the old lady was speaking to me:

'You are seeing the truth, but you must be careful.' Gill and I both felt it was time to go.

The car ran intermittently. It had good days and bad. Sometimes we'd get to town to buy food and other times, no matter what we did, it wouldn't start. I'm sure it wasn't just my vivid imagination that led me to think it monitored the importance of our trips! Our departure was obviously valid as it started first time. We threw the dogs in the car, left our stuff to pack up when we got back, and drove around to some friends who lived a few suburbs away. It was just a quick visit to say goodbye. I was keen to return to the community. All our stuff was still there, sitting out in the bush, and we hadn't been back for weeks. If it wasn't being eaten by mice, it would be rotting in the humidity.

After a quick cuppa, our friends walked out with us to wave us off. We got in the car and it wouldn't start. Gill and our friend Matt worked on it for hours and it still wouldn't go. I didn't even have my toothbrush with me.

I tried not to scream, to remember the lessons in letting go. *Trust Kye, we are obviously here for a reason.*

We stayed two nights with our friends before the car decided to run again. When we drove back onto the hill, we stopped at Jen's.

'You guys are so lucky; you've just missed the church.

They've been here the last two days!' All I could do was shake my head in astonishment. If our car wasn't so damn frustrating I could almost believe it was guided by an angel. There was no doubt that some unseen force was looking after us.

As we drove up the track to the sleep-out to pick up our gear, the engine died and would not start again. We had no option but to roll the car backwards down the track and park it outside Jen's. This was one of the most frustrating times of my life and I had never felt keener to leave my hill. As we walked back up the track I kept reminding myself to trust. It was all I could damn well do to maintain some sanity.

Lukey wasn't happy about the car being parked at Jen's, and every morning he would walk down the track to sleep in its shade, coming home at night. I hoped he wasn't obsessed with the car because he worried we'd leave him behind. It had been the story of Lukey's life, and there was no way that would happen to him again. Bad body odour and all, we adored him.

One morning I was picking tomatoes that grew prolifically on the fire site when I saw lying on the earth, pulsing with light, a crystal of mine that had been inside the house when it burnt down. It was a large chunk of the original and must have cracked in the fire. After the house had burnt down, Gill and I had spent days raking through the ashes of the house. The only things that hadn't burnt completely were envelopes of photos. They were unsalvageable, badly damaged, stuck together in a wad. If I peeled of the top photo, it uncovered a faded, water-damaged snapshot of my past.

I was delighted to find my black and grey snowflake obsidian that I used for protection. As I held it in my hand and felt its warmth, I knew it was significant that I'd found it. But I had no idea know why—yet.

Later that day, we called in to visit Jen. She had two rather remarkable Canadian women staying called Lindy Lou and Angelica. They were both psychic healers who, following their guidance, had flown across the world to heal some energy spots. Hubbies were left at home with the kids, an infrequent event judging by the phone calls from them. 'Where's Jake's clean school uniform?' and 'How long should I roast the chicken?' And these were not the only conversations going on around them. Lindy Lou was operating like a telephonist on a switchboard with half a dozen calls all happening at once, and only a few of them were on the physical realm.

It was the most interesting cuppa I'd ever had. Lindy Lou was a big, jovial woman, well and truly anchored on the Earth. She said what she thought and didn't curb her edges. She calmly sat there as if it was the most normal thing in the world to be chatting away to thin air.

'Oh, okay, that's why we're here? Yup, yup.' She was nodding her head. 'I understand.' Then she turned to face some other invisible entity. 'Oh, I've got it, makes more sense.' Then turning to someone else we couldn't see ... 'You reckon we use that stone? Perfect, yup. Angelica, can you get the stone? Give it to Kye.'

The next moment Angelica thrust a stone into my opened palm. It was an extraordinary shape, like a snake's backbone but made of rock in a pale mottled pink.

'That little babe's from another planet,' Angelica told me. 'Just let yourself go and it'll do what it needs to do.' While Lindy Lou was Earth, Angelica had the presence of a crystal wand and was really effervescent. Tall and skinny with brightly dyed red hair that grew from her head like a little bush, she jangled and dripped jewellery and oozed kindness and love.

With rainbow-emanating angels, cars that break down exactly where I'm meant to be and long-dead old ladies steering my life, unseen guests at the dining table, be they from another planet as we were told, now seemed quite normal. Lindy Lou was chatting away the whole time I was holding the rock. I was more interested in the rock, so she faded out for a while. But all of a sudden I heard her calling me, 'Kye, you've got to clear some energy on the top of the hill, where the house was, at sunrise tomorrow. You've found what you need today to do it with, haven't you?'

'The obsidian crystal?' I asked, feeling slightly incredulous at this amazing synchronicity. She was off again on her conversation with the unseen guest, nodding her head in agreement.

'Yup, that's the one,' she said looking at me. 'You'll know what to do. The obsidian will protect you.'

I was a little daunted by those last words. I'd already been chilled to my bones by the darkness released after the house fire. Rainbow Man had warned me I wasn't safe here anymore, and the ghost of the old lady had advised me to be careful. One way or another I seemed to be in need of rather a lot of protection recently.

Gill and I got up just before the sun. I held my obsidian in my hand as I walked over to the old house site. The sky was still dark; the birds were silent. I knew I had to do this with Gill. In an electrical circuit, he is my Earth. We sat down, clearing a space amongst the tomatoes.

It suddenly hit me. The house should never have been here. It's the highest point of the hill. A power point.

The house had capped energy that needed to flow free. No wonder it had been such a tumultuous place to live. Emotions were welling up inside me with this realisation. I felt choked up with the past and I began to cry. I'd often felt such a hypocrite living here. I believed in the power of love, yet I'd lived in a personal hell. Why had I ever thought my connection to the hill had helped keep it safe? I was overwhelmed with grief. My tears became a sob. The energy was building up inside me, rocking my body from side to side, like a baby in a crib being rocked by its mother. It was so comforting. I felt bathed in light and the tears I'd cried in sorrow turned to joy.

Why do I struggle so much to trust when I know that everything in life is perfect? Why do I constantly fight the flow of my life when I know that doors only open when I let go? For the first time I saw my pain for what it was—my own birthing into joy. My healing was entwined with the hills; the darkness I'd surrendered and the joy I'd embraced had helped heal this land I loved.

As the sun rose out of the Coral Sea and the birds began to sing, the energy surged through my body. It was so powerful that without conscious thought I rose and my body started spiralling like a twirling dervish, full of joy. When I finally opened my eyes, I could see Gill twirling beside me.

I'd completed what I'd come for. My life was once again my own. There was just one final thing I had to do—write a letter.

Gill felt unsure. He worried that would put me in danger. If I was right, there was reason to be cautious, but I still had to do it. I trusted in the same power that had kept me safe all through this so far. I went and sat on the rock with my pen and paper and I wrote a letter to who I considered to be the perpetrators of a crime. I told them all the reasons I believed they had burnt my home down. I didn't expect anything from them; I wanted them to know that truth, when it's hidden, will always struggle to get free and no one, however powerful they think they are, is beyond divine law.

I sent the letter with a return address of a post office box. When I posted it, I could feel a restless old lady, who I will call Mrs Blessings, was finally at peace. It was time to go. We packed up the car without a single doubt it would start. Suddenly everything was on green; the feeling of being released from the hill was palpable. I felt quite teary as we drove down the craggy winding track, all loaded up for the road ahead. How many times must I bear the wrench of leaving? I could see glimpses of ocean through the tall trees that had the elegance of dancers and in moonlight looked as if they'd been cast from silver. I wanted to hang on, turn back the clocks, re-erect the house and live always in the folds of this magical knoll.

I was still wiping away my tears when we broke down.

We were less than a kilometre away, in the midst of suburbia, conked out. Neither of us had expected this. Gill lifted the bonnet and waggled a few leads. We were certain it would start, but it didn't. We were trying to work out what to do when a couple of good old Aussie blokes stopped to help. Covered in tattoos and grease, they slid from their hotted-up ute, clutching their beers and Winnie blues fags.

'Must be beer o'clock again,' one of them said, handing Gill and I a beer each from the giant esky in the back of their ute. I'm not usually a drinker, but I skulled that beer and gratefully accepted another. Watching these two fix our car was like having a tooth extracted. There were constant exclamations. 'What the fuck's that doing there? You don't bloody well need that.' Crash, as it landed on the footpath, in amongst the growing pile of empty cans. 'We'll get rid of that bloody thing too and pull that out over there.'

Trust, the voice inside kept saying. *Trust?* When half the fucking engine's lying on the path? Surely we needed all that stuff they were pulling out of the car. If we didn't, why was it there in the first place? *Trust, Kye!*

Four cans later, our car was purring like never before. I picked up the cans and all the bits they'd thrown out, certain we'd need them again. We never did. Our tattooed angels brushed off my gushing praise with a lazy wave, bum cracks peeping from their drooping jeans, as they waddled back to their ute, on to more important things—at the local pub.

We took off, waving goodbye, relieved, happy, free. Our next destination—back to the community to pack up our stuff. I knew I couldn't live there anymore, but beyond that the future was unknown, and it didn't matter. I was slowly learning to trust and I was actually beginning to enjoy the adventure we were on.

Nineteen

The Pulse of the Song Lines

I didn't have a single doubt that Gill and I would manifest somewhere beautiful to live very soon. I was a firm believer that when one door shut, another opened, but even though we had left the community, nothing else was opening up for us. We had signs up everywhere. We'd advertised in the paper, had our name down with all the real estate agents, and still nothing came.

We had been living out of the car for six weeks, and the only potential offer of a home had come from Jen. She'd just returned from a trip into the mountains just north of Townsville and told us she had found our dream place to live. It was a rustic log cabin on an acre, and the owners loved dogs and would be happy for us to rent it. I had no plans to move over 300 kilometres away, and even though we'd told Jen we were not interested, she kept going on and on about it.

Nothing else was opening for us, but I still didn't like the sound of the log cabin.

We'd been moving from one place to another, sleeping on the beach and on the banks of creeks. One night we were camping on a property in the Daintree when life gave us a message we could not ignore.

To access this particular farm, you had to drive across a shallow stretch of the river. It was the wet season, and it had been raining continuously. The river had burst its banks, making access only possible by boat.

When we went to get the boat, usually moored on the edge, the river had risen so much it was now floating in the middle. It was already dark, and we only had a torch to see with. We finally found a surf ski that Gill said he could paddle out into the river with to get the boat. I was adamant I was going to and would not give in, despite Gill pleading with me to stay.

As we pushed off from the shore, the full force of the flooded river hit us and upturned the ski. We both disappeared under the water. Gill managed to get a grip on the ski before I did. I was bobbing up and down in the water as we were carried downstream. I was aware of Gill yelling at me to hold on, and I finally found an edge on the smooth surface of the board to cling to. It was all happening so fast there was no time to be afraid, yet there were many things to be afraid of. Not only was this river home to many crocodiles, trunks of trees and bits of debris were being swept downstream with such violence; if they hit us, we'd probably be dead.

Just before the river widened and became even more dangerous, we managed to grab hold of the tip of a tree sticking up out of the water.

It was a She Oak tree, Goddess of Fertility and New Beginnings, and I am forever grateful because she saved both our lives. She was the last tree to cling to before the river grew huge and swollen and swept out to sea.

I wrapped my arms around that tree and held on tightly while Gill launched himself into the water, towards the boat, a few feet downstream. I clung to that tree in total darkness, praying he'd make it, yet unable to see or hear anything above the roar of the river. I was freezing cold, crying and shivering and praying. I had no idea if my love had made it. When I saw the light of his torch coming through the darkness towards me, I sobbed with relief. I was so afraid and so cold my body had melded with the She Oaks, and Gill had to prise me from my tree.

I could not ignore that life was trying to tell us something. I don't believe in accidents. I'm a keen observer of the details of my life. Many years previously, I'd noticed that when I listened to what life was trying to tell me and acted from that guidance, accidents no longer happened to me, or if they did, I understood the minute they did why.

The message this time? We had been trying to manifest something that wasn't our path and were struggling against our flow.

I'd learnt in India that the path to follow is the one that made my heart sing. But I have come to understand that when you have given everything you can to manifest a goal, and it still doesn't come about, follow what presents. It may not be your path, but it could well be a stepping-stone to where you are meant to go. That's why it's so important to be open to synchronicities in life and have an open heart and mind.

After I had sent the letter to the church telling them of my suspicions, I had felt we needed to get away and go somewhere completely fresh, but I'd ignored my gut feeling. After all the excitement of Rainbow Man and ghosts of old ladies and following on the hot little trails of arsonists whilst being wrapped in blankets of protective energy, it had felt like we'd been well and truly dumped when we left the hill. It's certainly what I felt when we were dumped in that river—but I quickly realised the deeper meaning and chose to let go and go with the flow. And where had the flow been trying to send us? Through the only door that had opened so far—Jen's log cabin.

I wasn't enthusiastic, I confess, but we rang the owners, who sounded lovely. They gave us directions and told us the neighbour would give us the key. We loaded up our car, swags and baskets, and other household goods tied to the outside or on the roof. Our five dogs were tucked in air pockets in the back, their heads peeping out the canvas sides. I felt sad saying goodbye to the few friends I had left. I'd let go of so many people after splitting up with Dan, people that had broken my trust and let me down. I only had a few friends left, and I didn't want to leave them.

It took us four hours to drive there. We left the main highway and drove up the winding, snake-like road to the plateau at the top of the range.

'It's beautiful; you'll love it.' Jens's words echoed in my mind. The countryside we passed through was dry and sparse, with thin, whippy trees and shrivelled-up grass. Gone was the lush tropical paradise and the ocean views I had grown so used to.

Finally, we arrived at our dream home, and we sat in the car, staring in astonishment. The first welcome was a huge sign painted in dripping red that covered an entire wall of a shed. It was ugly and brutal and said TRESPASSERS WILL BE SHOT.

'There's a creek out the back,' Jen had told us excitedly. Yup, she was right, but it was dry and looked like it had been for a very long time. It was an acre of bleak, depressing land enclosed in a barbed wire fence. I was trying not to cry as I called into the neighbours for the key. A scrawny woman who was very stressed opened the door. When she heard we had dogs, she said, 'Don't let them get out. The farmer will shoot them.'

We returned to our new log cabin of a home and unlocked the door, praying desperately that what had failed to entice us on the outside would be within. We were greeted by a house full of furniture, and every cupboard had something in it. There was no room for us to make a home anywhere. Beds were all made up, and clothes were hanging in the wardrobe. There was even food in the fridge. With its fluffy toilet seat covers and crocheted toilet roll holders, this was the home of an elderly couple. It definitely wasn't ours.

Even with nowhere to go, we had no desire to stay, and after returning the key to our somewhat surprised neighbour, we sat in the car wondering what to do. I felt desperate and was bawling my eyes out. Life was really giving it to us tough, and I couldn't understand why. I had been so willing to trust and look where it had gotten us. Gill sat beside me, deep in contemplation. He is never a person for chatter, often silent and brooding. When he does speak, his words are always well thought out.

'Let's go to Broome,' he said, completely out of the blue.

'Broome?' I exclaimed. 'It's over 4,000 kilometres away!' *He has got to be joking.* We had hardly any money, and the tread on our tyres was beginning to peel. *We can't just up and leave like that, can we?*

As I sat and thought about it, a ray of sunshine burst through the clouds that had cast such a gloom on the day. The prospect of an adventure was certainly enticing, and what the fuck; we had absolutely nothing to lose.

'Let's go, Gill. We've nothing keeping us here.'

It took us five days to drive there, and our car flew across those desert miles as if it had wings—not a single tyre peeled. We arrived, hot and dusty from the long drive, with only fifty dollars left in the bank. To many, it would have seemed like craziness to have even undertaken a journey like that. But I've experienced so many times that in my greatest leaps of faith, I'm always caught, and this time was no exception.

I had never been to Broome and had no idea what to expect. I was not disappointed. It was like no other place I had ever been. It was magical and lazy and balmy and red. Red dirt, red rocks, a desert oasis on the edge of an ocean that sparkled azure.

It was almost dusk when we arrived. We decided to drive up the beach and find somewhere to camp. The sun was going down over the ocean, something neither of us had seen for a very long time. On the east coast of Australia, it rises over the sea. The tide was a long way out, and pools of water dappled with dusk shimmered in the last light. The sky was streaked with pinks and purples, and the red, bulbous sun was sinking low on the horizon.

We had entered a truly magical realm. When Gill noticed an eagle flying above the car, we decided to follow it. We knew we were being guided somewhere. The eagle suddenly flew up into the air and took off over the dunes, leading us to a track that ran alongside a beautiful lagoon. In the distance, we could see a few scattered houses sitting in the midst of coconut palms, frangipanis and mangos—the most idyllic setting overlooking the beach. 'That's where I want to live,' Gill exclaimed, and I had to agree. It was paradise.

The following day the market was on, and we strolled around the various stalls that were nestled in an exotic garden of hibiscus, frangipanis, baobab trees and a huge African sausage tree with its velvet burgundy flowers that were pollinated by the bats. It was a beautiful place for a market. I was chatting with one of the stallholders and asked her what it was like getting somewhere to rent.

'I've been here six months and still haven't found anything,' she snapped at me.

We were in such a vulnerable space, and I didn't want to fall into any negativity. We barely had enough to feed ourselves for the next few days. This little voice was going in my head. *Stay positive, Kye; things will work out. Look at what you CAN do and plant some seeds.*

We didn't have a phone. What could we do? The only thing we could think of was to write out some signs to put around town so people could leave a message. We were sitting outside the bakery, and I had finished writing the first sign when a guy approached.

'You looking for somewhere to rent? I might be able to help. I've got a place on the beach, and I'm hardly ever there. I wouldn't mind someone living there just to keep an eye on the place.' I was so damn nervous as I asked if he liked dogs. After everything I'd learnt about trust, I shouldn't have been, but I felt vulnerable. I'd cut things fine before, but this time we were really close to the edge.

'I *love* dogs,' he replied enthusiastically. 'Five?' I queried.

'No worries, I'm on five acres. There's plenty of room.'

'We also need to get some money together; we've only have a small amount left.'

'Look, it's not a problem,' he replied. 'Rent's paid for this month. Just pitch in for next month's.' I could barely believe our fortune. After searching so long for a home, believing, trusting, and staying positive, we had finally manifested one 4,000 kilometres from where we had looked.

I was so excited as we drove after our new housemate, twenty kilometres out of town down red corrugated roads. We both had an inkling where we were going and when we finally turned down a drive and came to a house surrounded by mango, coconut and banana trees with rose pink hibiscus, we knew for sure. Our eagle messenger had simply shown us the next place we would live.

When I rang one of my friends to let her know we were okay, she asked how the log cabin was. 'We're not there. We're in Broome.'

'What the fuck are you doing there, girl?' she'd replied, completely flabbergasted. I was blown away too. To make a decision to move over 4,000 kilometres in five minutes was a first for me.

Later, when we told a local indigenous man our story, he replied,

'Oh, you just followed that song line. It comes all the way from where you bin to here.' After so long, it was good to know we were finally back on track, following the pulse of song lines and listening to the eagle's call.

Twenty

Wunjo Crow

The ocean was just a short walk from our new home and the track that led there passed the Jigal trees, which had sweet red flowers that a friend showed us how to suck the nectar from. In the only bit of shade they cast were the raised nests of bowerbirds, piled with all their treasures. They had an attraction to blue and gathered every blue bit of glass, every blue bottle top or bit of plastic, even dead blue beetles and shells, bush pearls, (the seeds of a spikey vine) and little bits of wood.

Groves of stunted paperbark, with their white, peeling bark wooed us with their shade, but we soon discovered it was where the black scorpions lived and gave them a wide berth. Just before we reached the beach was a pristine lagoon, nestled behind the sand dune. Protected from the roar of the Indian Ocean, it was always serene and still. Often Aboriginal boys from a nearby community would be spear fishing in its shallows. I was always awed by their raw and powerful beauty.

Before my home had burnt down, I had just begun to get myself set up to create clothing to sell at the markets and festivals, like I'd been doing when I met Tui. I'd finally found a way of creating an income that I loved, and my clothes were always popular and there were several times my stall sold out! But it had taken me time to build up my business and buy all the things I needed. Only two days before the house fire, I'd proudly taken home a new sewing machine I'd saved all my pennies to buy. I hadn't even had a chance to use it, but it wasn't the only thing I lost in the fire. My fabric, my sewing threads, my dyes, as well as all my market gear and my overlocker too. Nothing was insured and I'd never been able to catch up enough financially to replace them though I was aching to create again. When some new friends, Lola and Jumille, offered to lend us six hundred dollars to get ourselves set up, I almost couldn't believe it. We had known them less than a fortnight and in that short time they had decided we were people they could trust.

Gill found some part-time work on a building site and I began to sew again. I loved it, but the dynamics between Gill and I began to change. While I was empowered by my days, Gill was not. He came home each night grumpy and exhausted, so when his job came to an end, I was very relieved. We had been doing the weekly market together on his day off and had been selling well enough to know we could do fine without his pay.

When Gill offered to dye the clothes for me, on many levels it seemed like the perfect solution. If we could work together, he would no longer need to look for a job. I was struggling to keep up as it was and between us we could get a lot more done—but I was hesitant. It took me so long to sew up the clothes, I worried he would spoil them. I had no doubts he was creative. He'd carved many beautiful bowls from burls, and when we had lived in the house in the clouds, I'd seen him carve the wounded stump of an old and ancient tree into an eagle. But he'd never dyed clothing before, though he was certain he could.

The day he took over dyeing, I was hovering over his every move, insisting he do everything my way. I didn't give him the room to breathe. I was certain all my beautiful clothes would be ruined. He finally insisted that if I wanted him to be creative, I had to stay inside. He was so forceful I had no choice.

Several anxious hours later, when he called me to show off what he'd done, I couldn't believe it. Our clothes line was full of the most stunning clothing, imbued with a vibrancy they'd never had before. They looked as if they'd been spun from the red dirt and dazzling tropical paradise we lived in. I was speechless. I should have known better, everything I had seen him do, whether it had been transforming a Coke can into a gasket, or carving a beautiful bowl, or even his green twig rack for cooking over an open fire, had all been impressive. It seemed there was nothing Gill couldn't do.

Gill loves to tell the story of how our market stall underwent a rebirth with all his new creations hung on display, and how each week, as delighted as I was, I had to sit through numerous markets where customers would innocently rub my face in it with their constant exclamations of how much my dyeing had improved! It was a humbling experience, but there was no doubt about it—we were a perfect team!

This was the tiny beginnings of our business that we called Wunjo Crow, clothing created with joy and celebration. While I loved and connected deeply with many animals, my greatest affinity had always been with the crow.

I had an old dog at the time, called Crow. She was a scruffy cross wolfhound with grey and black dreads who was so dark she brought up everyone's shadows, even mine! Her resemblance to an old crow was so strong, that I named her Crow. She appeared to sneer at everyone except me and it didn't matter how sweet the veneer, she'd scratch the surface and have them boiling with rage. A couple of times she'd snarled so viciously at people, I'd known immediately she was warning me to give them a wide berth. Even though I could see no evident reason, I trusted her completely, so I did.

Crow was my guardian dog, and while my theory, thankfully, was never tested, I didn't doubt she'd rip the throat out of anyone if they tried to harm me. I felt totally safe with her around. She alerted me to snakes, and while I didn't fear them, if it hadn't been for my Crow, there were several times I might have stepped on one, simply because it was so well hidden in the thick grass and I couldn't see it was there.

One day, when she'd really triggered some shit of mine by chewing up my favourite beaded top that I almost lived in, I'd sat down with my runes and asked for the reason why she was such a challenging dog. I pulled Wunjo, the rune for joy, and combining that with what I'd learnt about the crow, it began to make sense. Our greatest teachers are often those that provoke us the most, those that make us spew with rage and scream and shout. It's our own pain they are reflecting back at us to face and heal and the only path to joy is through releasing it. From that day on my treasured shadow dog was given the impressive title of Wunjo Crow but affectionately known as Wunji.

Those two words resonated so deeply for me, but I hadn't really thought about the implications of using that name for our clothing. I knew many people didn't like crows and judge them for the things they do, like pecking the eyes out of baby lambs that are still alive. However you look at that, it is not nice.

I wish they didn't do that too, but I also feel that they mirror us.

As human beings we do all sorts of heinous things, but we hide them away. We don't do them in the open. Crows teach us about being real and make us face our own reflection— not only in our deeds but in the way we live our lives. Are we living our lives honestly? Are we acting with integrity? Are we honouring ourselves and all of life? What are we supporting that is hidden? The journey with crow isn't an easy one, but trying to avoid it is like cancelling winter and replacing it with spring. If we did this, very little would sprout because, like us, seeds need darkness to germinate and grow.

I didn't think about the relevance of any of this when Gill and I decided on the name, Wunjo Crow, for our clothing, but I was soon shown it wasn't merely a whim. I'd felt the name Wunjo Crow emanated a strength and I liked that but it wasn't until shortly after, when we were at a market, that I realised the lessons my scruffy mutt of a dog had taught us were also relevant to our brightly coloured clothing creations.

A customer had picked up our newly hand-drawn swing tag and said, 'Oh wow, that's beautiful and so true. The Wunjo Crow reminds us that the journey to joy (Wunjo) is through the shadows with crow! And what a perfect representation of joy your beautiful clothing is!'

After all the dark times I did indeed feel joyful. I absolutely adored Gill and loved how our lives flowed so beautifully together. When I touched him, I couldn't feel where I ended and he began; there was no separation. I had never experienced this before. I had always believed a love like ours was possible, even when I was experiencing the exact opposite. There were times I'd said to Dan, 'Our love doesn't need to be like this. We could experience so much more together, I know we could.' But obviously neither of us were ready then.

Is Gill my one and only twin flame, my soul mate? I really don't know. I don't feel the need to label what we share, and I'm not even curious about understanding what it is. All the time it felt good and it worked; that was enough for me.

We had certainly journeyed through our shadows since those innocent days when we'd first met. But every tear I'd cried, every hurt I'd felt, had been well and truly worth it. People often told us they could feel the strength of our connection. When one gorgeous young woman had enquired about Gill to one of our friends, she'd replied, 'He's with Kye.' As far as she was concerned there was nothing else to say—our relationship spoke for itself!

Even in our early days together, people would ask me what I'd done to attract him and if there was anything they could do to bring a love like ours into their own lives. I always told them, absolutely, YES. My answer would be to stop looking for love in everyone you meet.

Instead draw up your bridges, secure your moats and prepare to bunker down.

The last thing I wanted when Gill cruised into my life was a relationship. While I was still feeling torn apart from the torment I'd experienced with Dan, I had reached a very crucial point in my life. I was not prepared to accept any more crap. I had told a friend that I had no interest in another relationship. 'I'm completely over men and I'm not prepared for any more bullshit in my life.'

'The one that breaks through your barriers is going to be very special,' she'd replied, and she was right.

While we continue to dally around with partners who don't touch us, heart and soul, who slough all our beauty away, we will not experience Sacred Love. It comes to us only when we truly and deeply realise that what we seek cannot be found in the mundane and we close that door forever.

Since I was a small child I have known I was on this earth because I had a mission to fulfil. As such, a life lived to old age that consisted of just sleeping, waking, eating and working in the daily grind of nine to five, with a few weeks' holiday scattered here and there, has never made sense to me. With all my heart and soul I desired more and I knew that every experience, however much it challenged me at the time was guiding me and teaching me so that I could fulfil on this earth what I had come to do. I didn't have the whole picture yet, because how can you see the full view from the top of the mountain, when you're still climbing up the side. I do know though that when I chose to close the door on the mundane, and to me a mundane life meant *not* living a life I loved, not only did Gill come but every aspect of my life began to synchronise as it moved swiftly into harmony.

Before Gill, my clothing creations had only been a hobby. I'd made pocket money from them, but they'd never supported me financially. Now they did, and not only that—they emanated with the vibration of everything I'd learnt on my quest so far. I was finally beginning to integrate the wisdom of India, of living from my heart and doing what I loved, instead of what I thought I should do. I was honouring myself by being loving to me and, at last, hallelujah, thanks to Philip I'd let down my barriers and was allowing others to love me! Combine that with the knowledge that Gill and I had gleaned from our time apart, when we'd each had to face our own shadows and by doing so, awakened a power that surged through us, my life was changing in every way.

Opening up like a rose in bloom.

One day, I was in our garden, sitting on the mattress under the shade of the mango tree that was heavy with young green fruit. I was taking some time out from sewing and was reading a book when I began to feel a familiar feeling. It had been such a long time since I had felt this angelic presence, and I had worried that he was gone for good. I could feel the energy building up inside me, becoming lighter and brighter, bathing me in intense rainbow light. But this time it did not take me to the edge, and his words came to me from a deeply meditative bliss.

'The strength of the love you share with Gill is only so because you did not run from the journey when the path you were on led into the darkness. You will help many others reach this sacred space.'

I was certainly aware of the wonderful ways my life was changing, but I wasn't feeling ready to help anyone else. I was still struggling with a few little wounds that I hadn't known were there until two people from my past had turned up to visit me. I answered him using my mind, with no spoken word. *I know I have faced many things that caused me pain, but I still feel so unable to forgive some people for the hurt they caused me.* I could feel myself welling up with tears.

'Why do you feel you have to forgive them? Why are you always giving to others instead of yourself?'

For a while I sat thinking about his words. *Wasn't this what I was meant to do? Isn't this what every book I read tells me? That the ultimate path to healing is through forgiveness?*

'But what does forgiveness mean to you,?' he asked, once again reading my mind.

Every time I thought of forgiving, I imagined myself with my arms around them, saying it was okay, and each time I shuddered and stopped because it wasn't.

'The only thing you need do is LET GO,' he replied. 'You don't need to take responsibility for the actions of others. Bless what you have learnt from those times then let them go. When you understand on the deepest level of your being that every experience has come into your life to awaken you, you will be overcome with joy at their gift.'

I want to let go, but there's a part of me that feels so wounded.

His next words came so softly, almost seductively, trance-like. 'Right now in this moment,' he answered, 'do you feel those wounds?'

Suddenly I was aware that nothing else existed but this moment. The moment I was in. I could smell the frangipani flowers with an intensity I'd never known before. Way off in the distance I could hear the sounds of children laughing, their voices sending ripples of delight that coursed through my body. I had never felt so alive.

An ant slowly walked across my bare, outstretched leg. I could feel its little legs tickling the surface of my skin and I didn't even think to brush it off. I could even hear the mangos on the tree above me growing. Everything was how it was meant to be and everything was perfect. When he spoke again, his words caressed me with the softness of a feather.

'There is only this moment now, and this is what it feels like when you are free of pain.' Once again I let his words sink in before I answered.

So how do I encourage others to face their shadow when there is only this moment?

'Unresolved shadows prevent you from being in this moment . Your pain and anger, your disappointments, your regrets and your fears, all keep you anchored in the past, and until they are faced, they will continue to manifest themselves in experiences you create in the now.'

I had experienced this myself when I first met Gill. After so much betrayal, I was terrified it would happen again. I had worried so much about it I had actually created that very scenario. But I had also ended the cycle by being willing to face it. Even though I was hurting so badly, I did not run when I saw him on the street with his new love.

'Yes, and you healed an old pattern in that moment; you did not need to dredge through old pain. That's how you transform your past, by facing what comes up in each moment, and, instead of suppressing— getting drunk, taking pills, eating chocolate, whatever it is you do to avoid facing what hurts— allow yourself to feel the pain, the anger. When you acknowledge it's there and give it the respect to express itself safely, without hurling it at others and creating more pain, it dissipates.

This is the pathway to joy.'

Shonteeha had given me a similar message when I had faced the prospect of returning home and dealing with the birth of Dan and Sheila's baby—*If you don't face it, it will always be with you.*

But when I faced the people that hurt me, I didn't feel any better.

'But did you face them in truth? Were you honest about how you felt, or did you suppress your feelings so they simmered under the surface?'

He had really struck a chord with that comment. It was exactly what I had done. I had welcomed them with a smile and not once in the two days they stayed did I say, 'This is how I feel'. I had been deluding myself if I thought I'd faced it.

'If you choose to change the integrity of your relationships then be honest. Those that can meet you in honour and love will value truth; those that don't will leave.'

Before Rainbow Man left he gave me a message which he said was a sacred key, and he asked me to give it out with our creations. 'Your clothes hold the energy of Joy, but it is through your own darkness that you found this light. Share this message. It will help others find their way through the shadows.'

Remember, said the Wunjo Crow,

You are a Sacred being,

Love yourself,

Embrace your shadows,

and you will find joy in who you are.

Once again I'd been uplifted and renewed by the presence of my rainbow-emanating angel, and I was so relieved he hadn't gone. After my time overseas, in India and England, then back to all the bizarre happenings on the hill, my life had slunk into normality. While that was just what I needed, I did enjoy the inexplicable aspects of my life, and I didn't want Rainbow Man to go.

Life had been intense for much too long. I had been tumbling from one major drama to the next for the last few years. It felt good to just hang out on the beach and not be emotionally wrung out. To sit with friends watching the sun sink into the sea, radiant with light, dazzled by the pools of dusk left by the tide, or sitting around a fire in the warm sand, watching the moonrise so bulbous and full, so achingly, cloyingly beautiful I felt I would burst.

The winter months of Broome were like living in the fragrant petals of a boab flower, every moment imbued with the charisma of our desert oasis. But it changed for me when the build-up to summer came. Every day was muggily hot and humid, and every afternoon huge clouds would rumble in, the sky would darken and turn black and lightning would crash down all around us—but no rain. Day after day. And no rain. It just got more and more humid. I felt as if I was being tortured.

When our absentee housemate moved back in, bringing his friends with him, our peaceful life was shattered with late night drinking and hooning in their cars. We both felt the urge to go. Some of the other stallholders from the markets were travelling south to Margaret River and Denmark to work the season there and we decided to do the same. I prayed we would find somewhere permanent to live, but I couldn't stop thinking about a hermit crab I'd seen!

I'd been sitting on the white sand on the edge of the salt-water lagoon, quietly meditating on the home I longed to find. When I opened my eyes, the first thing I saw was a hermit crab carrying his home, a salvaged empty seashell on his back. I'd felt very uneasy as I walked back up to the house.

Was life trying to tell me something?

It was only a crab. Why give it any meaning? Yeah, that's right, you're reading way *too much into it. You'll find a great home, Kye, just you wait and see!*

As we packed up the car for the long drive south I was still in denial of the magical little glimpse of my future that life had given me.

Twenty-One

The Miracle of Harry

That little hermit crab was wrong. We did get a house and, of course, it had a ghost! How could we attract anything less? It was an old stone cottage built by a one-armed fisherman one hundred and twenty years before. It sat on seventeen acres, just a short walk from the ocean where the water was crystal clear. But even on the hottest day it was always bitterly cold.

On the night before we moved in, I had a dream that I was being interviewed by a grumpy old lady who wasn't at all happy about sharing her home with us. She told me she was very upset about the transformer and wanted to know what electrical appliances we had and if there were any that would upset her. I had no idea what she meant, but she soon showed us.

We had an old electric clock that made a loud hum. Well, every time we switched it on, she would turn it off. At first we thought it was our imagination, but whether the clock was on or off soon became the focus of our day. We would turn it on and run back a minute later to find it once again off. I could almost hear the old lady tutting with disapproval every time we turned it back on. We had no intention of upsetting her and harmony was restored when we decided to leave it turned off.

The house was so picturesque from the outside, with its wide stone verandas and big old armchairs. But inside it was so angular, damp and drafty that whatever we did, it never felt cosy. It was always so cold we could never get warm. We had to sit huddled up over the pot belly stove, which Gill spent hours each day chopping wood for.

When we first moved in, we went to a local farmer to buy some chickens and ducks. He showed us a huge pen full and told us to pick the ones we wanted. Much to the farmer's amazement, we chose every bald chicken and every runty looking little duck. He kept asking us if we were sure, and we replied we were certain.

I'd had lots of chickens in my life before, but I connected with one of our new chooks as if she was my soul mate. I adored Harry. I didn't understand why I felt this love so intensely or so deeply, but I did, and it was obvious the feeling was mutual. One morning when I went down to feed the ducks and chickens and let them out, Harry was lying on the ground looking so unwell; my heart did the biggest lurch. I was sick with worry. Neither Gill nor I knew what was wrong, but she appeared to have a big lump on her rear end. I was so relieved by the response of the local vet when I rang and told him about Harry.

'The poor love; she must be in pain. Bring her in straight away.'

We drove to his place so fast and I prayed the whole way. When he examined her, he told us that in his opinion she had an abscess on her uterus and, and not only was she in pain, he'd never seen a chicken recover from this.

'Would you like me to put her to sleep?' he asked.

The grief I felt at the prospect of that was utterly overwhelming, yet I wanted to make a clear decision that would be in the absolute best interest of Harry. Should I hand her over and have her put down or should we take her home and give her a chance? I looked into Harry's eyes and I knew exactly what I had to do. This little love had only ever received the brunt of life. She had been so uncared for and looked so forlorn, she deserved a second chance. We needed to do all we could to heal her.

'She's coming home with us,' I said to the vet. 'We'll do everything we can for her.'

Every day after that—morning and night—Gill and I sat with Harry and sent her love. We sat one on each side of her and placed the palms of our hands gently against her. As we did so I could hear life speaking through me, telling me to let go of all doubt and to hold a vision of a healed Harry, so that's what we did.

Within a few days, we noticed a vast difference in her wellbeing. All the swelling had gone down and our little Harry soon became a radiant beacon of love. She grew new feathers and looked so healthy. She was the best little buddy and followed me everywhere like a dog. I was so overjoyed to see her looking so well and grateful for all I'd learnt about healing over the years.

I had been interested in different healing techniques for a long time. I had learnt Reiki, and for many years until I lost all my flower essences in the house fire, I'd treated patients with them and had many astounding results. My interest in alternative methods of healing had started in my early twenties when I'd spent time in the Philippines visiting several psychic surgeons. I'd even had an operation.

It was the final year of President Marcos and his wife Imelda's corrupt reign of that beautiful country and I flew in to meet an old man from Alaska called Uncle Frank who had spent his life investigating psychic phenomena. He was a friend of a friend and all I knew was that he'd spent a lot of time with the healers and he was going to show me around.

I have to say I was an incredibly naïve young woman. I had no idea what I was in for. I hadn't done any research; I'd gone to the Philippines on a whim. For a fortnight before we visited the healers, we stayed at the base of

Mount Banahaw, a three-peaked volcano known as a holy mountain and a sacred place for pilgrims.

Uncle Frank had been investigating a woman nearby who worked in the fields. Unlike other Filipinos, she had striking red hair and hypnotic green eyes. Despite having no education, under hypnosis she said she came from another planet and accurately identified its name as well as its exact location, which had all been verified. I didn't get to meet her, but I did climb up the holy mountain with Uncle Frank.

As we ascended this volcano every stage along the way was steeped in ritual as we purified ourselves, mentally, spiritually and physically. At one place two waterfalls fell, side by side. I had to bathe in the heavier one first and cleanse physically, and then move to the other fall that fell in a fine mist and cleansed me spiritually.

There were pilgrims all the way up the mountain and some were living in the shelter of caves. We came across a German woman who told us she was healing herself of cancer and had already been there several months. We rested for a while from the steep climb and she boiled some water on the fire to make us tea. She looked peaceful and accepting as she shared how her life had transformed overnight when she'd discovered she was ill. Suddenly her focus changed. From being a successful real estate agent earning lots of money, to living like a hermit in a cave on a holy mountain, but she was happier now than she had ever been. 'And that has to be a key to healing,' she added, with a sparkle in her eyes.

We continued our journey up the mountain and had just scrambled over some boulders blocking the path when Uncle Frank pointed to a small gap in the rocks below our feet, where there was a ladder descending into the darkness, he told me to climb down and submerge myself in the water. I had no idea what to expect. At the bottom of the ladder I found myself almost in total darkness, except for just a thin crack of light above my head from where I'd come. Water was trickling down the walls into the black icy pool and I would have felt cut off from the world completely if I hadn't been able to hear Uncle Frank ordering me around from above.

Yes, *ordering* ... he was such a pompous man and was starting to drive me nuts. I found him so rude and obnoxious. Several times he'd herded Filipino pilgrims out of the way as if they were cattle, waving his stick at them so that I could interrupt their ritual to do mine! I had been happy to wait my turn. I couldn't see anything holy in pushing others out of the way. Yet despite my insistence, he hadn't listened to a word I'd said. I should have just packed my bag and left, but I was young then. I wanted to see the world he had access to and didn't realise that I could have seen it without him and in a much more harmonious way.

'Now submerge yourself in the water and as you do, imagine letting go of all your negativity!' he shouted down at me. Instructing me in the ritual of the well as if we were doing military training. When I finally resurfaced, I didn't share with him that I hadn't been cleansed entirely of my negativity, or that I found him intensely annoying; he lacked any sensitivity to pick that up.

But the mountain was such a special place, even with this irritating man barking orders and pushing people out the way the whole climb up. As I ascended the mountain, delving deeper, releasing even more pain and sorrow, the radiance and love I began to feel soon eclipsed the petty tyrannies of Uncle Frank; I didn't doubt Mount Banahaw's majestic powers of healing.

Finally, at the summit, I felt as if my body was filling up with light. I had never experienced this before. It was streaming out of me with such force my physical body was on the verge of exploding into tiny particles and being lost in the ethers forever. I almost passed out and would have if my tyrannical saviour Uncle Frank had not sat me down with my head between my legs and got me to breathe deeply as I earthed myself!

One morning, he threw me a book about walk-ins to read. I had never heard of them before and while I certainly believed in reincarnation, I was sceptical about walk-ins. A walk-in happens, apparently, when a soul is needed urgently on the earth and, instead of being born into a new body, they take over an already dead body. The book was full of case studies of people who had been dead for days, about to be buried, and then woke up. While they would look the same as before, but they would behave radically different. They weren't the same person!

Later that day, we went to visit a spiritual community at the base of the mountain called 'Mystica'. While I was there, a bell rang and everyone on the community stopped what they were doing, sat down wherever they were and meditated. I was told this happened several times a day. I wish I had been able to speak Tagalog, as I would have learnt a lot more about this amazing community. Uncle Frank told me that their leaders were both men and women, but seven priestesses who were celibate held the priestly orders.

While I was there, an old lady, stooped yet radiant with love, beckoned me to follow her. She led me partway up the mountain to a bamboo shelter on the edge of a steep cliff and we sat meditating together. I felt blissful. In this sacred place I found it easy to lose myself in the divine.

Afterwards she told me in broken English the story of her brother. He had died and been dead for three days. 'He was stiff!' she exclaimed, stiffening her own fingers to demonstrate. 'We could not bend them, and his body was covered in flies. We were about to bury him and he woke up! My family was very frightened and went to run away, but my brother told them they had nothing to fear.'

I couldn't believe the synchronicity of her story, but I had no reason to disbelieve her.

'Something very strange happen when he come back,' she went on. 'He speak many new languages.' She was shaking her head from side to side. 'Before he only a simple farmer, now he work helping refugees!' It seemed incredible that so soon after I had been given the book I met someone who had experienced a walk-in. Good ol' synchronicity. It was still hard for me to believe, but one thing I was learning from the Philippines was that it was best to keep an open mind.

When we finally visited the healers, one in particular really stood out. He was Reverend Alex Orbito. There was a queue of people waiting to be healed that snaked around inside the room, filling it completely, and then continued out the door and down the street. He was standing at the front at a table and one by one people were lying down for a healing. With the room full to bulging, there was no way I could see what was going on. Uncle Frank was, as usual, jostling me to the front when the healer saw me and beckoned me to come closer to his table.

I was astounded by what I saw. His fingers seemed to disappear right inside the huge belly of a man he was treating, and I could see blood. It looked as if the wound he had his fingers inside had been cut with a knife. When he pulled his fingers out, there were dark, lumpy bits of tissue hanging from the very tips of his fingers. I was flabbergasted. I remember saying to Uncle Frank repeatedly, 'This is amazing, bloody hell. I can't believe it. It's absolutely amazing.'

Then I got that top-of-Mount Banahaw-about-to-leave-my-body feeling all over again. I felt so full of light and I was emanating it. The last thing I remember is standing with my back against a wall and a small Filipino women slapping my face and saying, 'Come back, come back, come back,' and inside I was saying,

No, No, No.

I woke up in a strange room being massaged by a strange man. I didn't know where I was. I had no recollection of getting there and I was hugely relieved to hear Uncle Frank's voice outside. As he led me back he told me that Reverend Orbito had seen brightly coloured lights streaming from me. Even though my experience of filling up with light had been blissful, it had left me feeling completely drained and I didn't feel I had any resilience to cope with much more. I was very low when I returned to the healing room. When Reverend Orbito saw me, he beckoned me over to the table and gestured for me to lie down. As he moved his hands over my body, he found himself drawn to my stomach. I watched the whole thing, absolutely flabbergasted—nothing had prepared me for this. I felt the pressure of the tips of his fingers on my belly. I was very tense and that may have been the reason why that initial probing hurt. As soon as he broke the skin, I didn't feel it as intensely. I could see the blood, and when he pulled his fingers out there was a small clot stuck to his fingertips.

Over the years I've had this experience picked apart by many unbelievers, but for me there was and is no doubt. I felt the energy in that room in the same way I felt it at the top of a sacred mountain.

I felt amazing after my session with the healer. I was full of energy once again and so was puzzled when, immediately after my spiritual surgery, Reverend Orbito told everyone there would be no more healing that day. I didn't understand what was happening or why. Then Uncle Frank told me that I had completely drained the reverend's energy and he couldn't heal anyone else that day! Apparently, the reverend had met his energetic match!

There was one thing that Reverend Orbito said that really stayed with me: 'Begin first to love yourself and you will know how to love others.'

While I was far from embracing the wisdom of his words at that time, I was finally taking steps in the right direction. Healing Harry through the vibration of love led me to look back over all I had learned in my life thus far, and I could see so many threads of my life finally weaving together— and the tapestry created was one of love. It was the lesson within every experience I had. When love had not been present, my life had been so dark and unhappy, and I had sunk so low that I almost gave up and died. Yet even that had been a potent time, because it was only when I reached the depths of my despair with nowhere else to fall, I realised I could wallow where I was or I could use the bottom of my pit as a platform to launch my way back up! I did have a choice and it was up to me.

Every step of my journey taught me the power of love and that it began with me. We are so programmed to *not* think about ourselves. We are told to stop being selfish and that life is a compromise. But we wrong ourselves deeply when we accept this as truth. How can we begin to teach children to live their dreams if we don't live ours?

When I'd been left penniless in poverty-stricken India, it was when I had loved myself and honoured every need as it arose, in that moment, without a fear of lack for the future, that I was looked after in miraculous ways for months on end. I experienced the amazing flow of energy that surges into our life when we surrender completely to the NOW and as a result embrace 'the space beyond asking' where there is no need for anything because it's already there.

That was the energy Gill and I held as we sat with Harry. In all my years of helping others to heal, I had never felt a more potent force. When we love ourselves, we build up the energy inside us that comes from our connection with the source of all life, up and up and up. Our frequency changes, we resonate at a higher pitch, and then that beautiful love energy overflows from us like a waterfall and seeps into everything in and around us. We cannot love others without loving ourselves, and we cannot hold space for others to heal, until we are healed. And the more we love, the further that love is felt, it even impacts places, people and animals that we have never met and may never do so.

I knew it was love that healed Harry and after so many years walking blindly through the darkness, it was wonderful to see that loving myself was not only creating miracles in my own life but in the lives of others. Even my little featherless chook with her big open heart felt its presence!

The home we shared with our uptight ghost was not meant to be. I began to get kidney infections and feel so run down I was finally guided to visit an old man everyone called The Wizard. He was well known for sorting everyone's health issues out. I was expecting a castle to match his name, yet he lived in an ordinary suburban house. However, as soon as we arrived I knew I was going to get to the roots of my problem.

He had just come in from the garden and carried a basket of freshly picked vegetables all brimming with health. He was an old man yet his eyes were so piercingly clear and blue; I could tell he practised what he preached. With his long, grey beard it was easy to see why he'd been called The Wizard.

As he reached out to get his pendulum I noticed his hands were still covered in dirt, but I found it reassuring. Like all the vegetables he grew, I was happy for him to garden me. He pulled lots of charts out onto the table and after getting me to hold the pendulum, he began testing for possibilities to explain my fading health—minerals, energy blocks, vitamins. All of a sudden he said, 'You're sleeping over the top of some underground water. No wonder you're not feeling good. Now just imagine moving your bed and I'll test and see if it's in a better spot.' No matter where I imagined moving our bed to, he found we were still sleeping above the water.

We didn't have many options. It was only a small two-bedroomed cottage and there was one bedroom we never went into. It was the front room of our home and had a menacing chill. Our grumpy bum of a ghost had told us if we left that room well alone, she'd wouldn't bother us. Was that a threat? Either way we gave her a wide berth.

'It's no good,' The Wizard said. 'You're on the top of water wherever you go and there's another problem coming up. Have you got a transformer outside your house?' I hadn't even known what a transformer was until then. When we worked out it was that huge box at the top of the power pole, right outside our idyllic little cottage, he said, 'Get out of there. You'll be sick forever if you stay.'

With his prognosis, I finally realised the cause of our ghost's miseries, and it was making me sick too!

Gill had been urging me to leave for quite a while. He was feeling trapped and our life was becoming mundane. It had been me that had clung on. I really wanted to have a home somewhere, but I'd known this wasn't the right place. Summer had been fine, but when autumn came and the weather began to get bitterly cold, we noticed that everyone around us was becoming miserable and depressed, whereas they'd been fine all through the summer. Not only that, there was no way Gill could chop enough wood to keep us warm. We both began to yearn for the warmth and freedom of the tropics. It was time to hit the road.

I had forgotten all about that hermit crab when Gill convinced me to sell our G60 Nissan and buy an old furniture truck with canvas sides and plenty of room for our bed and all our market gear, as well as the dogs in the back. My little home on wheels had manifested and we were to become gypsies for the next three years.

We found the most amazing seamstress in Perth called Rosie who took over a lot of our sewing and agreed to do all the cutting as well. We organised for the fabric to be delivered directly to her. She would sew it up into whatever we asked for and post boxes to us of ready-made clothes to wherever we were travelling through at the time. All we had to do was find a place to dye them.

As much as I could feel tinders of excitement at our new plan, I was overwhelmed with grief at leaving Harry. I felt as if my heart had been wrenched out of my chest every time I imagined leaving her behind, but I couldn't picture a good life for her being kept in a cage in the back of our truck. We had found a lovely woman to take over renting the house, who was delighted with the chickens and ducks and promised wholeheartedly to care for Harry, but I was still inconsolable with grief.

As Harry sat beside me, I kept explaining to her that soon I'd be gone and she sat beside me as if nothing was wrong, looking at me adoringly. It was heartbreaking. When I went to say goodbye to the friends we'd made I was crying so much that snot was running down my face, my eyes were thick and swollen and I couldn't get a grip on myself. They hugged me and said reassuringly, 'Don't worry, you can come back and see us,' but I couldn't even begin to find the words to explain that my heart was breaking, not because I was leaving them, but because I was leaving my beloved Harry behind, one of the hardest things I've ever had to do!

I would never forget my Harry.

Twenty-Two
Kundalini Crow

Our travels around Australia until then, and for the following three years, finally gave me the emotional break I had craved. I had so much time to relax and unravel and have a look at who I had become. My life had changed drastically since being with Gill. When we'd broken up, it wasn't only the loss of him in my life that I'd had to deal with; it was the loss of the lifestyle he'd bought with him too.

Before Gill my only visits in nature had been clumsy camping trips where my friends and I would struggle to erect tents, cook over a gas bottle and spend much time blowing up mattresses that I never slept comfortably on anyway. With all the paraphernalia, I was always going to be separate from what I was trying to enjoy—the simplicity and silence of nature.

With Gill there was no separation between him and nature. Just like the dream I'd had when I found him lying asleep by a waterfall in the rainforest, in nature Gill was totally at home. He opened up a world for me I had never seen before and showed me not only how to look after myself, but how to walk softly on our earth. I discovered how to light a fire when the wood is wet and numerous ways to cook our food on the fire without it getting burnt—though I burnt it several times as I perfected the art! Sleeping under the stars, tent free, was a balm for me, body and soul. I loved drifting off to sleep as I gazed up at the night sky.

Shonteeha had been right when she'd said to me, 'He will help you heal your pain.' He had. I'd needed to release the wounds I'd experienced with Dan and I'd needed to talk about it and I did. I talked and talked and talked until I was all talked out and I had no need to talk anymore. Having someone that validated my journey enough to listen played a huge part in my healing. So often people try to steer us away from telling our shadow stories. Certainly if we are going to get stuck in them that's wise, but there is a certain amount of telling we need to do before we can make peace with our pain.

And there were other things that helped too. Three years of travelling around Australia, in between markets and the business of clothes, with weeks of isolation where we bathed under waterfalls and camped by crystal clear creeks and watched the moon rise over the ocean on some white sand deserted beach, was so soothing for my pain, it finally dwindled away.

Gill helped me in many other ways too. From him I learnt about giving. He's a very humble man and never needs acclaim for the acts of kindness and caring he doesn't just do for me, but for everyone. He's very sensitive and honouring towards women and wherever we go, he gives. If there is a woman living on her own coping with a child and we are staying nearby, she'll wake up and find a big pile of wood chopped up for her, and he's done it silently, not seeking any praise.

Once when we were staying with a mother of four boys, their septic tank was backing up and their toilet was full to the brim with shit. Gill went out into their acreage, dug a massive hole and then bucketed their septic tank into the hole he'd dug and buried it. When I asked him why he was doing it—after all the father of this family was home playing computer games—he looked at me and said, 'I can't let those little kids go without a toilet, Kye.' This is my gentle lover and the man I love, and this is who I'd wept for when he'd so unexpectedly walked out of my life.

In many ways we had an idyllic lifestyle. When we were staying in the bush, we always slept outside by the fire, but when we were back on the market circuit, our truck made our nomadic lifestyle so much easier. My appreciation for our bed, all made up in the back, never waned.

Our migratory flow took us from the tropics down to the south-west to the desert and south to the snow. Everywhere we went we met new customers and found new shops to sell our Wunjo Crow creations. Many said our clothing was their fastest seller! Our business grew exponentially. There were many occasions we could be seen on some dusty outback road, pulled up in a lay-by, colourful collections of clothing festooned from the trees as we packed orders for our shops and I wrote out invoices on the tailgate of our old truck. If only they could have seen us!

Then, one day after we'd been travelling for eighteen months and were camping at a waterhole, we noticed Lukey struggling to get up. He'd been fine the day before. We helped him up for a pee and then settled him down on his bed.

He never got up again.

We sat with our dear Lukey the whole day as he faded from life. If you can have a magical death, that's what Lukey had. He left the world so peacefully, being held by Gill and me, with our other four dogs snuggled up beside him. Noble Luke, since being with us, had surged across oceans in boats, camped out on beaches all around Australia and shot the breeze in the back of our 4WD. He'd even chased wild pigs; something I found hard to believe but several people guaranteed they'd seen him. While we were in bed, sleeping, Lukey apparently lived a life of his own.

We buried him under a beautiful tree on the edge of one of our favourite waterholes. His last years were his best. Soar free beautiful Lukey.

When my dear Sprouty followed Lukey and died a year later, that was the end of travelling for me. An unhappy man at an outback service station had thrown a 1080 dingo bait into the back of our truck when all our dogs were in there. It was my curious little street dog who ate it. At first, I wrote this experience down to share with you, then I deleted it. Why draw out suffering any longer and why give one sick man any more of a feed? That's what it was. Some people feed on the sorrow of others; they are so unhappy inside and they want others to feel their pain. The agony of that experience is not one I want to share. It took me two years to be able to even speak of it, and even then it was in a flood of tears. With the loss of Sprouty, travelling for us both came to an end.

The death of two of my dearest dogs brought home to me how much I yearned for a safe haven. I just felt too vulnerable to remain on the road. The decision to return to Far North Queensland was made as swiftly as the one to leave it had been. All I could feel was relief that we were going home. I was really aching to be somewhere long enough to put down some roots.

I couldn't wait to watch the bulbs I'd planted in winter, bloom in the spring or eat the paw paws from trees I'd nurtured and grown myself. I wanted to get a horse, have a goat or two and settle blissfully down in some enchanted nook we could call home. Deep down I missed my hill and I hadn't found anywhere else I felt I belonged. Even though I had loved our travels in our old truck, secretly I'd hoped that every journey would lead us to a magical new home and it hadn't.

I felt like a tree being wrenched out of the ground every time we stayed somewhere for a while, started to settle, to see the cycles, make new friends, plant food in the earth and, as always, before it was ready to harvest, it was time to go, to travel to the sunshine, to the bustle of a market, where it didn't matter that we didn't have four sturdy walls to shelter us from the cold. Every time we moved on my fragile roots needed soothing.

But we had also gained so much from our travels, our business had grown, we were selling wholesale to many shops around Australia. We had made so many new friends and explored so many new places. I felt blessed by our time on the road; it was simply time for a change.

Once back in familiar territory we decided to go to the only place in Australia where I felt at home— my hill. I knew I couldn't live there anymore, but a few days camping whilst we looked for a new home, where was the harm in that?

I'd finally received a forwarded letter from the organisation I'd suspected had burnt my home down. It said the police had investigated the fire and if I had any suspicions to go and see them. While I was very aware that the police had not investigated the fire, I hadn't expected anything else, what could they say?

I still puzzled over why the hill had kept me hostage for almost two months and why had it been so important for me to know the truth if nothing could be done with the knowledge? Was it enough that what had been hidden was now known, even if it was only by us and was it enough that those who were responsible were aware we knew? I didn't know. I'd given up trying to make sense of it all. I wasn't returning for that.

Our truck struggled up the steep, washed out, old drive up to my former home overlooking the Coral Sea. Surges of energy raced through me. She was just as beautiful as ever. Apart from being very overgrown and tangled up with weeds, the garden was doing fine. I even preferred her wildness. The passion vine that I'd grown as a screen at the bottom of the garden, so that when you first drove in you didn't see the house, had taken off into the nearby trees and was loaded heavily with ripe fruit.

Seeing how well the passionfruit vine curtained the garden reminded me of a visitor who'd called around to see us a few days after the house had burnt down, when Gill and I were camping in the bus at the bottom of the garden. He lived several hundred kilometres up the coast and hadn't even heard about the fire. All that remained of the house were a few blackened stumps in a pile of still smoking embers. Our friend got out of his car and after greeting him I said brightly, 'We've been doing a spot of redecorating, Come and have a look.' I had led him around to the other side of the passionfruit vine and when he saw what had become of my home, he doubled up, holding his stomach as if he'd been punched.

It was certainly a shock for him, but after his initial response we were all doubled up—this time laughing so hard at the joke. If you can't see the funny side in life, you're in trouble!

We camped for a few days on the hill, and I would have loved to stay there, but I knew it wasn't possible. I was certain we'd manifest a home this time. After looking at many dull, suburban homes and not being roused by any of them, we saw an advertisement for a home that sat on the edge of a ten acre lake.

We dropped everything to rush around and see it for ourselves.

The house was so pretty. It was magical, just like my home on the hill had been. It was a Queenslander built up on stilts that sat overlooking a saltwater tidal lake where huge fish could be seen leaping out of the water. I could not believe our luck and I wanted to live in this house at any cost. I didn't ask questions; I didn't want anything to crack the veneer of my dream. I signed on the dotted line and agreed to honour and obey and pay the rent for the next six months. Little did I know...

The first sign that something wasn't right came from Jen. When I told her about our amazing find she replied (somewhat negatively I'd thought at the time), 'Oh God, check that out properly first. It's right under the flight path. It'll be hell!'

When I rang the woman who had shown us around and asked her if this was in fact true, she replied, 'Some pretty big planes flew over when you were here.' Well, I hadn't noticed them and that was good enough for me. What I had failed to observe was that this tenant was breaking her own six month lease and, in order to do so, she had to snare some innocent tenants to take over. If she told the truth, no one would move in. She had invited us to view the house in the only short space of time in the day when there was about forty minutes without a plane flying over.

Even though we struggled in this home, we never thought of sinking that low.

On our first night we were sitting in the big comfortable armchairs underneath the house, looking out over the lake and generally feeling like we'd landed in heaven. We noticed the bright lights in the distance heading towards us, but didn't really take any notice until they got too close to ignore.

We were like a couple of frightened deer caught in the headlights, not of a car, but of a Boeing 747. The plane was flying so low it looked as if it would hit the house. We were frozen in our comfy lounges with fear! Everything began to shake; all the glass in all the windows rattled. The roar of that plane consumed everything. Nothing else existed. There was no talking on the phone, no conversation of any kind; it was impossible to focus on anything else. We were completely unprepared for this experience; it was terrifying.

We found to our horror the following day that we were one of the last houses before the planes landed a few kilometres away at Cairns airport, and the only reprieve from the planes was from the hours of 11 pm at night to 4 am in the morning when the airport was closed. Each morning we were woken up with such brutality, I could never drift off to sleep again afterwards. I was always tense with expectation of the next plane.

Yes, our lovely temptress of a home had a very dark side!

For the first few weeks I lived in anxiety, never knowing when the next plane would fly over. One morning I was so angry I rang the airport screaming abuse. LOVE? What the fuck was that? I was a crazy woman. I kept trying to find my centre and calm down but then a plane would fly over and I'd lose it again. Nothing I'd learnt so far had prepared me for this. I felt I was going to crack!

We couldn't leave without losing our deposit and paying several months' rent in advance to break the agreement, and there was no way we were going to lie to someone else so they'd move in. I kept reminding myself we must have been put here for a reason. I knew I had to find a way of experiencing this in a more uplifting way.

One day a friend came to visit with her little boy. He was only two and when a plane flew over and the house began its rattle and shake, he screamed out in excitement and jumped up and down for joy. I remember watching him and thinking, *Okay, I'll see if I can experience the planes in the same way.*

It took several flights before I was able to move beyond feeling despair as they came into land. Finally ready as the plane approached, I ran out into the garden to get the full impact and right over the top of my head flew a 747 that had an aboriginal painting all over it. It was absolutely awesome and I yelled at Gill to come and look. I was jumping up and down with excitement, so charged up by the energy of the plane. But I wasn't at all sure I could do that every time. I was certain there had to be other ways to harness all that plane energy; and it was going to take a few more guests to show me what they were.

In between flights, our home was the prettiest place to be. It was nestled amongst coconut trees and mango trees, with the lake looking so serene. But we shifted polarities each time a plane came in to land. The next experience Gill and I had opened us up to new and completely unexpected possibilities! If we had been more entrepreneurial, we might have been able to milk it!

We were inside the house, had some gentle and serene relaxation music playing and were giving this beautiful young woman an energy healing. I didn't know the flight timetables, but I had hoped that we'd chosen a long enough break between planes to finish, without being disturbed.

She was lying on the table and we were in the final minutes of the healing when I heard the plane. There was no way we could rush what we were doing and neither of us wanted to alarm her. She knew that a plane may fly over, so all we could do was let go.

For a moment I saw our client stiffen as the house began its rattle and shake but as the plane flew above us I noticed the expression on her face change. Everything was vibrating—the table, us, the green ants that were walking across our washing line, the birds in the trees—nothing was exempt. When it was finally over, she got off the table and said to us both, 'That was bloody amazing; I just had the *best orgasm* ever!'

Both our mouths fell open in complete surprise. She then told us that when she'd heard the plane coming, her first reaction had been to protect herself, but then she thought, *No, let go, allow the energy to take you*, so she did. 'The energy of that plane was so amazing I climaxed!'

That really is a new way of experiencing the planes, I thought to myself. *I should try that for myself!* Gosh, we should have been more enterprising and charged for that experience!

When my father Philip and his wife Jill came out to spend a few weeks with us, our attitudes went through another transformation. I had been unnecessarily worried about how they would cope with the planes. I should have known they'd have a thing or two to teach us!

I soaked up every second we shared with Philip and Jill. I felt so earthed having my pa around. I remember one day when we were all at the market and someone asked me curiously who Philip was. He's very tall with big wide shoulders and they'd thought he was an Islander. I felt so proud when I told them he was my father.

Philip would erect his deck chair on the edge of the lake and fish with a rod that had no bait on its hook. Once he actually caught a fish and he got up so bothered by the inconvenience of having to get up, rescue it off his hook and throw it back in. He wasn't there to fish; he didn't want to catch anything. He was happy just to relax in the sun, but he had to be holding his bait-less rod.

Once I looked out of the window and saw him sitting on the edge of the lake, fishing. His little bald patch on the top of his head was berry brown. He looked deeply relaxed and very still, and I just felt so full of love for my pa. I continued to watch him as the next huge plane flew over. The smooth surface of the lake turned to waves, the reeds doubled over with the force of the wind, and the house was doing its rattle and shake; yet nothing about Philip outwardly changed. With his rod in his hand, he continued to sit serenely looking out over the water. But I was experiencing something amazing. I was feeling the energy of the plane surge through me and amplifying everything I was feeling. I was turbo charged with love! It was flowing through me and going out into the world with the full force of a Boeing 747! And it was probably flying out to all the destinations the plane was flying to; the power of it felt that strong.

But in the end it was Jill who showed us how to milk the flight path for all it was worth. This woman knew how to extract the honey from life and she harnessed all that 747 energy in a completely different way that opened us up to an even more sensual experience of the planes. She loved the planes so much that she joked with Philip they were moving to a flight path as soon as they returned to London, and if they hadn't only just bought a new home, I think she might have. As soon as the lights of a plane appeared in the distance Jill would put down her drink, recline her chair, close her eyes and, like our previous orgasmic guest, just let go. As the plane flew over the look on Jill's face turned to one of absolute ecstasy, as if she was in the throes of holy rapture, though knowing Jill, who is very down to earth, it was probably much more visceral and organic. She never did say exactly what happened, but we had a pretty good idea! If she had done all that preparation and the plane that flew over was only small, she'd look so disappointed and with a big sigh say, 'Oh, it was only a tiddler!'

As for me I still hadn't quite reached the same womanly ease that Jill had in dealing with the planes. She was certainly getting something out of these planes that eluded me. I was definitely curious, but it took me a lot longer to stop fighting them and surrender to their powerful force. As much as I was learning and finding new ways of coping or even reaping the harvest of all that energy they channelled, they were still challenging for me. It didn't help that I was woken at 4 am every morning and was often sleep deprived. I was often more irritable than normal, but one morning I made sure I was ready. I woke up really early and lay on my back in bed waiting in anticipation for that first plane.

I could hear it in the distance. Then as it approached I began to feel a tickling sensation in the tips of my toes. I had my eyes closed, my arms lay by my side, and my palms were open, facing the ceiling. I had no resistance left in me. As the plane got closer and the intensity of its energy turned into a roar, the whole house began its rattle and shake, and then it started. The almighty power of that plane charged from my feet and up into my legs. Nothing else existed but the plane, and as the sound of it got louder and louder and its energy began to build up inside me, reaching such intensity, I felt turbo charged with *joy*. I was emanating, resonating and pulsating joy, and as it skimmed our roof, the full force of that jumbo surged through my body and up my spine. Red lights erupted from my base chakra, bursting into orange, Catherine-wheeling into yellow as the energy moved up my spine and reached my solar plexus, up, up, up through green as my heart flowered like a rose in full bloom, up, up, up, through blue, then indigo as one by one my chakras opened, until the force reached my crown chakra. By then the energy was so rampant it blew off the top of my skull—that's how it felt. Magenta lights streamed from my crown.

I am bliss. I am love.

I was connected and one with everything. There was no feeling of separation. I could see myself lying on the bed yet I was the plane landing at the airport and I was all of the ants rebalancing themselves on the clothes line after the intensity of the rush. I was Rainbow Man, I was Mrs Blessings and I was the wounded man that had thrown the bait in the back of the truck and killed my Sprouty.

And I was Sprouty and full of love. I was the leaves on the trees and I was my shaking, still-trembling house.

The past had all gone, blown away. It was an illusion to think I had ever had anything to forgive. I finally got what Rainbow Man had told me: 'All you need to do is let go.'

I'd never felt so bloody good.

It took me a while to regain the use of my body. As I lay on the bed wriggling my toes and stretching my legs as my body tingled with energy, I heard an old friend calling me, and it was Crow. I had barely seen a crow since I'd been back in the tropics and I knew it was no coincidence he'd appeared to me then. My messenger bird had something to say.

When I finally made it to the window, I saw him sitting in the tree outside. His black feathers were flounced up as he shook himself sensuously, his body rippling from the tip of his tail feathers to his crown. I knew that, like me, he had surfed that wild plane energy, and I knew instantly what he'd come to tell me.

I became aware that every dark and shadowy path I had walked down, feeling utterly alone, and all those times I'd turned around and faced a fear when all I'd wanted to do was run, had led me here, to this point in time—when all I could feel was *joy*. The life we choose is up to us, but every time we step into our own darkness, we awaken a quality within that can only be ignited in the dark. The ecstasy of love, endless depths of compassion, the gift of healing and a life lived in utmost fulfilment are only available to those willing to trust in the brightness of their own sacred light as they journey into the darkness of their shadows.

I knew our journey under the flight path was almost over; our dark-hearted home had imparted her gifts.

Now you may have wondered where Gill was in the midst of all this Kundalini energy. He was lying soundly asleep beside me, sleeping through the early morning plane. You see, Gill's not a man of highs and lows; he calmly surrenders to the flow. He's not stubborn like me and doesn't feel the need to cling for dear life to every door jamb, as I so often do in my attempts to ward off change. He is much more likely to throw open the door and walk willingly through it. The lessons of life don't hit Gill in the same way they do me, they don't need to!

And even with everything I'd learnt when we got close to leaving that house I was trying to control things again. 'I'm not choosing to camp when we move out of here, Gill, I'm choosing to move straight into a new home.' I had chosen my words carefully; I knew the art of manifesting did not come from 'want'.

But I sometimes think I should begin to make statements that utter the exact opposite to what I'm choosing to manifest. It didn't matter how many times I affirmed that the perfect home was manifesting easily and effortlessly, that didn't happen. How long would it take me to realise, to finally get it? The answer was NEVER, or so it often seemed. I was on a spiritual quest and the mundane fripperies of life can never be my focus.

Still once again, emanating crown chakras, magenta lights or not, I continued to fight the flow. I wanted a home. The irony was not lost on me that all the time I'd lived in an unhappy relationship, I'd had a magical home and now I was with a man I adored, home was the one thing I struggled to find, my little haven where I could finally throw out the anchor! I knew that Gill would have loved that too, but it didn't matter to him and in truth, given the choice, it's Gill any day and every day, home or no home.

Even though we'd begun to look for a new home several months before our moving date, and despite many friends finding great spots for them to live, surprise, surprise—nothing manifested for us.

On our last night under the flight path, we were sitting in the armchairs having a beer, and I was wondering what was to become of us once again whilst Gill reassured me everything would be fine. I couldn't understand why, if the universe wanted us to go somewhere, do something, why didn't it damn well tell us? It could at least make it clear. All I knew was that we were moving out in the morning, and we would be living in the truck. But beyond that we hadn't got a clue. Why couldn't we at least get some cosmic itinerary? It would make our lives a whole lot easier.

I was sitting in the armchair mulling over the unknown once again when I felt something crawling up my leg. It had sturdy little feet and each time it moved a foot, I felt the tug on my pants and the grip of its foot—or was it feet?—as it climbed further and further up my leg.

Now I am not a person that gets freaked out by insects. If anything I can be rather intolerant of people who scream when they see a spider. I give the usual offerings, often spoken with a little disdain, 'They are more frightened of you than you are of them,' and in all the years I'd lived in the tropics I had experienced this to be true.

Despite sharing my home on the hill with numerous spiders and even allowing a bird eating spider, a mammoth Golden Orb Weaver, to spin a giant web in the corner of my sunroom that we contentedly shared like a couple of old biddies for years, I had never been crawled on.

I was afraid to look … Then when I did look down at my legs, I started to hyperventilate. Crawling up my leg was the biggest, hairiest spider I'd ever seen. I couldn't breathe. I couldn't speak. I was waving my arms around trying to attract Gill's attention. When he saw me as white as a ghost, having a panic attack, he rushed over to see what was wrong. I only began to breathe after he'd carefully gathered up the spider and taken it safely away. That will teach you to ask for clear guidance, Kye!

Little did I know that I was being spun into another web and I'd just been given a clue about our next destination. Be careful what you ask for! We were about to meet up with someone they called The Spider, and she was no daddy-long-legs either.

Twenty-Three

The Spider

I had a close friend that I hadn't seen for a very long time. He'd earned himself the colourful name of Mardi Gras, not only because he was such a queen, but because of his huge collection of holographic leggings that he wore for every occasion, even when he was working out in the garden.

He was often away travelling, so sometimes long periods of time would pass before I saw him again. Then he would turn up, out of the blue, in a shower of fairy dust and excitement, keen to share with me his latest spiritual awakening so we could try it out together. When I was with Mardi, I felt life as keenly as I had when I was a child. We explored so many new realms together. He always had something new to show me, whether it was a healing technique or some channelled writing, or his latest communication with the dolphins, whom he resonated with completely. He often travelled to far-flung places on the globe to especially experience close-up encounters swimming with his magical friends.

He'd once shown me a book he was writing, almost finished, that he kept locked away in a trunk under his bed. It contained all the conversations he'd had with not only the dolphins but the whales too. It was beautifully hand written and each page was decorated with pictures of these ocean messengers. It was a work of art and I often nagged him to get it finished, but I don't think he ever did.

For many years Mardi had been a dancer and his body was still lithe and athletic. He had a mop of bleached blonde hair from spending hours and hours in the sea. His eyes were huge and hazel and his skin the colour of honey. It wasn't just men that lusted after him, it was women too; though he'd told me once with a rather disdainful look on his face, 'No insult to you darling, but I never swim in that pond.'

We hadn't connected for several years. He'd been away in Hawaii then I'd gone to India. Then when the house had burnt down, neither of us knew where the other was living. But I remembered so clearly our last conversation because I had often wondered about its outcome. He had been unusually stressed and told me he had met a man he really liked and connected with, but he couldn't get over his repulsion for fat— and this man had a flabby belly. He'd shuddered as he told me. What should he do? Should he face it and tell the man to get fit? He was feeling quite lost about it. I couldn't think of anything to say that would help. I'd simply asked him if this was the only thing standing between him and love, and he replied it was.

'I really like him,' he'd said, 'but maybe I'm just too superficial.'

Gill and I had been floating around in the truck for several weeks and still no home had manifested. We were both feeling at a loose end and didn't have any clear idea what to do. When we pulled into a petrol station several hundred kilometres up the coast I got a really pleasant surprise. It was a dreary wet day and the first thing I noticed was some rainbow coloured holographic leggings. I was over the moon to see they belonged to Mardi. He was as effervescent as ever and after giving me the biggest hug, said cheekily when he saw Gill, 'Oh darling, we are going to have to duel at dawn for him.'

Mardi didn't say much about his new life. All he told us was he was very much in love and he lived nearby with his partner in a beautiful home in the rainforest.

'Come for a visit,' he said. 'We've been alone for much too long; it will be good to have some guests.'

I wondered all the way back to his place if he'd overcome his repulsion and if Mr Flabby Belly was the man we were about to meet. We finally turned off the road, following his Subaru as he drove across a shallow creek and down a long, dirt track. When we came to a stop, it was at a small wooden house with wide verandas wrapped all the way around. It sat on the edge of a dam that was full of reeds and resonant with the sounds of frogs croaking. Beside the house was a big garden full of flowering Birds of Paradise, with their stunning, rather alien looking red and yellow waxy blooms. It was very picturesque.

When we entered the house, there was a woman sitting on the settee, filling it up completely. I said hello as we came in, thinking she was visiting like us. I looked around expectantly, eager to meet Mardi's new man. Then he bent down and kissed her on the forehead, telling her he'd just bumped into an old friend. He turned to us. 'Meet my new love; this is Bella Rosa.'

For a moment I couldn't breathe. Throughout all the years I'd known Mardi, I had never seen him show any interest in women. Remember, he didn't swim in that pond. I'd often been asked about him by curious female friends, and as gorgeous as some of them were, I'd always told them to forget it because Mardi was one hundred per cent gay. But it wasn't only that aspect of Mardi's new relationship that intrigued me. Bisexual or not, in our very last conversation he'd been struggling with a slight case of tummy fat. But now he was with the biggest woman I'd ever seen.

I have to say, though, Bella Rosa was impressive. She was wearing a black shawl around her shoulders, covered with bright colourful embroidery that gave away her gypsy heritage. She had black hair silvered with grey that fell to her shoulders, and I noticed how her dark eyes had looked amused when she saw my initial reaction. She must have been used to that.

I got the feeling there was very little that passed Bella Rosa by, and I soon discovered I was right about that. Locally, she was known as The Strega—the Italian name for witch. Many people, despite her remote location, made the difficult journey to come and see Bella Rosa. She could tell if their partners were being unfaithful and who were carrying dark entities. She created spells to help infertile couples conceive and others to attract love. Many of her clients were people who had been abducted by extra-terrestrials and others needed protection spells because they were being abused.

If you asked her a question and she didn't know it, she would close her eyes, journey into the astral, retrieve the answer and come back and tell you. After all my crazy journeys and all my over-the-edge learnings, next to Bella I felt like a kindergarten kid with scuffed knees. She was so earthed; she was the earth and she emanated a power that was pure goddess, in all her phases. She spoke of Mother Earth and how it was up to women to awaken and embrace the magic and mystery of who they were.

'The divine feminine has been persecuted for far too long. Women have denied their true essence. They have sanitised their own natural cycles and given away their sacred moon power.' When she spoke, I could feel the soft rustling of the leaves on the trees like a breeze upon my face. Then she banged on the table with her fist and brought me back from my reverie. When I looked at her, she had shape-shifted into an Indian warrior with a feather headdress, and her face was covered in war paint. Her voice was like a crack of lightning crashing down from the sky. 'It is time to claim it back!'

Then suddenly her voice became gentle again, almost soothing, and when I looked, the Indian chief had gone and she was Bella Rosa again. 'The earth has been stained with the blood of wars; now it is up to women. Our mother needs their sacred moon blood to flow onto her earth and heal the tears of death.'

The room was reverberating with the truth of her words and listening to her was both hypnotic and sensual. She was emanating majesty as she spoke and looked awesomely beautiful. I felt there was a lot I could learn from her, but I had no idea how much she would help me shed light on much of what had happened in my life.

I hadn't seen Mardi since before the house had burnt down and I wasn't even sure he knew it had. 'I remember seeing it on the TV,' he said, 'but I thought you must have already moved out. It sounded as if the house was empty.'

'It wasn't though,' I replied. 'We were woken by rocks hitting our roof. It's a long story and most people think I'm mad, but I'm convinced it was deliberately burnt down.' I then told him who I thought had done it.

'Oh my goodness,' piped up Bella Rosa, 'now I know who you are. All I can say is you are right, they were responsible.' There was a part of me that wanted to sink into relief, but I needed to know how she knew. I'd had ghosts and dreams reassure me, now I needed something solid, not a witch out riding her broomstick in the astral, uncovering lies. I needed something credible. (As I write this, I realise how ridiculous it sounds given the unusual occurrences in my life to this stage!)

'I'm not at liberty to tell you who. All I can say is I have counselled someone who deeply regretted their involvement in the decision to burn it down,' she replied. 'It's your right to know that, but that's all I can say.'

'And they came to a witch?' I asked, incredulous that someone from a religious background would choose Bella as his or her counsellor.

'They came to me when I was working in my day job as a counsellor and not a witch. But remember that many organisations that present themselves as good have black magicians at their helm. Battles for power are being fought all the time in the astral.'

I could feel those words resonating with me and I knew Bella Rosa could help me understand some of the things that happened in Goa and I began to explain to her what had occurred. I had not been able to talk with anyone about what I'd experienced there, not even the people I'd shared that time with. It was a relief to now be able to do so.

'What I can tell you,' said Bella Rosa, 'is that Goa is the place where the art of siphoning energy on a mass scale was perfected. What you felt was going on, was.'

'But what do they do with all that energy?'

'They sell it,' she replied. 'They pass it on to anyone who's got the money to pay and who wants to gain power. But there is also a huge market for selling the techniques of how to extract that energy.'

'And how do they even begin to do that?' I asked, feeling like even my capacity for the paranormal was being stretched.

'Goa is the playground for black magicians everywhere. That's where they learnt not only to siphon it from unsuspecting people, but also to store it and sell it. A stock market exists that sells shares in this energy, and for a black magician who is successful at their art, it's a very lucrative market.'

I was astounded. Why had it never occurred to me that money would be involved too? I had been incredibly naïve. Gill asked her about an event we'd been to in Melbourne. It was a promotion for a huge clothing label and there had been about five stages with bands playing throughout the day. We had gone as marketeers, expecting to have a fun day. Instead the whole event had deteriorated into madness and we had ended up defending our stall from people coming in. The bands were screaming and yelling and had built the young crowd into such a frenzy. If we could have gotten out easily, we would have left immediately. At one point Gill went for a walk to see what was happening, but he didn't get far.

'The crowds were going crazy,' he said. 'When they saw me, I thought they were going to tear me apart. They all turned their attention on me. It was so freaky. I had to run to get away.'

When Gill had returned he'd been really worried and had picked up a big stick and stood out the front of our stall as if he was defending it. I actually felt afraid. I didn't go to the toilet all day; I knew it wasn't safe. It felt as if we were stuck in the middle of a crowd of zombies and at any minute they would turn on us and tear us apart. By the end of the day, there were mobs of youths upturning tables, screaming and fighting, and I'd recognised the same dark energy I'd experienced in Goa.

'Oh yes, that company,' said Bella Rosa. 'I don't even need to look them up; I've done it already. You're about the sixth person to ask me about them and, yes, they are siphoning energy. They have a very powerful black magician at their helm and that's how they make their money. They don't need to sell clothes.'

My brain was doing cartwheels. I knew I hadn't been mad and imagined my experiences in Goa. I had previously told Bella Rosa about how I'd felt terror when I'd become the focus of the dark forces' attention.

'You stood out from the party crowd in Goa, Kye,' she went on, 'because you were not prepared to grovel in the muck for a good time. And that's what happened to Gill when he went to have a look. You were both in a crowd of zombies.'

'But not every dance party was dark,' I replied. 'I knew many really wonderful people that were part of the dance scene.'

'Battles are fought in Goa,' she said, 'and there are many white magicians who go there too. While the dark forces harvest energy for power and self-gain, the forces of light channel it and send it out into the world to uplift and heal, to end wars and sickness and help people wake up. When people become aware of how their energy can be manipulated, they can at least make the choice to be a willing participant or not.

'Many white magicians travel to Goa every year, just to hold the energy of light and maintain balance. Without them there would be a lot more havoc wreaked and the dark forces would gain control.'

I realised in listening to Bella Rosa that I had only just scratched the surface of what had actually been going on in Goa and I was intrigued to know more, but Bella Rosa was winding down for the night. I had so many unasked questions but if I wanted to know more I was going to need to be patient.

Whatever choices Mardi had made, these two seemed to share a very special love, though it was not without its challenges. Simply because of Bella Rosa's size, she had very limited mobility and Mardi was not only her lover, he was her carer too. In the evening after Mardi had helped Bella Rosa to bed—she always went early; she'd told us that that's when she did her most work on the astral—Mardi, finally free to relax and unwind, went running for the bottle of port and three glasses and insisted we get drunk with him. He was obviously feeling quite celebratory and not only had his usual psychedelic holographic leggings on, but shocking pink stilettos too. 'We've got so much to catch up on,' he said.

For many years he'd been studying extra-terrestrials and since being with Bella Rosa, he'd had a chance to learn a whole lot more. She worked regularly with people who had been abducted and had had her own communications with several benevolent beings.

'Bella Rosa used to work as a psychic for the military,' he told us. 'She's had a lot of experiences communicating with extra-terrestrials. She even has one that comes and visits. It was captured by the military and when she heard its mother crying out for its baby, she helped it escape. It's been coming to see her for over twenty years. They're not all bad you know!'

I could tell we were in for a big night. Both Gill and I were constantly being blasted with information that stretched our perceptions of the world we lived in. I'd experience the Filipino healers; I'd spoken with angels; I'd communicated with ghosts; I'd battled dark forces and now it was ETs. How tiny our world is when we believe only in what we can see.

'I'm so curious to find out all about this, but I've gotta ask you, Mardi, what happened? I thought you were gay.' I didn't ask about his fat issues.

'Oooh I got spun into her wicked web,' he replied with a chortle. 'I was a willing victim. She is such a goddess and she's bisexual. We have so much fun.' Being the polite Kentish lass I was, I didn't ask Mardi to elaborate.

'But you know, everyone calls her The Spider,' he said. I nearly fell off my chair when he told us that! Thank you, universe, I muttered, for sending me that totally freaky sign! Now I understood why that spider had crawled on me! I told Mardi and he had laughed so much as I acted out the horror of my hairy visitor.

There was always someone calling in to seek Bella Rosa's advice. One was a middle-aged woman who looked really worn out and thought her husband was having an affair.

'There's not just one lover,' Bella Rosa had told her, 'there's a couple.' The poor woman had broken down in tears. She had a disabled child and was feeling very unsupported by her husband. The house was only small and it had been unavoidable to hear her crying. Gill and I had walked out into the garden and given them some space. Later that day after her distressed client had left, Bella Rosa excused herself telling us she had someone to bind up, which immediately got me curious.

'What do you mean by "binding up" Bella Rosa?' I asked.

'All I do,' she explained, 'is create a spell that stops that husband having his affairs, which frees him up to be more supportive of his wife and help more with their child. The poor woman needs some help; she's on the edge of a breakdown,'

I was puzzled by her answer. 'But isn't that interfering with Divine Will?' I could certainly see the women needed help, but if you let things run their natural course, don't they work out anyway? I thought that if the lady did have a breakdown, maybe then she'd get the help she needed. Her husband might wake up and realise what a selfish man he'd been, who knows? Something didn't feel right ...

Bella Rosa brushed me aside as if what I'd said was inconsequential ... as if I didn't know anything anyway. She completely ignored my question and then rapped her cane on the floor and said, 'There is no such thing as a powerful, skinny woman, Kye.'

POW.

I had been totally unprepared for an attack and what she said made absolutely no sense to me. Was I to eat really unhealthy food just to get fat and powerful? I had seen her diet and if I'd eaten what she did, I would be really fat too. I had certainly been open to seeing a new perspective, but I wasn't willing to be put down because I didn't agree. As interesting as this amazing woman was, after that comment I really felt like getting some fresh air and putting a bit of space between me and Bella Rosa. Spending time with her was like trying to relax on the edge of a volcano. She inhabited a totally different reality, and while I was soaking up *most* things she told me, in that moment I felt like doing something really normal for a change, like going to Kmart. I was sick of hearing about black magicians and alien abductions and people being possessed by demons. I just wanted to push my trolley up the aisles and pretend for a short while that I was a suburban housewife living the dream—even if it was a skinny one!

As we got ready to leave they both tried to convince us to stay longer. Bella Rosa was muttering something about how we had something to learn before we left and it wasn't time for us to go. We made vague promises to come back again, but as we drove out I had no immediate plans for that. I'd really appreciated the insight Bella Rosa had given me into some of my experiences and it had been a blessing reconnecting with me old mate Mardi Gras, but I wasn't prepared to be put down. I was always willing to learn, but if something didn't resonate for me as truth, even if the person telling me was a big and powerful witch who reeked of knowledge, I would not accept it.

Kmart was over two hundred kilometres away. Yes, I was serious. That's where I wanted to go. As we took the highway heading south, the wind blowing in our hair, feeling the illusion of freedom once again, I had forgotten how sticky a spider's web could be—and I had no idea we'd already been snared.

Twenty-Four
Beauty and the Beast

I can't say it came as a surprise when fifty kilometres down the road we received a phone call from Mardi. My messenger spider had been lurking in the back of my mind and even though I'd tried to ignore it, it hadn't gone away.

'Hey guys, we just found your guitar lying in the driveway. It must have fallen out of the back of your truck.'

It was only a three-chord wonder, but I couldn't do without my guitar, so with a slightly peed-off feeling, we turned the truck around and drove back the way we'd come. I was still feeling crushed by Bella Rosa's put-down and wasn't happy about having to return.

When we finally arrived, we pulled up beside the house and I ran in to get my guitar while Gill reversed the truck. As we took off down their driveway, wilful me was thinking that naughty spider had been wrong all along and we'd escaped. It was then we met a car on the drive coming towards us. There wasn't enough room for us both and the other car was obviously not going to leave the hard surface of the road, so we did. As soon as we pulled off the drive, we realised our mistake. The ground was still boggy from the recent heavy rains and the back of the truck sank into deep mud up to its axle.

We spent the next three hours trying to dig ourselves out. Mardi even came with his tractor and tried to drag our truck out but couldn't get enough traction. Despite everyone's best efforts, our truck did not want to budge and we were stuck.

Bella Rosa was still seeing a client when we went up to the house, so we sat in the garden with Mardi. 'No wonder you got driven off the road,' he said with a laugh. 'That's the woman Bella Rosa wanted you to meet. The one that carries all those demons around.'

There was never a dull moment in this house, and even though I felt so frustrated at being back, I couldn't help feeling intrigued by it all. Kmart could wait!

'So where do these demons come from?' I asked Mardi.

'People create them. Our thoughts manifest physically in this world. When someone lives in fear or anger, that energy has a life force; but it's the same with the light too,' he said.

'In what way?'

'Well, think of fairies and angels. They are only aspects of the Divine Force that separate and take on an identity so that they can express to us in a way we can understand.'

'So are you saying as a separate form, they don't actually exist?' I queried.

'They exist in the same way me and you exist,' he said with a laugh.

Talk about brainteasers; but I could understand what he was saying. Although I'd never been able to put it into words, I'd often had the feeling that nothing was as real as it seemed. If we are all sparks of the Divine Force, then any identity has to be an illusion.

Then Bella Rosa joined us, we were on our second glass of port and I was finally beginning to let go. Whatever I was here for, bring it on!

'I don't think I'll be seeing her again,' she said with exasperation. 'She's just wasting my time. I've said that's it. No more. If she calls them back in, she's on her own. It's up to her now. She's got to make the changes in her own life to keep them out. That's the third and last time I remove them for her.'

Bella looked at me and Gill. 'I keep getting told I have something to teach you. I don't know what it is at this present time, but if you're happy to stay, and you're welcome to, we can work it out.' She was very matter-of-fact, just stating things as they were. Whether we stayed or left, it was up to us.

I didn't actually feel I had much of a choice. Our truck was stuck up to its axle in mud. If there was something I needed to learn, yes, I was open, *but why is it that every time I need to learn something all my choices are taken away?*

But wouldn't you leave, Kye, if you could; you know how stubborn you are? I couldn't help recalling a time my mother had told me how one of my nieces reminded her so much of me.

'She's so... she's so...' Mum was stuck for words, struggling to find the right ones, and I waited on the end of the telephone, certain I was about to be showered with compliments. When the words finally came, they were not at all what I'd expected. 'She's so stubborn and pigheaded; she's just like you. You never listened. Whatever I tried to do, you did the opposite. If I put your shoes on you, you kicked them off. You always had to do your own thing.' When I'd gotten over the initial surprise, I burst out laughing. I hadn't changed; I was still trying to go the opposite way to my flow, almost every time! But, if I always tried to go against the flow and every time I did, my life fell in a heap, well, where's the free will in that? I couldn't help asking Bella Rosa. If I had to be here, I may as well get some answers! She answered with a question.

'So what are you here on this planet for, Kye?'

'I don't know exactly what it is,' I replied. 'But ever since I was a child I've always known there was something in this world I had to build; it feels like my driving force.'

'Do you think you will find it going against the flow? And how can you build anything without tools?' she replied, looking at me directly with an amused look on her face.

'Okay, I get it; I surrender,' I said, playfully.

'I understand,' she said. 'Mardi told me we share the same birthday and there is nothing worse for a Libran than feeling trapped.' As Bella said this, her voice was full of pain. I realised then that in her own way she was letting me see her vulnerability, which was her big cumbersome body and this was her way of making amends for what she'd said. She could barely walk, let alone dance and she spent most of her days sitting in a chair. When she needed something, Mardi was there. She had a lot more reasons to feel trapped than I did.

I can't say that my relationship with Bella Rosa was easy. I have always struggled with teachers. I don't accept everything I'm told, I like to ask questions if I don't understand and I guess that even though Bella Rosa had shown me her pain, there was still a line in the sand I felt I couldn't cross. I would learn what I needed to but I could not absorb everything I was taught as truth unless it chimed in my heart. Her relationship with Gill was one of kindred souls; they connected with an ease I didn't share and when I asked Gill why he felt I had problems with Bella Rosa, he suggested it was because she felt threatened by me. I couldn't understand this; she often waved away something I was trying to say as if it was inconsequential, as if nothing of value could come from my mouth and often treated me as if I was stupid. Yes, I found it frustrating. I couldn't wait to leave but I knew that wouldn't happen until I'd got what I'd come for so I may as well settle down, put aside what I thought I knew, and learn!

One morning, Bella Rose taught us a meditation to cleanse and purify our energy and we visualised bathing under different coloured lights. She asked us to visualise the colour yellow. When we began to do so, she said to Gill, 'No, not like that Gill—more like a waterfall ... Ah, yes, that's better.' Gill and I both caught our breath. We realised that Bella not only saw our energetic bodies but our thoughts as well. She later told us that when she was a child, the doctors had thought she was blind. All she could see was energy; she couldn't make out any individual forms. She would see the lights of someone standing in front of her, but there was nothing separating them from the table or anything else in the room; everything merged together as one. It had been her grandmother who had eventually realised that Bella was seeing energetically, not physically, and had helped her learn how to separate and define what she saw.

The story I loved the most was when Bella Rosa was a little child, she'd asked her grandmother what she would be when she grew up, and her grandmother had told her she'd be a sweeper. 'You will sweep away all the rocks and stones on the path and make it easier for those that come behind. You will really have to value yourself and know that what you do is important. Some will appreciate what you do, but there will be many who complain at the little pebble you missed, that they tripped on!"

I often felt Bella Rosa's loneliness and I understood that even with Mardi, as conscious as he was, none of us came anywhere close to her experience of life. Mardi, after two years of being with Bella Rosa, was still often blown away by the experiences that occurred in his everyday life, just because he was with her.

Each night, after Bella Rosa had retired early for her night journeys into the astral, Mardi enthralled us with tales of alien abductions, guardians from other realms and the black magician they'd found stalking them. Our hair would stand up on our heads!

Bella Rosa was barely fifty years old, yet she was recognised by many other elders as one of them. She had only just returned from a gathering of indigenous elders from all around the world, which was held every year in a different location, and that year it had been in Australia.

She'd found herself sitting in a circle of women elders, who, just like her were all big women, round like the earth; but they had a lot more than that in common. They all had gun shot wounds or had been stabbed, they had all experienced sexual abuse or been raped. They had all lost children and all in their own ways had a very tough life. 'How can we help others if we don't know their pain?' she said.

One day Bella Rosa commented on the shape of my eyes. 'They are so unusual. I can see something tribal in you.'

I laughed. 'My father is an Irish, African, Jew.'

'Three races of persecuted people,' she replied. 'As you heal the pain in your own life, you heal the wrong done to your ancestors. Their pain walks with you.'

In that moment something very liberating happened. All my life, since I was a child, I'd had cramps in my legs. For many years, after seeing numerous specialists, I was told it was growing pains and they would eventually go. But they never did. My legs felt as if they'd been bound tight with ropes, round and round and round, as if all my circulation had gone. As I stood in front of Bella Rosa I felt those ropes around my legs loosen and slip down to my ankles, and then fall away. The tight feeling in my legs had miraculously gone.

When I explained to her what had happened, she replied, 'The ropes were all the untruths you were told as a child. Everyone in your life wanted to do the best, but they didn't realise the impact of their actions.'

I could feel all this emotion welling up inside me, and I began to cry as I asked her how lies can impact like that.

'Nothing can be suppressed. When we try to hide something, it bursts out another way. Every thought, every deed, has a life force. When the truth about your heritage was denied you, it made its presence known in the form of pain. It was the only way it could express to you that something was wrong. It's your African heritage that keeps your feet firmly anchored on the earth.'

I had to laugh at that. I'd grown up cursing my big feet. I remembered a girl at school who had such small feet and always wore the latest shoe fashion. I nagged my mother to buy me the same shoes I'd seen her wear. When I put them on my big feet they looked ugly, whereas on hers they had looked so cool. It didn't help that I had such skinny legs. It had taken me a long time to accept my feet and love the way they kept me anchored on the earth.

'The pain you felt from those secrets,' Bella Rosa continued, 'manifested in your legs and it prevented you from moving forward in life, but now you are free.'

Gill and I were both learning so much from Bella Rosa. We had just had a very intense week learning how to create mirrored shields and we both felt like taking a short break. But Bella Rose felt we would be too sensitive after all the energy work we'd just done and advised us to put it off for a week or two. However, we were both really keen to go.

There were several reasons for this; the main one was our dogs. They'd been kept on a very tight rein because Mardi had a cat that was terrified of them. We all needed to relax, and they'd been so good; they deserved a good run around. We were also finding the intensity of the rainforest claustrophobic. We were both craving blue sky and wanted to spend a few days on our own.

When Gill got a phone call from a man that regularly let him cut down the coconuts from his trees, telling him his neighbours wanted their coconuts removed as well, it seemed like perfect timing. We could take a break and return with a full load of green coconuts to drink that would last us a couple of weeks.

We both felt incredibly excited as we drove out. I couldn't wait to swim in the sea and camp on the beach and have a fire. It felt like we were all heading off on our holidays. I also had a friend who'd just returned from overseas I wanted to see. Gill had hand carved a wooden bowl for her as she'd let us stay in her home for a couple of weeks when we'd moved out of the forever-to-be-known Orgasmic Kundalini House.

Our first call was the coconut tree, which was all very straightforward. It was a small tree and the coconuts were easy for Gill to collect. When he finished, the owner of the tree directed Gill to a tree in his neighbour's driveway and told Gill that there was no one there at the moment, but they'd asked him to get Gill to remove the nuts. It was fast approaching the wet season with its threat of cyclones and coconut trees could be very dangerous if they were full of nuts. In the strong winds they were likely to be blown from the trees and could easily hit someone on the head.

Gill climbed up the tree and was lowering the first bunch of green coconuts down on a rope when the man that lived there returned. When he saw Gill up his tree, he went berserk. He was a dark-skinned man, perhaps an Islander, and he screamed at Gill. 'You f......g racist, come down you coward.' He went on and on. He was so mad he was spraying spittle. I ran and found the neighbour who'd told Gill it was okay to climb the tree, and he came back and settled everything down. We couldn't leave fast enough. We got in the truck and drove off. He could get his own bloody nuts down for all we cared.

We were totally stunned by what had happened and were shaking so much we decided to call around and see our friend. I couldn't wait to see Trudy. She'd been working overseas as a nurse for two months in a remote part of Africa, and I was so keen to hear about her adventures. When she answered her door, we got the biggest shock. We had no idea that we were jumping head first into another fire.

Trudy was absolutely livid; she was frothing at the mouth. What was it with froth and spittle that day? She accused us of doing all sorts of damage to her place while she'd been away, and when we calmly asked her to tell us what we'd done, she couldn't name a thing.

We had no idea what she was angry about. Nothing made any sense. We had left her place looking beautiful, and Gill had even spent days outside, cleaning up her garden and mowing all her lawns so that it would look lovely for her return.

I felt shaken to my core as we walked back to the truck.

We drove down the coast and pulled up to spend a couple of nights on an isolated tropical beach, lined with tall coconut trees. It was paradise; the ocean was as flat and clear as glass. Brightly coloured parrots were squawking in some nearby trees, but nothing touched me. We had been so looking forward to this experience but I was totally unable to enjoy it. I shook and trembled the whole two days. I felt deeply shocked by the attacks, most of all from Trudy. On the third day we decided to begin the journey back to the rainforest to Bella Rosa and Mardi's. Even with Bella Rosa's dismissive attitude towards me, their home was looking like a safe haven! Halfway back we stopped for a night at a beautiful creek that we often went to when we needed to recharge. This creek was wide with lots of smooth, round boulders sitting in the water, with pockets of deep water where we could swim. I had been completely unable to let go of what had happened. I sat on a boulder in the river, in the midst of the rainforest with all its moist, warm beauty, and I was huddled up with grief. I also felt angry at how Trudy had abused us.

My thoughts were going round and round my head. I was consumed with trying to work it out and exhausted by the process. We had left her place looking beautiful, and I had expected her to be delighted. I felt like I was suffering from the trauma of a bomb blast.

For a long time I had my head resting on my knees as my thoughts went *why, why, why?* When I finally looked up, I got another surprise ... but this time a pleasant one. On the adjacent boulder beside me sat a leprechaun, and when he saw that I'd finally noticed him he gave me a cheeky wink.

This little fellow emanated life and vitality. He was like a fresh, new sprout and everything about him was bright, luminous green—his trilby hat, his suit, even his face. When he began to speak, his words were charged by the river and I heard them booming above its roar.

'You are the rock and not the river. Why do you still hold on to what has passed and is now downstream? Let go,' he said. I could hear his words repeating like an echo ... *You are the rock, not the river, let go, let go, let go* until they faded away and I noticed he had gone. I shook my head. Had I imagined that? Whatever that little being was, he had reminded me of a powerful truth and I was finally able to shake myself free of what had occurred. It had been three days since it had happened and I had let all the beauty in life pass me by because I couldn't let go. Well not anymore!

It was actually a relief to arrive back into the safe folds of Bella Rosa's and Mardi's world, however insane it sometimes appeared to be. When we told them both what had happened, Bella Rosa just shook her head with an amused look on her face that said, 'I told you so!'

'You know what happened,' she rapped, back into business as the powerful witch. 'They saw themselves reflected in your mirrors and they didn't like what they saw.'

'But why would a friend react like this and accuse us of things we didn't do and not even notice all the things we had done?'

'And what was it you did?' she asked, with a bemused look on her face.

'I cleaned her house and Gill tidied her garden.'

'You did more than that,' she retorted. Bella Rosa knew the person I was talking about and had not been at all surprised by the attack. 'Nothing moved in that house, nothing ever changed. The energy was stagnant and you breathed fresh air and life into it. You disturbed her demons; that's what you did.'

It just hadn't occurred to me that Trudy would be anything less than pleased, but Bella Rosa was right. Nothing ever did change in that house and it had felt stifling being there. In order for us to stay, I'd had to clean it up a little.

Bella Rose explained some more. 'When you begin to do this work, your sensitivity is so amplified. That's why I didn't want you to leave when you did. In a few weeks it will settle down and you won't attract this to yourselves again.

'When people stir you up, they can energetically feed off you. You are vulnerable. When you lose your centre and allow someone to get inside you, your energy is drained.'

I had seen this so many times in Goa, and not only experienced it but defended myself from it too. But I had been wide open with Trudy because I had thought I was safe with her. Even that had been a little naïve for someone as sensitive to energy as me. I knew she didn't look at her own stuff and she left many things to fester away in her past. In many ways we had a lot in common, but I'd always known I couldn't share with her my spiritual path. She just didn't get it and could even be a little condescending.

All the signs had been there; I just hadn't chosen to read them. It was a big lesson in not leaving myself so wide open.

Most days Mardi worked out in the garden. He was such a fairy himself; it was no surprise to hear him speak of the nature spirits and fairy folk that guided him in caring for the plants. His garden looked so healthy and abundant, and he was always coming inside with a big basket of home-grown vegetables he'd just picked. Everything was grown from old heritage seeds. He had three fridges full of packets of seeds, extracted from what he'd already grown. Many of the seeds were extremely rare vegetables and fruit that were on the edge of extinction. Until spending time with Mardi, I had never even thought about what was happening with our seeds. Mardi was very passionate about educating people.

'We are giving up our power,' he said fiercely. 'People don't realise they are becoming dependent. All these new hybrid varieties don't produce fertile seeds so you have to keep purchasing new ones from the seed companies each year. That's just where they want you because then they are making more money. They don't taste as good either and we lose the wonderful genetic diversity we had. We have to keep these old strains alive. We have lost too many already to extinction.'

It was hard to get him to stop once he'd started, but I was really interested in what he had to say. There were many nights we spent with Mardi, counting out seeds smaller than a pinhead and sealing them away in packets. Mardi treated them like gold, and I had begun to understand why.

Over the next few weeks, Bella Rosa taught us how to cleanse energetically, how to remove blocks and how to build up our energy. She was very insistent on the necessity of protection. After what had occurred with the crazy coconut man and then with my friend Trudy, I was in no position to argue that I didn't need it, and I did want to learn her techniques. But when I wanted to discuss the lessons I had received in India, she would wave my words aside as inconsequential and didn't want to hear about it.

I didn't absorb everything they told me without seeing if it worked for me, and while some things did, others didn't. And it seemed to me that every relationship should be cyclical, giving and taking, learning and sharing. As wise and wonderful as Bella Rosa was, I couldn't help thinking that some of her actions meandered into the dark and left her psychic doors wide open—which made protection for her always an absolute necessity. How could you not attract repercussions in your own life when you regularly bound up the lives of so many others?

There were times I was awed by her majesty and hypnotised by the power and truth of her words. She could transform from a judgemental, middle-aged, dour-faced woman with greying black hair, to an Earth Goddess garlanded with spring—but I never knew who she would be on any given day.

In Bella Rosa I saw Beauty and the Beast.

One day, she and Mardi were teaching us a healing technique they'd never shown anyone else. It basically involved Gill and I both working on someone, both in sync but on opposite sides, as we moved our hands along their energy field. The intensity of both of us working together soon broke down any energy blocks. We had just finished when Bella Rosa began to communicate with some being we couldn't see.

'Oooh,' we heard her say. 'Okay, I'm being told, Kye, that you should never work on men, only women.' Then she smiled as if she'd finally understood something. 'You're a sensitive, Kye. That's what you're here for.'

I looked at her, puzzled. I had never heard of the expression before, let alone understood what it meant. Then I suddenly felt as if my entire existence had shrunk down to that room. Nothing else existed. Bella Rosa was looking directly at me, holding my gaze as she lifted her arm and pointed. As I followed the direction she was pointing I could hear some crows way off in the distance.

The velvety caws of my forever-to-be-known Kundalini Crows drew me to them, and all of a sudden I had left my body behind and was flying through the air towards them. Yet as I did so I could hear Bella Rosa's voice in the wind. 'What are they saying?'

'They are telling me to remember who I am,' I replied.

When I woke up back in my body, back in the room, Bella Rosa was leaning towards me, waiting for me to open my eyes.

'That's your gift,' she said. 'As a sensitive, you feel energy; you experience life on a deeper level than most. You understand the silent language of the universe that speaks to you through the birds and the animals, the sacred rocks and the beings that reside in the stones. You are here to work with nature and the animals. That is your gift ... and that's what I am to show you.'

There had been so many times I'd felt almost blasted out of my own body by the intensity of light I was experiencing—by Rainbow Man, by the Filipino healers, at the top of Mount Banahaw—and this was another occasion. But this time I also felt deeply exhausted. I felt so overloaded. I couldn't take anymore; I needed to rest. I felt quite dizzy as I made my way back to the truck with Gill holding my arm, guiding me. He had obviously felt concerned about me, and I'd been vaguely aware of Bella Rosa telling him I would be okay.

Over the next five days, I sank into a fever. All I could drink was water and the herb teas prepared for me by Bella Rosa and picked from her magical herb garden, which was planted in a giant mandala and cared for by the fairies.

'There's nothing to worry about. You're only being rewired. After, you will be able to hold more energy and your reality will feel even more heightened,' she told me one day.

'But life feels pretty intense most of the time already!' I exclaimed, not sure if I could deal with much more.

'Most people don't get shown how to nurture their gift, Kye, and you have already done a lot of clearing of stagnant energy, past pain, whatever you want to call it, which will make it easier for you now. When a sensitive experiences the world through their own pain, they can become so emotional they are unable to use their gift.'

'Even so, I still feel the pain and sometimes it overwhelms me,' I replied.

'That's why you must cleanse your energy field every day. It will get easier. You will still feel the pain, but instead of being disabled by it you will be motivated.'

It was certainly a relief to understand why I felt life so keenly. I was often so moved by the tiniest little thing, and often found my tears embarrassing and difficult to explain. They weren't only triggered by the pain in the world, I could well up and overflow at seeing an old couple on the street, whom I had never met, sharing a moment of tenderness and giving each other a kiss; or a car passing by on a long stretch of lonely road and its passenger giving me a wave. I was so moved by fleeting moments when two people who may never see each other again collide and connect, even for the briefest of moments.

I had so much to learn from Bella Rosa, I could have spent my entire lifetime with her and still not have known everything she knew.

'Kye always needs a haven,' she said to Gill one day. 'Even us Roms when we are on the road have a bolt hole, somewhere to escape ... And always make sure she has water. It's vital for a sensitive. The best thing you can do for Kye is to set her up a bath in nature, somewhere that's totally private.'

One day over tea, she told us about the gypsy king who acted like a decoy. He always walked in front, leading his clan, and if there was any trouble he dealt with it, keeping the attention well away from the wise old women, the witches in the back.

'The clan knew that it was the old women who carried the knowledge and the power, and they knew the importance of keeping them safe.' she said. 'So much knowledge is lost today because people have forgotten the wisdom of the elders.' Her words were full of sadness.

Every day, she came down to see me in her electric wheelchair and brought me another cup of her sweet herbal brew. 'You're going to feel very different when you leave here, so you must build up your strength; so drink this. I've made this tea from the roots and the larger branches of the herb. It will make you strong.' Bella Rosa could be so derisive and yet so tender. It wasn't an easy love, but I did love her!

On the day I felt ready to return to the house, she came down to see me in her electric wheelchair and escorted me back. I was walking slowly, still feeling quite weak, and we paused for a moment at a sacred circle that had been created by Mardi and some other men for their magic and rituals.

It was a sweet little fairy circle and emanated 'gay'. Bella Rosa sat looking at it for a moment then burst out in a gust of laughter that made me laugh too.

'What a poofy little circle that is,' she said, affectionately. 'But don't tell the blokes that.' She looked at me conspiratorially. Her own circle was so robust it could have withstood a tornado.

Both Mardi and Bella Rosa made crystal wands that they sold, and Mardi's were light, playful little fairy wands while Bella Rosa's were huge, masculine staffs. Once, when I'd been living on the hill, Mardi had come to stay a night and we'd decided to walk along the beach and buy a pizza. I just hadn't been prepared for his outfit; when he walked out all he had on was the teeniest pair of bathers and was carrying a crystal wand, which he held out in front, waving it around like a fairy. He even went into the pizza shop like that too. I couldn't help notice the rumble of the Aussie blokes within, who weren't used to displays of masculine femininity like this. But that's what I loved about him. He was always uncompromisingly himself.

When it came time for us to leave, we were spat out like a piece of gum.

One morning Mardi turned up at our truck early and woke us. 'You two have to get out of here. There's a cyclone coming in on the coast. If you don't leave now, you won't get out until after the wet.' We went up to the house and shared a final cuppa with them as we watched the news on TV about the impending disaster. Then we quickly hugged them goodbye, tears streaming down all our faces as we thanked them for everything, words all seeming much too small. Relief and sorrow that we were leaving, everything merged into one. We called the dogs into the truck and we drove out of there.

The road north was a dirt road through the wilderness, impassable in the wet. Our only route out was south, towards tarmac and town, and the path of the incoming cyclone that was due to hit the coast the following day!

Twenty-Five
Place of the Heart

The closer we got to town, the wilder the weather became. It was a miracle we made it out of the rainforest. The last river we crossed broke its banks and flooded the road within minutes of us getting through. Our flow was taking us into the heart of a cyclone, and after everything we'd already experienced, I had to let go. I was even feeling quite excited by the wild weather.

There was no doubt it would be dangerous for us to park out in the open, so we drove around to a friend's place that had a big shed out the back that we knew we could drive the truck into if it was free. We had to leave it parked at the bottom of the drive while we went to speak with our friends. As we walked to the front door, the wind was so strong we had to lie completely flat on the earth so we didn't get blown away and wait until it had passed. The trees were all doubled up, limbs breaking with the force of the cyclonic gusts, and the normally busy suburban street was utterly deserted. Not even a parked car could be seen.

We must have appeared quite mad when we knocked on our friend's front door. The three people who shared the house had barricaded themselves into their bathroom with all their cyclone supplies—their radio, spare batteries and water bottles—and were communicating to us from the small frosted glass window above the toilet.

'Don't you know there's a cyclone coming?' they yelled. 'Get yer truck in the shed, for God's sake.' All we saw was a mouth at the tiny window. We fought the wind back to the truck and managed to drive it into the shed.

We at least were lucky that night. The cyclone downsized and came in fifty kilometres north and hit a small town we had driven through the previous day. Even so, it did a lot of damage. Trees had fallen, power poles were down, and buildings had lost their roofs. Somehow we'd managed to sleep through the night, and we were woken in the morning by sunlight filling the shed when one of our friends opened up the double doors to see if we were okay. It was chaos outside.

You don't usually see waves in the tropics, but they were pounding on the shore, and the ocean was almost a solid platform of driftwood. As far as the eye could see, the beach was piled high with debris. There were plastic bottles, thongs and driftwood, and in amongst it all, the macabre bodies of drowned cane toads that had blown up to the size of footballs.

What saddened me most, though, were all the poor cows. They'd been washed out to sea in the swollen rivers and then dumped back on the shore where they sat on leys of land, traumatised. It choked me up to see them. It seemed cruel and compassionless to me when I heard on the news that the farmer was waiting for the roads to clear before he brought his trucks in and took them to the abattoir. After everything they'd been through, how could anyone justify that? If I hadn't been such a young gypsy, albeit a reluctant one, I would have bought the lot of them and taken them home to heal, and they would have lived out their lives in safety and love with me.

There were many flooded roads, and people were travelling through the suburbs by canoe. In the days after the cyclone, and with all the rain, the humidity built up with such an intensity we were constantly battling plagues of mosquitos. Our bed in the truck was always damp and on the verge of going mouldy, and I developed a tropical ear infection that was so painful I longed to be somewhere dry. I had no idea where dry was.

'You know, even if we got a house now,' I said to Gill, 'I wouldn't want it. I'm over living here.' Nothing could have tempted me to stay.

Four days after the cyclone had passed, I woke up with the tail end of a conversation I'd had in my dream. I couldn't remember the whole thing. Just *Go to the heart*, *go to the heart.* I didn't even know what it meant. Was it a physical thing? Gill and I discussed it as we sat in the back of our truck. I felt we'd been given a vital clue as to where the treasure was, but neither of us could figure it out. We had our tattered map unfolded on the bed and were trying to avoid the drips that plopped through the worn-out, canvas-covered back.

In the past, when we'd been travelling and were unsure where to go next, we would often open the map and, sitting with our back to it, toss a coin over our shoulder to see where it landed. We never actually followed up on any of our coin destinations. It always landed on some dustbowl in the wheat belt out west or 200 kilometres off the coast of Darwin. So it just turned into a game. Sometimes we'd do the best of three to see if we could get a better outcome. But we never got anything that felt like the hand of God had been present in the fall of the coin.

This day, we sat looking at the map, feeling a little lost as to where to go next. We were wondering if we should try the hopelessly inefficient toss of the coin when our attention was drawn to that tiny town right in the middle of the map.

In the dampness and humidity, with the wind buffeting the sides of our truck, there was a moment of clarity. It was as if the letters A-L-I-C-E-S-P-R-I-N-G-S had been written on the map larger than anywhere else.

And honestly, I'm not telling a lie, but they looked as if they were pulsing. We both looked at each other. There wasn't even the need for words. Neither of us had ever felt more certain about something. We were going to Alice, that small desert town right in the very centre of Australia, 500 kilometres north or south from its nearest tiny town neighbours and much further across the desert, east or west.

We had only been there briefly on our travels once before, but we'd liked it. It's a dynamic and exciting place, full of creative people, and home to an eclectic mix of Aboriginals, locals, government workers, artists and bush men. It also has Australia's highest per capita population of lesbians, and because of the US Pine Gap Space Base, it is home to many Americans.

I couldn't get to Alice soon enough, but I had one last thing to do before we left. I needed to visit the hill and say goodbye. I didn't know when I'd be back or if I ever would, and I had this strong feeling there was something I needed to pick up.

We hadn't been up there since the cyclone. We drove the truck to the start of the dirt track that led up the hill to the old house site and walked the rest of the way. It was a rough clamber up; the track had deep gullies from all the rain and was blocked by trees that had fallen in the cyclone. It was still raining heavily when we finally got to the top. Papaya trees still gave lush fruit, and gardenias peeped out from the buffel grass. The whole garden was moist and beautiful and dripping with the rain. Without the people, without the pain, it was an enchanted place to be. I knew exactly what it was I needed to get. Right by what was once the front door of the house were three rocks. Our vehicle was a mile away. It would be a hard haul back, but I knew I had to take the biggest.

'Won't the little one do?' Gill asked, looking apprehensive. We were both dripping wet, and my ear infection was causing me a lot of pain. Yes, I wanted it to be the little rock too. I didn't want either of us to have to lug that big rock over and under all those fallen trees back to the truck. But it wasn't the little rock; the feeling inside me was so strong. I couldn't ignore it. *We have to take the big rock.*

'I'll help carry it,' I offered consolingly.

After all the years of living with the ghosts and ghoumas of my magical knoll, I was finally leaving. My work here was done. There were no more old bones to dig up, and all the old ghosts were now dancing in the light whilst I stood at a pivotal point. Whatever occurred now would be new and not seared out of the sorrows of the past, but the strength and wisdom of those lessons would always be with me.

Gill wouldn't accept my help; he struggled all the way down the track, carrying that big rock, and only let me take it from him once when he was scrambling under a fallen tree. He was on his hands and knees when I heard an exclamation.

'Wow. Look what I've found.'

He finally emerged and held out to me a perfectly clear quartz crystal. I'd always known the hill was made of crystal and often found broken shards, but never anything as pretty or whole as this. I held it up. Sunlight was streaming through the clouds, and as I looked inside the crystal, I could see a tiny rainbow. We stood in the sunshine, feeling its warmth, shaking a little from being wet and cold. On every blade of lush green grass and on every leaf on every tree, droplets of rain plopped. Caught by the sunlight, they glistened and sparkled like diamonds; what a beautiful gift the hill had given us.

I knew we had got what we came for. I didn't understand why we had to take the rock or what unseen force was guiding this act. I just knew it had to come.

Gill and I had often spoken about the ghoumas, the sacred travelling stones that find all sorts of ways to reach their destination. Some may be picked up and carried there by people, and others will move in floodwaters. Some even travel in the belly of a bird, helping them grind their food before being pooped out in a new location.

Indigenous people from all over the world use them, and they have different names in different cultures. They are used by medicine healers, witches and wizards to see visions from the past, present or future. The powerful rays of the ghoumas not only help people heal, but they are also a potent protection. The most powerful magician would not go near anyone when they have the protection of their ghouma. I didn't know if our giant ghouma was coming because we faced danger or if it just needed to be placed somewhere else on the earth, but coming it was!

Gill had his own way with the ghouma and often carried little stones around, leaving them in different places. If someone was having a hard time, he'd pull one out from his pocket and say,

'Ah, that's why I got this. This is for you.'

He'd always had a strong connection with all the sacred stones, not just the ghoumas and always seemed to find some invisible trail that led him to those hidden away. Used in ceremonies, these stones should never be moved or even touched. Some would be sitting on the earth for all to see, others hidden away. Often it would be secret women's places, their painted stones tucked away in a hole in the rock on the edge of a cliff. They were never in easy places to find, but Gill would amble through the bush following a current that led him to them. When he saw them, he'd back away respectfully.

But he didn't the first time and learnt a big lesson. He pulled out one of the stones to look closer, and as he did, he was bitten. Giant red Hoppy Joe ants were crawling all over his body, and they began to bite him, and their bites were like electric shocks. He never took one of the ceremonial stones from its secret places again. He knew about the power of the stones and rocks and understood why mine had to come.

It was a long haul down, and the whole way, I felt mixed emotions about leaving the hill once again, the future an invisible screen. *There is nothing certain in my life. We are heading off into the unknown once again, hauling up fears so that we can fly free, and it's scary sometimes ... being reborn again every time you reach a new place ... But I've got what I came for. My rock, our crystal, some anchor to my home, to the place where I walked through shadows yet grew strong. I came here with so little, yet I'm leaving with so much.*

It was two more days before the flooded roads cleared, and we could escape. Ours were the first tracks in the drying mud. I was in so much pain with my ear infection that I lay on the bed in the back of the truck, groaning, while Gill drove the three hundred and fifty kilometres south to Townsville. It wasn't until then, until we turned west and began to climb The Great Dividing Range, leaving the wet of the tropics behind, that the agony of my ear began to abate. We were finally in the desert with its big open spaces and huge blue skies. It felt so exhilarating.

It suddenly occurred to me that we were driving right into the heart of Australia. 'Do you think that's what those words meant?' I asked Gill as we rattled over the corrugations on the rough dirt road. I couldn't stop thinking about how those letters on the map had appeared to pulse.

'Who knows, but we're going to find out!' and I could tell he felt as excited by our destination as me.

It took four days of travelling in our worn-out truck. We arrived early in the morning. The day was already beginning to swelter with the heat. Driving down through rocky outcrops, the desert already dried to ochres and browns, and seeing Alice Springs nestled by the deep terracotta of the McDonnell Ranges that throbbed like a living beast, with the sky so blue, so big... I couldn't help but feel a wave of optimism.

We had come on a whim, driving 2,850 kilometres just because it felt right. We had barely a hundred dollars to our name, and our truck was running like shit. Yet I knew we'd made the right choice.

The crystal Gill had found was sitting on the dash. My big ghouma rock, and my anchor, sat on the floor under my feet. The words of Rainbow Man echoed in my ear, *'You and Gill have something to create together.'*

Was this it, the place where it would all happen?

I had no idea, but I felt full of love for the journey we were on. I was finally getting it! The source of everything flows through me. When I open up to the highest expression of who I am and embrace the sacred truth that I am a being of love, my life flows in miraculous and beautiful ways.

Oh, I was sure there would be challenges up ahead, but I hoped now that I would see them as the tool-gathering exercises they were and look for their treasures. For in every challenge lies a gift, but it's only those with an open heart that can see them: wisdom, divine knowing, revelation, self-reliance, healing, strength, the unveiling of our own sacred light, for who is going to light the path of our own darkness if we don't?

Other people's lights, however well-intentioned, can never shine as brightly for us as our own.

I am the source. I AM LOVE

Dearest Readers

I am a self published author & all profits from this book help us to continue to care for not only ourselves, but an already large family of previously rescued animals.

The more books we sell, the more we can do to help even more animals & build our vision of kindness.

If you have enjoyed this book please let your friends know.
Share it on social media and PLEASE leave feedback on Amazon

Gift it to your friends.

And if you know anyone I can send this book to that can help me get this epic and beautiful journey of trust out there into the world in a much bigger way, beyond the realms of little me, let me know.

I am often so busy caring for animals, or trying to write

my next book while bottle feeding an orphaned lamb, mucking out the horse poop, or welcoming the latest animal that's arrived worn down from abuse with their trust in people broken. Finding time to focus on building sales, attracting media, getting interviews, all of which would be an enormous help gets lost in the midst of all these animals.

If you can help and be part of our beautiful network - even if it's just by letting others know about my books.
We thank you
We appreciate you
and so much LOVE

Kye & Gill

& all the animals.

www.kyecrow.love

About Kye Crow

Formerly from the UK, Kye grew up steeped in the magic and wisdom of the animals, her greatest love. She was only five when she was first shown a vision of the sanctuary she would one day build: a healing haven for the weary and footsore of the animal realms and a centre of learning where people could come and share in the wisdom and healing of the animals.

Often called stubborn, Kye refuses to accept spiritual truths unless she can see them working in her own life, which has led to all sorts of adventures. Kye's request to Spirit is simple: if something is a Sacred Truth, please teach it to me in a way I can understand.

The dynamic laws of prosperity were taught to her in India after all her money was stolen, yet despite this, she stayed there for six months learning how to manifest, without asking a soul for help (Wild Holy Love). Kye has never chosen to walk the well-worn tracks and one of her ultimate lessons in TRUST was when spirit guided her to let go of her home and all her possessions and head out on a journey, destination unknown, travelling

in a camel wagon pulled by eight camels with over fifty r
escued animals coming a long for the trip, and more b
eing rescued along the way. You can read about this p
henomenal adventure in 'Love We Live', {Book one} and '
Tracks of Love'. {Book two}

Kye is a sacred seamstress, a visionary, artist, writer and cares for hundreds of rescued animals and is a wise voice to a more conscious relationship with our animal friends.

She is passionate about helping others unveil their Sacred Path through retreats, courses and storytelling.

Other publications by Kye

Kye's second book, is '**Sacred Journey into the Animal Realm**".

While Kye was writing '**Love We Live**', the adventure that follows '**Wild Holy Love**', the animal messengers began appearing to her. They told her there was a completely new and unexpected book to birth, and this is it. Hear the voices of the animals as they guide us on a journey into a mystical and enchanted realm. They know that only when we heal our pain will their suffering end forever. This book, full of wisdom, sacred tools and healing, is their gift to us. When we choose compassion and love for ourselves we naturally give it to others. It's now time to create a world of love for us all.

'The path we travel together, with the animals as our guides and teachers, traverses the open plains of the desert where we experience a stillness and a clarity we have not felt before. It weaves through enchanted flower-filled glades where the fairy folk live. It touches briefly on the realms of the dragons, but it also weaves through the shadowy heart of the deepest part of the forest where only the wise wood folk go, for they have lived for many moons in the folds of this magical realm and they know of its treasures.

So gather around my friends. Our fire burns brightly and the billy boils, infusing the golden blossoms from the sweet bride of the meadows that grows lush along the banks of the nearby lake for a heart-opening nectar of a tea. For, many worlds weave through this and whilst there will be times we are striding across the arid plains of the desert as we converse with our friends the emus, in the blink of an eye we can be in the soft and mossy garden of an ancient oak wood with a fairytale lake within sight, watching squirrels scamper along the gnarled branches of a nearby tree. The beauty is that all things are possible in the realms of love'.

If you loved 'Wild Holy Love', and would like to read more of Kye's inspirational and heartfelt adventures-

'**Love We Live**' {Book One} and '**Tracks of Love**', {Book two} share an extraordinary journey of Love and trust.

Kye and her partner Gill were guided by Spirit to sell their home, let go of all their possessions and prepare for a journey, destination unknown.

They had no idea when they set off in their camel wagon (built from old scrap by Gill, pulled by a team of eight previously rescued, much-loved camels and accompanied by almost fifty other rescued animals: dogs, goats, pigeons, doves, parrots, a donkey, chickens and their adored rooster "The Colonel") that their journey would take them over 2,200 kilometres through the desert of Australia.

This journey of challenge and ultimate transformation is brimming with the wisdom and guidance of the animals, the magic of the stones and trees, and an awareness that only comes from slowing our lives down to the pace of a walk, living simply on our earth, cooking on an open fire and gazing at the stars as you drift off to sleep.

Join Kye and Gill on the ultimate journey of trust as they discover it wasn't the animals that needed training, it was them!

Thank You and Acknowledgements

I would like to thank so many people for helping me learn and grow on my journey and become the much happier and more joyful soul I am today.

I recognise that some of my darkest moments were triggered by people that ultimately offered me some of my greatest gifts and like me, many of those people were learning and growing too. The people they are today is very different from the people they were when we were all trying to make sense of our pain and find our way out of the shadows.

I have of course changed some people's names simply for privacy, but they will know who they are.

I have so much gratitude for my former partner Dan, who over twenty years on is now the father of three gorgeous daughters, a drug and alcohol counsellor and a much loved AWESOME yoga teacher. When I told him I had shared many aspects of our relationship that didn't always put him in a great light, he replied, "Go for it Kye!

Absolutely no problem." Wow, that's inner peace! Thank you Dan!

Thanks also to Bonnie and Tui, our paths have never woven together since but I still feel the gifts.

And heartfelt appreciation for my friend Smithy who now lives with his phenomenal wife and son in Wales and is given free rein by appreciative clients to create the magical gardens he is known for. And in his spare time lovingly tends his bonsai trees created from roots he finds on the tip! Smithy let me dive into the past and describe a scene when he too was working things out!

In a bid to contain this adventure to one book a few deeply significant relationships were left out. Jules, thank you my friend, you have been an anchor for me and in many of my fragile moments the reason I didn't lose it completely was because you were there. Your beloved brews of earl grey and the ritual of spinning the pot three times before pouring soothed many a tear, as did your way of slicing through the crap to get to what was real. Thank you!

Monica, you are part of this story too. I had no idea that when I was struggling to stay afloat, you were too. It's hard to see what's happening when you're going under but you have been this stoic, wise, beautiful woman in the background of so many of these adventures. Thank you.

My thanks also go to Alan Nixon for his early support and constructive advice that took a while to filter through my resistance but eventually I turned it into great compost.

To Seanara for believing in me and Karen for her early editing of a manuscript that still had a long way to go. Knowing you were both there supporting me kept me going when I felt like giving up! Thank you both.

Thanks go to Ailsa for listening to the latest chapters and being the greatest one woman cheerleading team in the entire universe!

And to Lindy for believing in us. You have shone a light that's been so bright, it kept us warm on some of our darkest days.

Thanks also to Wendy Millgate from "Wendy and Words" for being an awesome editor and making such fabulous suggestions. Thanks also to Verity from The Outsourcing Queen for all your expert advice and wonderful assistance with our latest publishing venture.

And now my book is flying out into the world and you have all made this possible. Thank you all so much!

And of course, this book would never have been birthed without the support of Gill. I give thanks every day for having such a kind and loving and wise man in my life. Not only has he been the rock in the background during the seven years of birthing this story, he has soothed and encouraged me through numerous rejections. He has fed and watered me when I have been so immersed in writing I can't function on this earth. He has kept all the animals at our sanctuary cared for and loved, built endless fires to warm up water for a hot bath and every time I have come close to giving up, he has cheered me on. He also gave me the freedom to write openly about the time our own path wove into the shadows and got so dark, we both lost our way.

Over twenty years together and our love still grows.

Heartfelt thanks my beloved Gill for everything.

www.ingramcontent.com/pod-product-compliance
Lightning Source LLC
Chambersburg PA
CBHW011147290426
44109CB00023B/2517